PREFACE

Article I, Section 8, of the Constitution vests in Congress the power "to declare War." Pursuant to that power, Congress has enacted 11 declarations of war during the course of American history relating to five different wars, the most recent being those that were adopted during World War II. In addition, Congress has adopted a number of authorizations for the use of military force, the most recent being the joint resolution enacted on October 16, 2002, authorizing the use of military force against Iraq. To buttress the nation's ability to prosecute a war or armed conflict, Congress has also enacted numerous statutes which confer standby authority on the President or the executive branch and are activated by the enactment of a declaration of war, the existence of a state of war, or the promulgation of a declaration of national emergency.

This book examines a number of topics related to declarations of war and authorizations for the use of military force by the United States. It provides historical background on each of the declarations of war and on several major authorizations for the use of force that have been enacted; analyzes the implications of declarations of war and authorizations for the use of force under both international law and domestic law; lists and summarizes the more than 250 standby statutory authorities that can come into effect pursuant to a declaration of war, the existence of a state of war, and/or a declaration of national emergency; describes the procedures in Congress governing the consideration of declarations of war and authorizations for the use of force, including the procedures under the War Powers Resolution; and sets forth in two appendices the texts of all of the declarations of war and the major authorizations for the use of force that have been enacted.

GOVERNMENT PROCEDURES AND OPERATIONS

Additional books in this series can be found on Nova's website
under the Series tab.

Additional e-books in this series can be found on Nova's website
under the e-book tab.

CONTENTS

Additional color graphics may be available in the e-book version of this book.

Library of Congress Cataloging-in-Publication Data

ISBN: 978-1-63482-987-8

Published by Nova Science Publishers, Inc. † New York

GOVERNMENT PROCEDURES AND OPERATIONS

ENACTMENT OF WAR AND THE USE OF MILITARY FORCE

BACKGROUND AND LEGAL IMPLICATIONS

CRAIG PEREZ
EDITOR

nova publishers
New York

GOVERNMENT PROCEDURES AND OPERATIONS

ENACTMENT OF WAR AND THE USE OF MILITARY FORCE

BACKGROUND AND LEGAL IMPLICATIONS

In: Enactment of War and the Use of Military Force
Editor: Craig Perez ISBN: 978-1-63482-987-8

Chapter 1

DECLARATIONS OF WAR AND AUTHORIZATIONS FOR THE USE OF MILITARY FORCE: HISTORICAL BACKGROUND AND LEGAL IMPLICATIONS*

Jennifer K. Elsea and Matthew C. Weed

SUMMARY

From the Washington Administration to the present, Congress and the President have enacted 11 separate formal declarations of war against foreign nations in five different wars. Each declaration has been preceded by a presidential request either in writing or in person before a joint session of Congress. The reasons cited in justification for the requests have included armed attacks on United States territory or its citizens and threats to United States rights or interests as a sovereign nation.

Congress and the President have also enacted authorizations for the use of force rather than formal declarations of war. Such measures have generally authorized the use of force against either a named country or unnamed hostile nations in a given region. In most cases, the President has requested the authority, but Congress has sometimes given the President less than what he asked for. Not all authorizations for the use of force have resulted in actual combat. Both declarations and authorizations require the signature of the President in order to become law.

In contrast to an authorization, a declaration of war in itself creates a state of war under international law and legitimates the killing of enemy combatants, the seizure of enemy property, and the apprehension of enemy aliens. While a formal declaration was once deemed a necessary legal prerequisite to war and was thought to terminate diplomatic and commercial relations and most treaties between the combatants, declarations have fallen into disuse since World War II. The laws of war, such as the Hague and Geneva Conventions, apply to circumstances of armed conflict whether or not a formal declaration or authorization was issued.

---

* This is an edited, reformatted and augmented version of a Congressional Research Service publication RL31133, prepared for Members and Committees of Congress dated April 18, 2014.

With respect to domestic law, a declaration of war automatically triggers many standby statutory authorities conferring special powers on the President with respect to the military, foreign trade, transportation, communications, manufacturing, alien enemies, etc. In contrast, no standby authorities appear to be triggered automatically by an authorization for the use of force, although the executive branch has argued, with varying success, that the authorization to use force in response to the terrorist attacks of 2001 provided a statutory exception to certain statutory prohibitions.

Most statutory standby authorities do not expressly require a declaration of war to be actualized but can be triggered by a declaration of national emergency or simply by the existence of a state of war; however, courts have sometimes construed the word "war" in a statute as implying a formal declaration, leading Congress to enact clarifying amendments in two cases. Declarations of war and authorizations for the use of force waive the time limitations otherwise applicable to the use of force imposed by the War Powers Resolution.

This report provides historical background on the enactment of declarations of war and authorizations for the use of force and analyzes their legal effects under international and domestic law. It also sets forth their texts in two appendices. The report includes an extensive listing and summary of statutes that are triggered by a declaration of war, a declaration of national emergency, and/or the existence of a state of war. The report concludes with a summary of the congressional procedures applicable to the enactment of a declaration of war or authorization for the use of force and to measures under the War Powers Resolution.

INTRODUCTION

Article I, Section 8, of the Constitution vests in Congress the power "to declare War." Pursuant to that power, Congress has enacted 11 declarations of war during the course of American history relating to five different wars, the most recent being those that were adopted during World War II. In addition, Congress has adopted a number of authorizations for the use of military force, the most recent being the joint resolution enacted on October 16, 2002, authorizing the use of military force against Iraq. To buttress the nation's ability to prosecute a war or armed conflict, Congress has also enacted numerous statutes which confer standby authority on the President or the executive branch and are activated by the enactment of a declaration of war, the existence of a state of war, or the promulgation of a declaration of national emergency.

This report examines a number of topics related to declarations of war and authorizations for the use of military force by the United States. It (1) provides historical background on each of the declarations of war and on several major authorizations for the use of force that have been enacted; (2) analyzes the implications of declarations of war and authorizations for the use of force under both international law and domestic law; (3) lists and summarizes the more than 250 standby statutory authorities that can come into effect pursuant to a declaration of war, the existence of a state of war, and/or a declaration of national emergency; (4) describes the procedures in Congress governing the consideration of declarations of war and authorizations for the use of force, including the procedures under the War Powers Resolution; and (5) sets forth in two appendices the texts of all of the declarations of war and the major authorizations for the use of force that have been enacted. The report does not address the issue of the constitutionality of Presidential uses of military force absent a declaration of war or authorization for the use of force.

Previous Declarations of War

From the Washington Administration to the present, there have been 11 separate formal declarations of war against foreign nations enacted by Congress and the President, encompassing five different wars—the War of 1812 with Great Britain, the War with Mexico in 1846, the War with Spain in 1898, the First World War, and the Second World War.[1] In each case the enactment of a formal declaration of war has been preceded by a presidential request to Congress for such an action, either in writing or in person before a joint session of Congress. In each such message requesting a war declaration, the President has cited what he deemed compelling reasons for doing so. These reasons have included armed attacks on United States territory or its citizens, and attacks on or direct threats to United States rights or interests as a sovereign nation. In the 19th century all declarations of war were passed by the Congress in the form of a bill. In the 20th century all declarations of war were passed by the Congress in the form of a joint resolution. In every instance the measures were adopted by majority vote in both the House and the Senate and were signed into law by the President.[2] The last formal declaration of war was enacted on June 5, 1942, against Rumania during World War II.[3]

The circumstances of President McKinley's request for a declaration of war against Spain in 1898 stand in singular contrast to all the others. McKinley's request for a declaration of war on April 25, 1898, was approved by a voice vote of both Houses of Congress on that date. His request was made after Spain had rejected a U.S. ultimatum that Spain relinquish its sovereignty over Cuba and permit Cuba to become an independent state. This ultimatum was supported by a joint resolution of Congress, signed into law on April 20, 1898, that among other things, declared Cuba to be independent, demanded that Spain withdraw its military forces from the island, and directed and authorized the President to use the U.S. Army, Navy and militia of the various states to achieve these ends. The war with Spain in 1898, in short, was not principally based on attacks on the United States but on a U.S. effort to end the Cuban insurrection against Spain, bring about Cuban independence, and restore a stable government and order on the island—outcomes that were believed by the United States to advance its interests.[4]

In the 20th century, without exception, presidential requests for formal declarations of war by Congress were based on findings by the President that U.S. territory or sovereign rights had been attacked or threatened by a foreign nation. Although President Wilson had tried to maintain U.S. neutrality after the outbreak of the First World War, he regarded the German decision on February 1, 1917, to engage in unrestricted submarine warfare against all naval vessels in the war zone, including those of neutral states, to be an unacceptable assault on U.S. sovereign rights which the German Government had previously pledged to respect. Wilson's request to Congress for a declaration of war against Germany on April 2, 1917, stated that war had been "thrust upon the United States" by Germany's actions. Congress passed a joint resolution declaring war which the President signed on April 6, 1917. Wilson delayed requesting a war declaration against Austria- Hungary until December 4, 1917. He did so then because that state, a German ally in the war, had become an active instrument of Germany against the United States. Congress quickly passed a joint resolution declaring war which the President signed on December 7, 1917.[5]

President Franklin D. Roosevelt requested a declaration of war against Japan on December 8, 1941, because of direct military attacks by that nation against U.S. territory, military personnel and citizens in Hawaii and other outposts in the Pacific area. The House and the Senate passed the requested declaration and the President signed it into law that same day. After Germany and Italy each declared war on the United States on December 11, 1941, President Roosevelt asked Congress to respond in kind by recognizing that a state of war existed between the United States and those two nations. Congress passed separate joint resolutions declaring war on both nations which the President signed on December 11, 1941.[6] On June 2, 1942, President Roosevelt asked that Congress declare war on Bulgaria, Hungary and Rumania, nations that were under the domination of Germany, were engaged in active military actions against the United States, and had themselves declared war on the United States. Congress passed separate joint resolutions declaring war on each of these nations. The President signed these resolutions on June 5, 1942.[7]

There is a striking similarity of language in the eight declarations of war passed by the Congress in the 20th century. They all declare that a "state of war" exists between the United States and the other nation. With the one exception of the declaration of war against Austria-Hungary on December 7, 1917, the other seven declarations characterize the state of war as having been "thrust upon the United States" by the other nation. All eight of these 20th century declarations of war state in identical language that the President is

> authorized and directed to employ the entire naval and military forces of the United States and the resources of the Government to carry on war against [the 'Government' of the particular nation]; and to bring the conflict to a successful termination all of the resources of the country are hereby pledged by the Congress of the United States.

The complete texts of the 11 declarations of war are set forth in **Appendix A**.

KEY STATUTORY AUTHORIZATIONS FOR THE USE OF MILITARY FORCE

From the Administration of President John Adams to the present, there have been various instances when legislation has been enacted authorizing the use of military force by the President instead of formally declaring war. In most cases such legislation has been preceded by a specific request by the President for such authority. During the Presidencies of John Adams and Thomas Jefferson, these Chief Executives noted in messages to Congress that congressional authorizations for use of force would be appropriate to enable the United States to protect its interests from predatory actions by foreign powers, in particular attacks on U.S. commercial vessels and persons on the high seas by France and by Tripoli. Congress responded with specific authorizations for the use of force under the President's direction in 1798 against France and in 1802 against Tripoli. In 1815 President James Madison formally requested that Congress declare war against the Regency of Algiers in response to its attacks on U.S. citizens and commerce in the Mediterranean. Congress responded with an act authorizing the President to utilize U.S. armed vessels to be used against Algerian naval attacks but did not declare war.

In the period following World War II, Presidential requests for authority to use military force, when made, have usually been for broad authority to use U.S. military force in a specific region of the world in order to defend U.S. interests or friendly states as the President deems appropriate. More recently, due to an expansive interpretation of the President's constitutional authority as Commander-in-Chief of the Armed Forces and of his inherent powers to use force without congressional authorization, the President has welcomed support from the Congress in the form of legislation authorizing him to utilize U.S. military forces in a foreign conflict or engagement in support of U.S. interests, but has not taken the view that he is required to obtain such authorization.

What follows is a brief overview of key legislative authorizations of the use of military force by the President from the Administration of John Adams to the present.[8] **Appendix B** provides the complete text of these specific authorizations.

France 1798

The United States during the 1790s had remained neutral in the conflict in Europe between France and Great Britain and had only begun to develop a Navy. During the Administration of President John Adams, relations with France deteriorated as American commercial ships were frequently seized by French naval vessels. In response, in his message to Congress on May 16, 1797, President Adams argued that it would be prudent for the Congress to enact legislation that would address the actions of the French by authorizing, among other things, the use of U.S. naval vessels to defend against attacks on American shipping and citizens engaged in lawful commerce abroad. President Adams reiterated, in a message of March 19, 1798, his view of the necessity for congressional action on his recommendations for the adoption of measures to protect American seafaring citizens and commerce.[9]

Congress subsequently responded to the President's recommendations by passing legislation "more effectually to protect the Commerce and Coasts of the United States" authorizing the President to instruct commanders of U.S. armed vessels to act against any "armed vessel" found to have committed or attempting to commit "depredations on the vessels" belonging to United States citizens, and to retake any ship or vessel of United States citizens that may have been captured by non-U.S. armed vessels.[10] The legislation was signed into law on May 28, 1798, Congress passed additional legislation, signed into law on July 9, 1798, that authorized the President to instruct commanders of U.S. Navy warships to "subdue, seize and take any armed French vessel which shall be found within the jurisdictional limits of the United States, or elsewhere, on the high seas...." The President was further granted the authority to grant special commissions to "owners of private armed ships and vessels of the United States," to permit them to lawfully subdue, seize, and capture "any armed French vessel," and to recapture U.S. vessels, goods and effects of U.S. citizens with the same authority as U.S. Navy vessels, subject to instructions given by the President.[11]

Table 1. Key Dates and Actions Related to Formal U.S. Declarations of War

1812—Great Britain	Madison asked June 1, 1812. House passed on June 4, 1812 (79-49). Senate passed on June 17, 1812 (19-13). President signed on **June 18, 1812**. Act of June18, 1812, ch. 102, 2 Stat. 755. Terminated by Treaty of Ghent, which entered into force on February 17, 1815. 8 Stat. 218, Treaty Series 109.
1846—Mexico	Polk asked May 11, 1846. House passed on May 11, 1846 (174-14). Senate passed on May 12, 1846 (40-2). President signed on **May 13, 1846**. Act of May 13, 1846, ch.16, 9 Stat. 9. Terminated by Treaty of Guadalupe Hidalgo, which entered into force on May 30, 1848. 9 Stat. 922, Treaty Series 207.
1898—Spain	McKinley asked April 25, 1898. Senate and House passed on April 25, 1898, by voice votes. McKinley signed on **April 25, 1898**. Act of April 25, 1898, ch. 189, 30 Stat. 364. The bill made the war date retroactive to April 21, 1898. Terminated by Treaty of Paris, which entered into force on April 11, 1899. 30 Stat. 1754, Treaty Series 343.
1917—World War I (Germany)	Wilson asked April 2, 1917. Senate passed on April 4, 1917 (82-6). House passed on April 6, 1917 (373-50). President signed on **April 6, 1917**. Act of April 6, 1917, ch.1, 40 Stat. 1. Terminated by Act of July 2, 1921, ch. 40, 42 Stat. 105, which declared the state of war between the U.S. and Germany to be at an end. Formally recognized by the Treaty on Establishment of Friendly Relations, which entered into force November 11, 1921. 42 Stat. 1939, Treaty Series 658.
1917—World War I (Austria-Hungary)	Wilson asked December 4, 1917. House passed on December 7, 1917 (365-1). Senate passed on December 7, 1917 (74-0). President signed on **December 7, 1917**. Act of December 7, 1917, ch.1, 40 Stat. 429. Terminated by Act of July 2, 1921, ch. 40, 42 Stat. 105, which declared the state of war between the U.S. and the two successor states and governments to the Austro-Hungarian monarchy—Austria and Hungary—to be at an end. Formally recognized by the Treaty on Establishment of Friendly Relations with Austria, which entered into force November 8, 1921 (42 Stat. 1939, Treaty Series 658) and the Treaty on Establishing Friendly Relations with Hungary, which entered into force December 17, 1921. 42 Stat. 1951, Treaty Series 660.
1941—World War II (Japan)	Roosevelt asked December 8, 1941. Senate passed on December 8, 1941 (82-0). House passed on December 8, 1941 (388-1). President signed on **December 8, 1941**. Act of December 8, 1941, ch. 561, 55 Stat. 795. Terminated by Treaty of Peace with Japan, which entered into force April 28, 1952. 3 UST 3169, TIAS 2490.
1941—World War II (Germany)	Roosevelt asked December 11, 1941. Senate passed on December 11, 1941 (88-0). House passed on December 11, 1941 (393-0). President signed on **December 11, 1941**. Act of December 11, 1941, ch. 564, 55 Stat. 796. Terminated by Act of October 19, 1951, ch. 519, 65 Stat. 541.
1941—World War II (Italy)	Roosevelt asked December 11, 1941. Senate passed on December 11, 1941 (90-0). House passed on December 11, 1941 (399-0). President signed on **December 11, 1941**. Act of December 11, 1941, ch. 565, 55 Stat. 796. Terminated by Treaty of Peace with Italy, which entered into force September 15, 1947. 4 UST 311, 61 Stat. 1245.
1942—World War II (Bulgaria)	Roosevelt asked June 2, 1942. House passed on June 3, 1942 (357-0). Senate passed on June 4, 1942 (73-0). President signed on **June 5, 1942**. Act of June 5, 1942, ch. 323, 56 Stat. 307. Terminated by Treaty of Peace with Bulgaria, which entered into force September 15, 1947. 4 UST 429, 61 Stat. 1915.

1942—World War II (Hungary)	Roosevelt asked June 2, 1942. House passed on June 3, 1942 (360-0). Senate passed on June 4, 1942 (73-0). President signed on **June 5, 1942**. Act of June 5, 1942, ch. 324, 56 Stat. 307. Terminated by Treaty of Peace with Hungary, which entered into force September 15, 1947. 4 UST 453, 61 Stat. 2065.
1942—World War II (Rumania)	Roosevelt asked June 2, 1942. House passed on June 3, 1942 (361-0). Senate passed on June 4, 1942 (73-0). President signed on **June 5, 1942.** Act of June 5, 1942, ch. 325, 56 Stat. 307. Terminated by Treaty of Peace with Rumania, which entered into force September 15, 1947 4 UST 403, 61 Stat. 1757.

Tripoli 1802

President Thomas Jefferson, in response to attacks on U.S. commercial shipping in the Mediterranean Sea by vessels under the control of the Bey of Tripoli, noted in his message to Congress of December 8, 1801, that it would be prudent for Congress to authorize the use of U.S. Navy forces to protect U.S. shipping against Tripoli, including permitting them to take offensive action against Tripolitan vessels.[12] Congress responded by passing legislation, enacted on February 6, 1802, that authorized the President to "equip, officer, man, and employ such of the armed vessels of the United States as may be judged requisite by the President of the United States, for protecting effectually the commerce and seamen thereof on the Atlantic ocean, the Mediterranean and adjoining seas." The President was also authorized to utilize the U.S. Navy "to subdue, seize and make prize of all vessels, goods and effects belonging to the Bey of Tripoli, or his subjects ... and to cause to be done all such other acts of precaution or hostility as the state of war will justify, and may, in his opinion, require." The President was further granted the authority to grant special commissions to "owners of private armed vessels of the United States," to permit them to lawfully subdue and seize "any Tripolitan vessel, goods or effects" with the same authority as U.S. Navy vessels, subject to instructions given by the President.[13]

Algeria 1815

President James Madison, after the conclusion of a peace treaty with Great Britain ending the War of 1812, sought authority to use the U.S. Navy to take action against vessels of the ruler and Regency of Algeria that had been seizing U.S. commercial vessels in the Mediterranean area. Due to acts of "overt and direct warfare against the citizens of the United States," President Madison, on February 23, 1815, recommended that Congress declare the "existence of a state of war between the United States and the Dey and Regency of Algiers."[14] Congress did not declare war but did pass legislation, enacted on March 3, 1815, that authorized the President to use the U.S. Navy, "as judged requisite by the President" to protect the "commerce and seamen" of the United States on the "Atlantic Ocean, the Mediterranean and adjoining seas." The President was also authorized to utilize the U.S. Navy to seize "all vessels, goods and effects belonging to the Dey of Algiers, or to his subjects ... and to cause to be done all such other acts of precaution or hostility as the state of war will justify, and may, in his opinion, require." The President was further granted the discretionary authority to grant special commissions to "owners of private armed vessels of the United States," to permit them to lawfully subdue, seize, and capture "any Algerine vessel, goods or effects" with the same authority as U.S. Navy vessels, subject to instructions given by the President.[15]

Suppression of Piracy 1819-1823

During the years after the War of 1812, there was a notable increase in the number of attacks on U.S. commercial shipping vessels in and around the Caribbean and Latin American coastal waters. Some of this was stimulated by the chaotic conditions attendant to the struggles for independence by South American colonies of Spain. Pirates attacked not only Spanish vessels in the region, but vessels of other nations generally. In response to calls for action against these predatory attacks on their vessels, American shippers petitioned Congress for action to protect them from pirates. In response, on March 3, 1819, legislation was enacted "to protect the commerce of the United States, and punish the crime of piracy." This legislation authorized the President to employ "the public armed vessels" of the United States as he deemed necessary to protect "the merchant vessels of the United States and their crews from piratical aggressions and depredations." This legislation further authorized the President to instruct the commanders of the "public armed vessels of the United States" to take various actions to combat piracy, including attacking and seizing pirates and their vessels. The legislation also authorized U.S. vessels attacked by pirates to take actions against their aggressors and seize their ships. The legislation further established penalties for those that engaged in piracy. This 1819 statute was subsequently made permanent law on January 30, 1823. It has been amended, but the current text, found in Title 33 of the *United States Code*, contains substantially the same language as was enacted in March of 1819.[16]

Formosa 1955

In a message to Congress on January 24, 1955, President Dwight Eisenhower, detailed a series of "provocative political and military actions" by the Chinese Communist government that he believed established a "pattern of aggressive purpose." That purpose was the "conquest of Formosa." This situation, said Eisenhower, posed a "serious danger to the security of our country and of the entire Pacific area and indeed to the peace of the world." The President believed that the U.S. should not wait for the United Nations to take steps to deal with the situation but should be prepared to use its own armed forces "to assure the security of Formosa and the Pescadores." President Eisenhower stated that authority for "some of the actions which might be required would be inherent in the authority of the Commander-in-Chief." He noted that, pending congressional action, he "would not hesitate, so far as my Constitutional powers extend, to take whatever emergency action might be forced upon us to protect the rights and security of the United States." However, he stated that a "suitable Congressional resolution would clearly and publicly establish the authority of the President as Commander-in-Chief to employ" the U.S. armed forces "promptly and effectively" as he deemed necessary to deal with the circumstances. Such a resolution would "make clear the unified and serious intentions of our Government, our Congress and our people."[17]

In response to the President's request, Congress passed legislation on January 29, 1955, that authorized the President to "employ the Armed Forces of the United States as he deems necessary for the specific purpose of securing and protecting Formosa, and the Pescadores against armed attack...." The President was also authorized to take "such other measures as he judges to be required or appropriate in assuring the defense of Formosa and the Pescadores." The resolution stated that it would expire when the President determined and reported to Congress that the "peace and security of the area is reasonably assured...."[18] The resolution was subsequently repealed in 1974.[19]

Middle East 1957

In a special message to Congress on January 5, 1957, President Dwight D. Eisenhower requested congressional support for a program of military and economic cooperation with nations in the general area of the Middle East to "deal with the possibility of Communist aggression, direct or indirect" against nations in that region. As one component of this military and economic assistance program, President Eisenhower sought authority to employ the "armed forces of the United States to secure and protect the territorial integrity and political independence of such nations, requesting such aid, against overt armed aggression from any nation controlled by International Communism." The President emphasized that such authority would not be utilized by him "except at the desire of the nation attacked."[20]

In response, the Congress passed legislation, enacted on March 9, 1957, that, among other things, authorized the President "to undertake, in the general area of the Middle East, military assistance programs with any nation or group of nations of that area desiring such assistance." The joint resolution further provided that "if the President determines the necessity thereof, the United States is prepared to use armed forces to assist any such nation or group of such nations requesting assistance against armed aggression from any country controlled by international communism: *Provided*, that such employment shall be consonant with the treaty obligations of the United States and with the Constitution of the United States." The President was also to report to Congress on his action under the joint resolution between January and July of each year. The joint resolution further provided that it would expire when the President determined that the "peace and security of the nations in the general area of the Middle East" was "reasonably assured" or should Congress terminate it earlier by passage of a concurrent resolution.[21] The resolution has not been formally repealed.[22]

Southeast Asia 1964

In the early 1960s the United States had been providing military assistance and support to the government of South Vietnam. Over time tensions, associated with the U.S. military presence in Southeast Asia and support for the South Vietnamese government, grew between the U.S. and the communist government of North Vietnam. On August 2, 1964, a U.S. destroyer, the U.S.S. Maddox, while in international waters off the coast of North Vietnam (the Gulf of Tonkin) was attacked by North Vietnamese torpedo boats. The attack was repulsed. The State Department protested to the North Vietnamese government and noted that grave consequences would follow additional offensive actions against U.S. forces. Subsequently, on August 4, further attacks by North Vietnamese vessels against U.S. destroyers were reported to Washington. President Lyndon Johnson responded on August 4 by sending U.S. military aircraft to bomb "gunboats and certain supporting facilities" in North Vietnam that had allegedly been used in the actions against U.S. naval vessels. After meeting with congressional leaders, President Johnson on August 5, 1964, formally requested a resolution of Congress that would "express the support of the Congress for all necessary action to protect our armed forces and to assist nations covered by the SEATO Treaty."[23]

Congress responded to President Johnson's request by passing a joint resolution to "promote the maintenance of international peace and security in southeast Asia." This legislation has come to be popularly known as the "Gulf of Tonkin resolution." This joint resolution, enacted on August 10, 1964, stated that "the Congress approves and supports the determination of the President, as Commander-in-Chief, to take all necessary measures to repel any armed attack against the forces of the United States and to prevent further aggression." The joint resolution further stated that "[c]onsonant with the Constitution of the United States and the Charter of the United Nations and in accordance with its obligations under the Southeast Asia Collective Defense Treaty, the United States is, therefore, prepared, as the President determines, to take all necessary steps, including the use of armed force, to assist any member or protocol state of the Southeast Asia Collective Defense Treaty requesting assistance in defense of its freedom." The joint resolution stated that it would expire whenever the President determined that the "peace and security of the area is reasonably assured" or if Congress chose to terminate it earlier by concurrent resolution.[24] Congress repealed the resolution in 1971.[25]

Lebanon 1983

On July 6, 1982, President Ronald Reagan announced he would send a small contingent of U.S. troops to participate in a multinational force for temporary peacekeeping in Lebanon. When the forces began to land on August 25, President Reagan reported this action to Congress but did not cite Section 4(a)(1) of the War Powers Resolution,[26] and said the agreement with Lebanon ruled out any combat responsibilities. After overseeing the departure of the Palestine Liberation Organization force, the U.S. Marines in the first Multinational Force left Lebanon on September 10, 1982. The second dispatch of Marines to Lebanon began on September 20, 1982. President Reagan announced that the United States, France, and Italy had agreed to form a new multinational force to return to Lebanon for a limited period of time to help maintain order until the lawful authorities in Lebanon could discharge those duties. The action followed three events that took place after the withdrawal of the first group of U.S. Marines: the assassination of Lebanon President-elect Bashir Gemayel, the entry of Israeli forces into West Beirut, and the massacre of Palestinian civilians by Lebanese Christian militiamen.

On September 29, 1982, President Reagan submitted a report to Congress that 1,200 Marines had begun to arrive in Beirut, but again he did not cite Section 4(a)(1), of the War Powers Resolution, stating that the American force would not engage in combat. As a result of incidents in which U.S. Marines were killed or wounded, there was controversy in Congress on whether the President's report should have been filed under Section 4(a)(1). In mid-1983 Congress passed the Lebanon Emergency Assistance Act of 1983 requiring statutory authorization for any substantial expansion in the number or role of U.S. Armed Forces in Lebanon. It also included a section that stated:

> Nothing in this section is intended to modify, limit, or suspend any of the standards and procedures prescribed by the War Powers Resolution of 1973.[27]

President Reagan reported on the Lebanon situation again on August 30, 1983, still not citing Section 4(a)(1), after fighting broke out between various factions in Lebanon and two Marines were killed. The level of fighting heightened; and as the Marine casualties increased and the action enlarged, there were more calls in Congress for invocation of the War Powers Resolution. Several Members of Congress said the situation had changed since the President's first report and introduced legislation that took various approaches. Senator Charles Mathias introduced S.J.Res. 159 stating that the time limit specified in the War Powers Resolution had begun on August 31, 1983, and authorizing the forces to remain in Lebanon for a period of 120 days after the expiration of the 60-day period. Representative Thomas Downey introduced H.J.Res. 348 directing the President to report under Section 4(a)(1) of the War Powers Resolution. Senator Robert Byrd introduced S.J.Res. 163 finding that Section 4(a)(1) of the War Powers Resolution applied to the present circumstances in Lebanon. The House Appropriations Committee approved an amendment to the continuing resolution for FY1984 (H.J.Res. 367), sponsored by Representative Clarence Long, providing that after 60 days, funds could not be "obligated or expended for peacekeeping activities in Lebanon by United States Armed Forces," unless the President had submitted a report under Section 4(a)(1) of the War Powers Resolution. A similar amendment was later rejected by the full body, but it reminded the Administration of possible congressional actions. On September 20, 1983, congressional leaders and President Reagan agreed on a compromise resolution invoking Section 4(a)(1) of the War Powers Resolution and authorizing the Marines to remain for 18 months. The Multinational Force in Lebanon Resolution became the first legislation to be handled under the expedited procedures of the War Powers Resolution. On September 28 the House passed H.J.Res. 364 by a vote of 270 to 161. On September 29 the Senate passed S.J.Res. 159 by a vote of 54 to 46. The House accepted the Senate bill by a vote of 253 to 156 later the same day. The President signed the joint resolution into law on October 12, 1983. As passed, the joint resolution contained four occurrences that would terminate the authorization before eighteen months: (1) the withdrawal of all foreign forces from Lebanon, unless the President certified continued U.S. participation was required to accomplish specified purposes; (2) the assumption by the United Nations or the Government of Lebanon of the responsibilities of the Multinational Force; (3) the implementation of other effective security arrangements; or (4) the withdrawal of all other countries from participation in the Multinational Force. Congress also determined in the joint resolution that the requirements of Section 4(a)(1) of the War Powers Resolution became operative on August 29, 1983.[28]

In a statement made on signing S.J.Res. 159 on October 12, 1983, President Reagan expressed appreciation for the support for the U.S. presence and policies in Lebanon he believed were embodied in the legislation. He sharply differed, however, with various "findings, determinations, and assertions" by the Congress on certain matters. He stated his concerns about the practical problems associated with Section 4(a)(1) of the War Powers

Resolution, and the wisdom and constitutionality of Section 5(b). President Reagan noted that in signing the Lebanon resolution it was important for him to state

> that I do not and cannot cede any of the authority vested in me under the Constitution as President and as Commander in Chief of United States Armed Forces. Nor should my signing be viewed as any acknowledgment that the President's constitutional authority can be impermissibly infringed by statute, that congressional authorization would be required if and when the period specified in section 5(b) of the War Powers Resolution might be deemed to have been triggered and the period had expired, or that section 6 of the Multinational Force in Lebanon Resolution may be interpreted to revise the constitutional authority to deploy United States Armed Forces.[29]

Iraq 1991

On August 2, 1990, Iraqi troops under the direction of President Saddam Hussein invaded Kuwait, seized its oil fields, installed a new government in Kuwait City, and moved toward the border with Saudi Arabia. A week after the invasion, on August 9, President George H.W. Bush reported to Congress "consistent with the War Powers Resolution" that he had deployed U.S. armed forces to the region prepared to take action with others to deter further Iraqi aggression. He noted that he did not believe involvement in hostilities was imminent. Throughout the rest of 1990, President Bush continued to work to establish an international coalition opposed to Iraq's aggression, while continuing to deploy additional U.S. military reinforcements into Saudi Arabia and the Persian Gulf region. By the end of the year approximately 350,000 U.S. forces had been deployed to the area.[30]

As the prospect of a war without congressional authorization increased, on November 20, 1990, Representative Ron Dellums and 44 other Democratic Members of Congress sought a judicial order enjoining the President from offensive military operations in connection with Operation Desert Shield unless he consulted with and obtained an authorization from Congress. On December 13, Judge Harold Greene of the federal district court in Washington, D.C. denied the injunction, holding that the controversy was not ripe for judicial resolution because a majority of Congress had not sought relief and the executive branch had not shown sufficient commitment to a definitive course of action.[31]

By January, 1991, President Bush had secured the support of the United Nations and an international coalition to use force, if necessary, to free Kuwait from Iraqi occupation. U.N. Resolution 678 of November 29, 1990, authorized all U.N. member states "to use all necessary means" to implement various U.N. resolutions seeking to end Iraqi occupation of Kuwait. It set a January 15, 1991 deadline for Iraq to implement fully all relevant U.N. resolutions relating to its invasion of Kuwait. On January 8, 1991, President George H.W. Bush, in a letter to the congressional leaders, requested a congressional resolution supporting the use of all necessary means to implement U.N. Security Council Resolution 678. He stated that he was "determined to do whatever is necessary to protect America's security" and that he could "think of no better way than for Congress to express its support for the President at this critical time." It is noteworthy that the President's request for a resolution was a request for congressional "support" for his undertaking in the Persian Gulf, not for "authority" to engage in the military operation. In a press conference on January 9, 1991, President Bush reinforced this distinction in response to questions about the use of force resolution being debated in Congress. He was asked whether he thought he needed the resolution, and if he lost on it would he feel bound by that decision. President Bush in response stated: "I don't think I need it.... I feel that I have the authority to fully implement the United Nations resolutions." He added that he felt that he had "the constitutional authority— many attorneys having so advised me."[32]

On January 12, 1991, both houses passed the "Authorization for Use of Military Force Against Iraq Resolution." Section 2(a) of that joint resolution authorized the President to use U.S. Armed Forces pursuant to U.N. Security Council Resolution 678 to achieve implementation of the earlier Security Council resolutions. Section 2(b) required as a precondition that the President would first have to report to Congress that the United States had used all appropriate diplomatic and other peaceful means to obtain compliance by Iraq with the Security Council resolution and that those efforts had not been successful. Section 2(c) stated that it constituted specific statutory authorization within the meaning of Section 5(b) of the War Powers Resolution. Section 3 required the President to report every 60 days on efforts to obtain compliance of Iraq with the U.N. Security Council resolution.[33]

On signing H.J.Res. 77 into law, President Bush said the following:

> As I made clear to congressional leaders at the outset, my request for congressional support did not, and my signing this resolution does not, constitute any change in the long-standing positions of the executive branch on either the President's constitutional authority to use the Armed Forces to defend vital U.S. interests or the constitutionality of the War Powers Resolution.

He added that he was pleased that "differences on these issues between the President and many in the Congress have not prevented us from uniting in a common objective."[34] On January16, 1991, President Bush made the determination required by P.L. 102-1 that diplomatic means had not and would not compel Iraq to withdraw from Kuwait. On January 18, he reported to Congress "consistent with the War Powers Resolution" that he had directed U.S. forces to commence combat operations on January 16.[35]

Terrorist Attacks against the United States (World Trade Center and the Pentagon) 2001

On September 11, 2001, terrorists hijacked four U.S. commercial airliners, crashing two into the twin towers of the World Trade Center in New York City, and another into the Pentagon building in Arlington, Virginia. The fourth plane crashed in Shanksville, Pennsylvania near Pittsburgh, after passengers struggled with the highjackers for control of the aircraft. The death toll from these incidents was nearly 3,000. President George W. Bush characterized these attacks as more than acts of terror. "They were acts of war," he said. He added that "freedom and democracy are under attack," and he asserted that the United States would use "all of our resources to conquer this enemy."[36]

In the days immediately after the September 11 attacks, the President consulted with the leaders of Congress on appropriate steps to take to deal with the situation confronting the United States. One of the things that emerged from discussions was the concept of a joint resolution of the Congress authorizing the President to take military steps to deal with the parties responsible for the attacks on the United States. Between September 13 and 14, draft language of such a resolution was discussed and negotiated by the President's representatives and the House and Senate leadership of both parties. Other members of both Houses suggested language for consideration. On Friday, September 14, 2001, the text of a joint resolution was introduced. It was first considered and passed by the Senate in the morning of September 14, as Senate Joint Resolution 23, by a vote of 98-0. The House of Representatives passed it later that evening, by a vote of 420-1, after tabling an identical resolution, H.J.Res. 64, and rejecting a motion to recommit by Representative John Tierney that would have had the effect, if passed and enacted, of requiring a report from the President on his actions under the resolution every 60 days.[37]

President Bush signed the measure into law on September 18, 2001.[38] The joint resolution authorizes the President

> to use all necessary and appropriate force against those nations, organizations, or persons he determines planned, authorized, committed, or aided the terrorist attacks that occurred on September 11, 2001, or harbored such organizations or persons, in order to prevent any future acts of international terrorism against the United States by such nations, organizations or persons.

The joint resolution further states that Congress declares that this resolution is intended to "constitute specific statutory authorization within the meaning of section 5(b) of the War Powers Resolution." Finally, the joint resolution also states that "[n]othing in this resolution supersedes any requirement of the War Powers Resolution."

A notable feature of P.L. 107-40 is that, unlike all other major legislation authorizing the use of military force by the President, this joint resolution authorizes military force against not only nations but also organizations and persons linked to the September 11, 2001, attacks on the United States. This authorization of military action against organizations and persons is unprecedented in American history, with the scope of its reach yet to be determined. The authorization of use of force against unnamed nations is more consistent with some previous instances where authority was given to act against unnamed states as appropriate when they became aggressors or took military action against the United States or its citizens.

President George W. Bush in signing S.J.Res. 23 on September 18, 2001, stated that the Congress had acted "wisely, decisively, and in the finest traditions of our country." He thanked the "leadership of both Houses for their role in expeditiously passing this historic joint resolution." He noted that he had had the "benefit of meaningful consultations with members of the Congress" since the September 11 attacks and that he would "continue to consult closely with them as our Nation responds to this threat to our peace and security." President Bush also asserted that S.J.Res. 23 "recognized the authority of the President under the Constitution to take action to deter and prevent acts of terrorism against the United States." He also stated that "in signing this resolution, I maintain the longstanding position of the executive branch regarding the President's constitutional authority to use force, including the Armed Forces of the United States, and regarding the constitutionality of the War Powers Resolution."[39]

The Bush Administration interpreted P.L. 107-40 broadly, to confirm the President's authority as Commander-in-Chief to conduct antiterrorism operations anywhere in the world, including within the United States.[40] In 2004, the Supreme Court affirmed the President's powers to detain "enemy combatants" captured in Afghanistan as part of the necessary force authorized by Congress, but found that detainees could challenge their detention in federal court.[41] In light of the Supreme Court decisions, the Bush Administration interpreted the joint resolution to authorize any measures that can be characterized as fundamental incidents of the conduct of war, even where such measures are otherwise prohibited by statute (at least so long as the statute in question contemplates a statutory exception). Thus, the Administration cited the joint resolution to support the President's power to detain persons he has deemed to be "enemy combatants" (whether citizens or aliens and without regard to the location or circumstances of their capture)[42] and to conduct electronic surveillance of communications within the United States without following the procedures prescribed in FISA.[43] The Supreme Court in 2006 held that P.L. 107-40 does not override the Uniform Code of Military Justice (UCMJ) as it pertains to the trial of captured combatants for violations of the law of war.[44]

Authorization for Use of Force against Iraq 2002

In the summer of 2002, the Bush Administration made public its views regarding what it deemed a significant threat to U.S. interests and security posed by the prospect that Iraq had or was acquiring weapons of mass destruction. Senior members of the Bush Administration cited a number of violations of U.N. Security Council resolutions by Iraq regarding the obligation imposed at the end of the Gulf War in 1991 to end its chemical, biological and nuclear weapons programs. On September 4, 2002, President Bush met with congressional leadership and stated that he would seek congressional support, in the near future, for action deemed necessary to deal with the threat posed to the United States by the regime of Saddam Hussein. The President also indicated that he would speak to the United Nations shortly and set out his concerns about Iraq.

On September 12, 2002, President Bush addressed the U.N. General Assembly, explaining U.S. concerns about Iraq's actions since the end of the 1991 Gulf War, including numerous instances when Iraq had violated various U.N. Security Council resolutions, including those related to disarmament. He stated that the United States would work with the U.N. Security Council to address the threat to international peace and security posed by Iraq. He emphasized, however, that if Iraq refused to fulfill its obligations to comply with U.N. Security Council resolutions, the United States would see that those resolutions were enforced.[45]

Subsequently, on September 19, 2002, the White House proposed legislation to authorize the use of military force against Iraq. This draft would have authorized the President to use military force not only against Iraq but "to restore international peace and security in the region." Subsequently introduced as S.J.Res. 45 on September 26, the Senate from October 3 to October 11 debated the desirability, necessity, and scope of the proposed legislation.

The President's proposal was not formally introduced in the House. Instead, Speaker of the House Dennis Hastert and Minority Leader Richard Gephardt introduced H.J.Res. 114 on October 2, 2002, which included generally accepted modifications to the President's proposal. The House International Relations Committee reported out a slightly amended version of the joint resolution on October 7, 2002 (H.Rept. 107-721). The House adopted the rule governing debate on the joint resolution (H.Res. 474) on October 8, 2002; and debated the measure until October 10, when it passed H.J.Res. 114 by a vote of 296-133. Subsequently, the Senate passed the House version of H.J.Res. 114 on October 11 by a vote of 77-23, and President Bush signed the Authorization for Use of Military Force against Iraq Resolution of 2002 into law on October 16, 2002.[46]

In signing H.J.Res. 114 into law, President Bush stated that by passing this legislation the Congress had demonstrated that "the United States speaks with one voice on the threat to international peace and security posed by Iraq." He added that the legislation carried an important message that "Iraq will either comply with all U.N. resolutions, rid itself of weapons of mass destruction, and ... its support for terrorists, or will be compelled to do so." While the President noted he had sought a "resolution of support" from Congress to use force against Iraq, and appreciated receiving that support, he also stated that "... my request for it did not, and my signing this resolution does not, constitute any change in the long-standing positions of the executive branch on either the President's constitutional authority to use force to deter, prevent, or respond to aggression or other threats to U.S. interests or on the constitutionality of the War Powers Resolution."

President Bush went on to state that on the "important question of the threat posed by Iraq," his views and goals and those of the Congress were the same. He further observed that he had extensive consultations with the Congress in the past months, and that he looked forward to "continuing close consultation in the months ahead." He stated his intent to submit written reports to Congress every 60 days on matters "relevant to this resolution."[47]

The central element of P.L. 107-243 is the authorization for the President to use the armed forces of the United States "as he determines to be necessary and appropriate in order to—(1) defend the national security of the United States against the continuing threat posed by Iraq; and (2) enforce all relevant United Nations Security Council resolutions regarding Iraq."

As predicates for the use of force, the statute requires the President to communicate to Congress his determination that the use of diplomatic and other peaceful means will not "adequately protect the United States ... or ... lead to enforcement of all relevant United Nations Security Council resolutions" and that the use of force is "consistent" with the battle against terrorism. Like P.L. 102-1 and P.L. 107-40, the statute declares that it is "intended to constitute specific statutory authorization within the meaning of section 5(b) of the War Powers Resolution." It also requires the President to make periodic reports to Congress "on matters relevant to this joint resolution." Finally, the statute expresses Congress's "support" for the efforts of the President to obtain "prompt and decisive action by the Security Council" to enforce Iraq's compliance with all relevant Security Council resolutions.

P.L. 107-243 clearly confers broad authority on the President to use force. In contrast to P.L. 102-1, the authority granted is not limited to the implementation of previously adopted Security Council resolutions concerning Iraq but includes "all relevant ... resolutions." Thus, it appears to have incorporated resolutions concerning Iraq that were subsequently adopted by the Security Council at least up to the expiration of the UN mandate on December 31, 2008, as well as those resolutions adopted prior to the enactment of P.L. 107-243. The authority also appears to extend beyond compelling Iraq's disarmament to implementing the full range of concerns expressed in those resolutions. Unlike P.L. 107-40, the President's exercise of the authority granted is not dependent upon a finding that Iraq was associated in some direct way with the September 11, 2001, attacks on the United States. Moreover, the authority conferred can be used for the broad purpose of defending "the national security of the United States against the continuing threat posed by Iraq." Nevertheless, P.L. 107-243 is narrower than P.L.

107-40, as well as President Bush's originally proposed authorization, in that it limits the authorization for the use of force to Iraq. It also requires as a predicate for the use of force that the President determine that peaceful means cannot suffice and that the use of force against Iraq is consistent with the battle against terrorism.[48] P.L. 107-243 further limits the force used to that which the President determines is "necessary and appropriate." Finally, as with P.L. 107-40, the statutory authorization for use of force granted to the President in P.L. 107-243 is not dependent for its exercise upon prior authorization by the U.N. Security Council.

The Bush and Obama Administrations relied on P.L. 107-243's authorities to maintain the presence of U.S. armed forces and to conduct military operations in Iraq until the withdrawal of U.S. armed forces in December 2011. After initial invasion operations and the removal of the Saddam Hussein regime from power, U.S. military operations in Iraq continued under P.L. 107- 243 authority. Both the Bush and Obama Administrations considered Iraq a continuing threat to U.S. national security interests; in addition, U.S. armed forces were enforcing relevant U.N. Security Council resolutions regarding Iraq. Relevant U.N. resolutions included the creation in 2003 of the Multinational Force in Iraq (MNF-I), of which U.S. armed forces made up the significant majority. The United Nations Security Council ultimately terminated the MNF-I on December 1, 2008.[49] Beginning January 1, 2009, U.S. armed forces remained in Iraq pursuant to an agreement between Iraq and the United States that set the date for withdrawal of such forces on December 31, 2011.[50] At the time of the U.S.-Iraq agreement, it was argued that the end of the U.N. mandate required a new authorization for continued U.S. military presence in Iraq, and that the agreement itself needed congressional approval either by submission to the Senate as a treaty for advice and consent, or by general legislative approval.[51] Congress continued to provide funds for military operations in Iraq, however, and legislative efforts to repeal P.L. 107-243 or otherwise bring about an end to the U.S. military presence in Iraq did not succeed.[52]

P.L. 107-243 does not include provision for automatic termination of its use of force authorization, and Congress has not repealed the legislation. Thus P.L. 107-243 remains current U.S. law, although its continued effectiveness is questionable. Arguably, the President could rely on P.L. 107-243 to reintroduce U.S. armed forces into Iraq if he determined that Iraq once again posed a threat to U.S. national security, or in order to enforce relevant U.N. resolutions, as the legislation provides in its authorization language. Nevertheless, any presidential decision to again utilize the authority for use of military force in P.L. 107-243 would likely meet renewed resistance from some Members of Congress, as well as other observers who have argued for repeal of open-ended use of force authorizations such as this.

IMPLICATIONS UNDER INTERNATIONAL LAW

Traditionally, peace and war have been deemed under international law to be distinctive forms of relations between states. Thus, peace has been defined as "a condition in which States maintain order and justice, solve their problems by cooperation, and eliminate violence. It is a condition in which States respect each other's sovereignty and equality, refrain from intervention and the threat or use of force and cooperate with one another in accordance with the treaties which they have concluded."[53]

War, in contrast, has been described as "a condition of armed hostility between States,"[54] "a contention, through the use of armed force, between states, undertaken for the purpose of overpowering another."[55] War has been said to terminate or suspend the laws and customs that prevail in peacetime and to substitute for them the laws of war. Under the traditional laws of war enemy combatants can be killed, prisoners of war taken, the enemy's property seized or destroyed, enemy aliens interned, and other measures necessary to subdue the enemy and impose the will of the warring state taken.[56] Moreover, the existence of a state of war traditionally has been deemed to terminate diplomatic and commercial relations and most of the treaty obligations existing between the warring States.[57] A state of war also has brought into play the law of neutrality with respect to relations between the belligerent and non-belligerent States.

In this traditional understanding a declaration of war has been deemed, in and of itself, to have the effect of creating a state of war and changing the relationship between the states involved from one of peace to one of war. That has been the case even if no hostilities actually occur. Some question exists as to whether international law traditionally deemed a declaration of war to be a necessary prerequisite to the existence of a state of war;[58] but it is clear that under international law a declaration of war has been viewed as "creating the legal status of war ... [and giving] evidence that peace has been transmuted into war, and that the law of war has replaced the law of peace."[59]

Authorizations for the use of force, in contrast, have not been seen as automatically creating a state of war under international law. The U.S. Court of Claims, in construing the statutes authorizing the limited use of force against France in 1798, described how their effects differed from those that followed in the wake of a war:

> [Our naval vessels] might seize armed vessels only, and only those armed vessels which had already committed depredations, or those which were on our coast for the purpose of committing depredations, and they might retake an American vessel captured by such an armed vessel. This statute is a fair illustration of the class of laws enacted at this time; they directed suspension of commercial relations until the end of the next session of Congress, not indefinitely ...; they gave power to the President to apprehend the subjects of hostile nations whenever he should make "public proclamation" of war ..., and no such proclamation was made; they gave him authority to instruct our armed vessels to seize French "armed," not merchant, vessels ..., together with contingent authority to augment the army in case war should break out or in case of imminent danger of invasion....
>
> If war existed, why authorize our armed vessels to seize French armed vessels? War itself gave that right, as well as the right to seize merchantmen which the statutes did not permit. If war existed why empower the President to apprehend foreign enemies? War itself placed that duty upon him as a necessary and inherent incident of military command. Why, if there was war, should a suspension of commercial intercourse be authorized, for what more complete suspension of that intercourse could there be than the very fact of war?
>
> There was no declaration of war; the tribunals of each country were open to the other—an impossibility were war in progress; diplomatic and commercial intercourse were admittedly suspended; but during many years there was no intercourse between England and Mexico, which were not at war; there was retaliation and reprisal, but such retaliations and reprisals have often occurred between nations at peace; there was a near approach to war, but at no time was one of the nations turned into an enemy of the other in such manner that every citizen of the one became the enemy of every citizen of the

other; finally, there was not that kind of war which abrogated treaties and wiped out, at least temporarily, all pending rights and contracts, individual and national.[60]

Whether this traditional understanding of war and of the effect of a declaration of war continues to be viable is a matter of considerable dispute among scholars. The right of a state to initiate war, many contend, has been outlawed by such international agreements as the Kellogg-Briand Peace Pact and the Charter of the United Nations. In the Kellogg-Briand Peace Pact,[61] for instance, the Parties stated that they "condemn recourse to war for the solution of international controversies, and renounce it as an instrument of national policy in their relations with one another."[62] After World War II the Nuremberg Tribunal gave teeth to this commitment by ruling that the Pact rendered aggressive war illegal under international law and makes those who plan and wage such a war guilty of a crime.[63] The Charter of the United Nations, in turn, states one of its purposes to be "to save succeeding generations from the scourge of war," and it requires its Members "to refrain from the threat or use of force against the territorial integrity or political independence of any State, or in any other manner inconsistent with the Purposes of the United Nations."[64] Moreover, it provides for a system of collective security through the Security Council as the primary means of maintaining or restoring international peace and security.[65] Both instruments, it is contended, recognize that the concept of war as a legal right of states, except in self-defense,[66] has been superseded. (The United States, of course, is a Party not only to the Charter but also to the Pact, and it still regards the latter as continuing to be in force.[67]) Whether the traditional concept of war remains valid has been further complicated by the increasing participation in armed conflict of non-State actors such as insurgents, freedom fighters, and terrorists.

The clarity of the consequences of a state of war in traditional international law has also become muddied in the modern era. Most States since 1945, even when engaged in armed conflict, have resisted describing the conflict as a war.[68] States so engaged have not always automatically terminated diplomatic and commercial relationships,[69] and the discontinuance of treaty obligations has increasingly been deemed to require a treaty-by-treaty examination.[70] Moreover, conventions that attempt to regulate the means used to wage war, such as the Hague Conventions and other more recent agreements,[71] and those that attempt to ameliorate the consequences of war for certain categories of persons, such as the Geneva Conventions,[72] are deemed to apply to armed conflicts regardless of what label the Parties attach to them. A state of war still gives rise to "a mutual right to kill in battle,"[73] triggers application of the various conventions regulating the means of waging war as well as of the general principles of necessity and proportionality, and brings into play the Geneva Conventions. But its other legal consequences seemingly have become less determinate.

Perhaps as a consequence of these developments, declarations of war have fallen into disuse and are virtually never issued in modern conflicts. One commentator asserts that since 1945 "[t]here are no cases of a formal declaration of war having been delivered by one state to another through diplomatic channels...."[74] As noted above, the United States last declared war in 1942 against Rumania and has since adopted only authorizations for the use of force.

Thus, declarations of war may have become anachronistic in contemporary international law. The legal right of States to engage in war has seemingly become constrained (for other than defensive purposes), and the most salient international laws regarding the means of waging war and the protection of certain categories of persons apply to the circumstance of armed conflict regardless of whether war has been declared. That circumstance can arise in the wake of an authorization to use force as well. States likely still retain a right to issue declarations of war, at least in exercising the right of self-defense; and such a declaration seemingly would still automatically create a state of war. But it is not clear that the legal consequences under international law that would flow from a declaration differ dramatically from those that occur if an armed conflict comes into being pursuant to an authorization for the use of force.

IMPLICATIONS UNDER DOMESTIC LAW

Early American jurisprudence drew a distinction between general, or perfect, war and limited, or imperfect, war, and understood a declaration of war under Article I, Section 8, of the Constitution to commit the nation to a general war. Justice Washington, in *Bas v. Tinghy*,[75] described the distinction as follows:

> It may, I believe, be safely laid down, that every contention by force between two nations, in external matters, under the authority of their respective governments, is not only war, but public war. If it be declared in form, it is called *solemn*, and is of the perfect kind; because one whole nation is at war with another whole nation; and *all* the members of the nation declaring war are authorised to commit hostilities against all the members of the other, in every place, and under every circumstance. In such a war all the members act under a general authority, and all the rights and consequences of war attach to their condition.
>
> ... [H]ostilities may subsist between two nations more confined in its nature and extent; being limited as to places, persons, and things; and this is more properly termed *imperfect war*; because not solemn, and because those who are authorised to commit hostilities, act under special authority, and can go no farther than to the extent of their commission. Still, however, it is *public war*, because it is an external contention, by force, between some of the members of the two nations, authorised by the legitimate powers.[76]

Justice Chase, more simply, stated: "Congress is empowered to declare a general war, or congress may wage a limited war; limited in place, in objects, and in time."[77]

Thus, at least in the 18th and 19th centuries, authorizations for the use of force were understood to be included within Congress's power to declare war and to have narrower legal consequences than declarations of war. Declarations were reserved for general war against particular countries and empowered the President "to use the whole land and naval force of the United States" (United Kingdom in 1812), "to employ the militia, naval, and military forces of the United States" (Mexico in 1846), or "to use the entire land and naval forces of the United States" (Spain in 1898) to prosecute the war. Authorizations, in contrast, allowed the President to use the American navy against the vessels of France, the Bey of Tripoli, and the Dey of Algiers, or against piracy generally.

In the modern era authorizations have sometimes been quite broad[78]; and some have, arguably, been equivalent in scope to a declaration of war. But the domestic legal consequences that flow from such authorizations still are substantially more limited than those that would flow from a declaration of war.

Both declarations of war and authorizations for the use of force have the effect of eliminating the time limits otherwise imposed on the President's use of the armed forces under the War Powers Resolution; and both may legitimate the killing of foreign officials that might otherwise be prohibited by the executive order on assassinations. The capture of enemy combatants on the battlefield and their detention until hostilities have subsided is implied in an authorization to use ground forces,[79] just as it would be included in a formal declaration of war.

But a declaration of war automatically brings into effect a number of statutes that confer special powers on the President and the Executive Branch, especially concerning measures that have domestic effect. A declaration, for instance, activates statutes that empower the President to interdict all trade with the enemy, order manufacturing plants to produce armaments and seize them if they refuse, control transportation systems in order to give the military priority use, and command communications systems to give priority to the military. A declaration triggers the Alien Enemy Act, which gives the President substantial discretionary authority over nationals of an enemy state who are in the United States. It activates special authorities to use electronic surveillance for purposes of gathering foreign intelligence information without a court order under the Foreign Intelligence Surveillance Act. It automatically extends enlistments in the armed forces until the end of the war, can make the Coast Guard part of the Navy, gives the President substantial discretion over the appointment and reappointment of commanders, and allows the military priority use of the natural resources on the public lands and the continental shelf.

An authorization for the use of force does not automatically trigger any of these standby statutory authorities. Some of them can come into effect if a state of war in fact comes into being after an authorization for the use of force is enacted; and the great majority of them, including many of the most sweeping ones, can be activated if the President chooses to issue a proclamation of a national emergency. But an authorization for the use of force, in itself and in contrast to a declaration of war, does not trigger any of these standby authorities.

On the other hand, the authorization to use force in response to the terrorist attacks of 2001 has been asserted as legal authority for executive actions in the domestic context, the validity of which remains unresolved. The executive branch asserted that the authorization permits detention without trial of persons arrested in the United States on suspicion of Al Qaeda related terrorism, which it regarded as bolstered by the Supreme Court's Hamdi decision finding the detention of enemy combatants captured in Afghanistan to be authorized as "a fundamental incident of waging war."[80] While there is limited authority to support military trials of enemy soldiers captured within the United States, in previous wars the Alien Enemy Act would likely have been the chief means of interning suspected enemies domestically.[81] Under the executive branch view, the authorization to use force could be construed as broader than a declaration of war in that it is seen to authorize detention powers without any of the few rules or restrictions specified in the Alien Enemy Act, and to authorize the detention of U.S. citizens as an exception to the Non-Detention Act.[82] Similarly, the executive branch argued that the authorization to use force must also be read to permit the conduct of certain types of electronic surveillance outside of the strictures of the Foreign Intelligence Surveillance Act, even though that act provides for only a two-week exception triggered by a declaration of war.[83] Accordingly, it is possible that any similarly broad authorization to use force may be read to authorize any power that may properly be regarded as "a fundamental incident of waging war" under the circumstances, at least as implied exceptions to statutes that admit of statutory exception.

The following subsections give an overview of some of the more salient domestic legal consequences of a declaration of war or authorization for the use of force. They are followed by a section setting forth a detailed list of the standby statutory authorities that can be triggered by a declaration of war, a state or war, and/or a proclamation of national emergency.

The War Powers Resolution

Both a declaration of war and an authorization for the use of force have significant implications with respect to the War Powers Resolution (WPR).[84] The WPR was enacted over President Nixon's veto in 1973 purportedly to restore a congressional role in authorizing the use of force that was thought by many to have been lost in the Cold War and the Vietnam War. To that end the WPR mandates that the President consult with the Congress "in every possible instance" prior to introducing U.S. armed forces into hostilities and regularly afterwards. Section 4(a) of the WPR further requires the President, "in the absence of a declaration of war," to report to Congress within 48 hours in any case in which United States Armed Forces are introduced—

(1) into hostilities or into situations where imminent involvement in hostilities is clearly indicated by the circumstances;
(2) into the territory, airspace or waters of a foreign nation, while equipped for combat, except for deployments which relate solely to supply, replacement, repair, or training of such forces; or
(3) in numbers which substantially enlarge United States Armed Forces equipped for combat already located in a foreign nation.

Section 5(b) of the Resolution, in turn, requires that if a report has been submitted or was required to be submitted under Section 4(a)(1) above, the President shall terminate the involvement of U.S. forces unless Congress

(1) has declared war or has enacted a specific authorization for such use of United States Armed Forces;
(2) has extended by law such sixty-day period, or
(3) is physically unable to meet as a result of an armed attack upon the United States.[85]

Thus, congressional enactment of either a declaration of war or an authorization for the use of force pursuant to Section 5(b) has the effect of tolling the 60-90 day withdrawal mandate of the WPR.

Each of the last three authorizations for the use of force enacted—the 1991 Gulf War authorization, the September 18, 2001, authorization with respect to terrorist attacks, and the October 16, 2002, authorization with respect to Iraq—have explicitly stated that they constitute the authorization required by Section 5(b) of the WPR. Each, in other words, has tolled the 60-90 day limitation that the WPR otherwise would impose on the use of military force by the President. All three authorizations have further specified that "[n]othing in this resolution supersedes any requirement of the War Powers Resolution." That appears to mean that the consultation and reporting requirements of the WPR still apply.

Trading with the Enemy Act and the International Emergency Economic Powers Act

Two related statutes, the Trading With the Enemy Act[86] (TWEA) and the International Emergency Economic Powers Act[87] (IEEPA), grant the President extraordinary powers to control foreign- owned property and foreign trade transactions with designated countries under certain exceptional circumstances. TWEA comes into effect upon a declaration of war or the existence of a state of war, while IEEPA is triggered solely by a presidential declaration of national emergency. Neither statute is triggered by an authorization for the use of force (unless, in the case of TWEA, the authorization eventually leads to the existence of a state of war). IEEPA is the authority most commonly invoked to freeze or block the assets of foreign states, companies, or individuals located within the jurisdiction of the United States.

Until 1977 the broad range of economic authorities granted by TWEA could be exercised both in times of war and in times of national emergency. However, in 1977 Congress limited the prospective application of TWEA to times of declared or undeclared war only and enacted IEEPA to apply during times of a national emergency declared by the President. Under TWEA the President may

(A) investigate, regulate, or prohibit, any transactions in foreign exchange, transfers of credit or payments or payments between, by, through, or to any banking institution, and the importing, exporting, hoarding, melting, or earmarking of gold or silver coin or bullion, currency or securities, and

(B) investigate, regulate, direct and compel, nullify, void, prevent or prohibit, any acquisition, holding, withholding, use, transfer, withdrawal, transportation, importation or exportation of, or dealing in, or exercising any right, power, privilege with respect to, or transactions involving, any property in which any foreign country or a national thereof has any interest, by any person, or with respect to any property, subject to the jurisdiction of the United States; and any property or interest of any foreign country or national thereof shall vest, when, as, and upon the terms, directed by the President, in such agency or person as may be designated from time to time by the President, and upon such terms and conditions as the President may prescribe such interest or property shall be held, used, administered, liquidated, sold, or otherwise dealt with in the interest of and for the benefit of the United States....[88]

IEEPA replicates many of TWEA's powers to regulate international transactions,[89] but it does not include TWEA authorities relative to purely domestic transactions, the regulation of bullion, and seizure of records.[90] It also does not contain TWEA's general authority to take title to foreign assets. But Congress did amend IEEPA in the "USA PATRIOT Act" in 2001 to authorize the President to confiscate and take title to

> any property, subject to the jurisdiction of the United States, of any foreign person, foreign organization, or foreign country that he determines has planned, authorized, aided or engaged in ... hostilities or attacks against the United States....[91]

Congress further amended both IEEPA and TWEA in the "Terrorism Risk Insurance Act of 2002" to provide that the assets of foreign terrorist states that have been frozen in the U.S. pursuant to either statute may be used to satisfy certain civil judgments against them.[92]

As noted, IEEPA is triggered solely by a declaration of national emergency, while TWEA applies in time of war. Thus, TWEA is not dependent upon a declaration of war, but it can be triggered by such a declaration. Neither appears to be triggered by an authorization for the use of force, unless and until, in the case of TWEA, a state of war actually develops.

Other Economic Authorities

As noted, a declaration of war gives the President full authority over trade relations with the enemy. Other statutes triggered by a declaration give the President the authority to order plants to convert to the production of armaments and to seize those that refuse to do so,[93] to take control of the Tennessee Valley Authority in order to manufacture explosives or for other military purposes,[94] to assume control of transportation systems for military purposes,[95] to condemn land for military uses,[96] to have the right of first refusal over natural resources,[97] and to take control of communications facilities.[98] It also gives the President full power over agricultural exports.[99] An authorization for the use of force, in itself, does not trigger any of these authorities.

Alien Enemy Act

First enacted in 1798, the Alien Enemy Act[100] broadly authorizes the President to deport, detain, or otherwise condition the stay of alien enemies in the U.S. in cases of "declared war" or "any invasion or predatory incursion ... perpetrated, attempted, or threatened against the territory of the United States by any foreign nation or government...." The act implements the internationally recognized right of every nation to protect itself during times of war from individuals whose primary allegiance lies with a hostile foreign power. Given this premise, the Supreme Court has observed that "[e]xecutive power over enemy aliens, undelayed and unhampered by litigation, has been deemed, throughout our history, essential to war-time security."[101]

The President must publicly proclaim the event that gives rise to activation of the act and make regulations regarding the treatment of those aliens. But once he does so, his power to "apprehend, restrain, secure, and remove" enemy aliens extends to all "natives, citizens, denizens, or subjects of the hostile nation or government, being of the age of fourteen years and upward, who shall be in the United States and not actually naturalized."[102] The President may intern or remove enemy aliens or set lesser restraints on them, and may adopt any "regulations which are found necessary in the premises and for the public safety."[103] Thus, President Woodrow Wilson, for example, barred alien enemies during World War I from possessing firearms and explosives, coming within a half a mile of a military facility or munitions factory, residing in certain areas, possessing certain communications equipment, and publishing certain types of materials. President Franklin D. Roosevelt authorized similar restrictions during World War II and, additionally, set up over 100 community hearing boards to make internment recommendations to the Attorney General.[104]

The procedural rights of aliens who are subject to the Alien Enemy Act are drastically restricted compared with those that aliens otherwise enjoy, including hearing rights under the removal provisions of the Immigration and Nationality Act.[105] The scope of judicial review is equally circumscribed.[106] Among the few rights recognized under the act, alien enemies subjected to removal may, if not chargeable with "actual hostility" or other crime against public safety, be entitled to the time allowed by applicable treaty or order to wind up his or her affairs here.[107] A very limited right to judicial review under a petition for a writ of habeas corpus also is recognized. Generally, however, the power of the President to control alien enemies under the act is extraordinary.

As noted, the act does not appear to be triggered solely by an authorization for the use of force.

Criminal Law

There are a number of civilian federal criminal law provisions that apply explicitly to specified conduct in time of war. They do not appear to distinguish between circumstances involving a declaration of war and other situations in which a state of war may exist absent a declaration of war, although courts (and Congress) have in some cases construed "time of war" or "at war" to require a formal declaration by Congress. Thus, these statutes may be triggered by a declaration of war, but they also may apply in circumstances where a state of war is deemed to exist.

Consequently, these criminal prohibitions do not appear to be triggered by an authorization for the use of force, unless and until a state of war develops. These statutes include, for example:[108]

(a) 18 U.S.C.A. Section 443 (willful secreting, mutilating, obliterating or destroying records of a war contractor, that is, a holder of a prime or subcontract connected with or related to the prosecution of a war);
(b) 18 U.S.C.A. Section 757 (procuring the escape of a prisoner of war held by the United States or any of its allies or the escape of an apprehended or interned enemy alien held by the United States or its allies; aiding or assisting such escape or assisting the prisoner of war or enemy alien after his escape; or attempting or conspiring to do any of the above);
(c) 18 U.S.C.A. Section 792 (harboring or concealing persons known or believed to have committed or to be about to commit an offense under 18 U.S.C. §§793 or 794);
(d) 18 U.S.C.A. Section 793 (gathering, transmitting or losing information related to the national defense with the intent or reason to believe that it is to be used to the injury of the United States or to the benefit of a foreign nation. Includes, among other things, such actions with respect to information on any place in which any vessel, aircraft, arms, munitions, or other materials or instruments for use in time of war are being prepared, repaired, stored, or are the subject of research or development; or with respect to any prohibited place so designated by the President by proclamation in time or war or in case of national emergency in which anything for the use of the Army, Navy, or Air Force is being prepared, constructed, or stored);

(e) 18 U.S.C.A. Section 794 (gathering or delivering information relating to the national defense with the intent or reason to believe that it is to be used to the injury of the United States or to the advantage of a foreign nation. Subsection (b) deals with recording, publishing, or communicating or attempting to elicit information regarding movements, numbers, condition or disposition of Armed Forces, ships, aircraft or war materials, with the intent that the information be communicated to the enemy in time of war. It also covers communicating to the enemy in time of war information on plans or conduct of naval or military operations or defense measures.)[109]
(f) 18 U.S.C.A. Section 1038 (making a false statement, with intent to convey false or misleading information, about the death, injury, capture, or disappearance of a member of the Armed Forces of the United States during a war or armed conflict in which the United States is engaged);
(g) 18 U.S.C.A. Section 1091 (genocide in time of peace or in time of war);
(h) 18 U.S.C.A. Section 1653 (aliens who are found and taken on the sea making war against the United States or engaging in piracy against U.S. vessels or property);
(i) 18 U.S.C.A. Section 2153 (when the United States is at war or when a national emergency has been declared, willful destruction of war material, war premises, or war utilities, with intent or reason to believe that such actions may injure, interfere with, or obstruct the United States or associate nations in their war or defense activities; and conspiracy to do so);
(j) 18 U.S.C.A. Section 2154 (in times of war or national emergency, willfully producing defective war material, war premises, or war utilities with intent to injure, interfere with, or obstruct the war or defense activities of the United States or associate nations);
(k) 18 U.S.C.A. Section 2381 and U.S. Constitution, Art. 3, Sec. 3, Cl. 1 (while owing allegiance to the United States, levying war against the United States or adhering to its enemies, giving them aid and comfort. Constitution requires confession in open court or testimony of two witnesses to the same overt act to convict for treason);
(l) 18 U.S.C.A. Section 2382 (misprision of treason);
(m) 18 U.S.C.A. Section 2384 (seditious conspiracy to overthrow or destroy by force the Government of the United States or to levy war against the United States);
(n) 18 U.S.C.A. Section 2388 (willfully engaging in certain activities in time of war with intent to adversely affect armed forces of the United States or to obstruct enlistment or recruitment; conspiracy to do so; harboring a person knowing or having reason to believe that the person has engaged in such conduct);
(o) 18 U.S.C.A. Section 2389 (recruiting soldiers or sailors within U.S. jurisdiction to engage in armed hostilities against the United States); and
(p) 18 U.S.C.A. Section 2441 (war crimes).

It should also be noted that other federal and state criminal law provisions,[110] which do not draw distinctions between conduct in time of war and at other times, also apply during wartime.[111] For example, 18 U.S.C.A. Section 175 prohibits knowing development, stockpiling, acquisition, possession or retention of any biological agent, toxin, or delivery system for use as a weapon, or knowing assistance to a foreign state to do so. 18 U.S.C.A. Section 229, with certain exceptions, prohibits similar conduct with respect to chemical weapons. 18 U.S.C.A. Section 831 prohibits specific transactions or actions involving nuclear materials, while 42 U.S.C.A. Section 2284 deals with sabotage of nuclear facilities or fuel. 18 U.S.C.A. Section 2332a prohibits certain uses of weapons of mass destruction. Other explosives offenses are covered in 18 U.S.C.A. Section 844. Hostage-taking is addressed in 18 U.S.C.A. Section 1203, while kidnapping is covered by 18 U.S.C.A. Section 1201. 18 U.S.C.A. Section 1116 deals with murder or manslaughter of foreign officials, official guests, or internationally protected persons. 18 U.S.C.A. Section 1114 addresses the murder or attempted murder of federal officers and employees, including members of the uniformed services, while they are engaged in or on account of the performance of official duties.

It also covers murder or attempted murder of any person assisting an officer or employee of the United States in the performance of those duties or on account of that assistance.[112]

Statutes of limitations, which preclude prosecutions after a specific amount of time has lapsed (typically five years), may also be affected during wartime. When the United States "is at war" or Congress has authorized the use of military force within the meaning of the War Powers Resolution, the Wartime Suspension of Limitations Act ("Suspension Act"), codified at 18 U.S.C. Section 3287, extends the statute of limitations for the prosecution of certain crimes against the United States for five years beyond the termination of hostilities. Originally enacted during World War II, the Suspension Act previously extended the statute of limitations in relevant cases until three years after the end of hostilities only "when the United States is at war." One court had construed this language to refer only to a war declared by Congress, and held that the 1990-91 Persian Gulf conflict, although authorized by Congress, did not qualify.[113] Apparently also construing the phrase "is at war" to mean pursuant to a declaration of war,[114] Congress amended the provision in 2008[115] to trigger its application also upon the enactment of an authorization to use military force "as described in section 5(b) of the War Powers Resolution (50 U.S.C. 1544 (b))."[116] (The military counterpart to the provision, found in 10 U.S.C. §843(f), was not amended. It continues to suspend the applicable statute of limitations for three years beyond the end of hostilities, and applies "when the United States is at war.")

There are other criminal law provisions applicable to the military in the Uniform Code of Military Justice, 10 U.S.C.A. Sections801 *et seq.* Some of these provisions apply specifically in times of war. These will be treated separately in the subsequent section of this report on "Military Personnel."[117]

Foreign Intelligence Surveillance

The Foreign Intelligence Surveillance Act (FISA), as amended, in pertinent part, authorizes electronic surveillance, physical searches, and the use of pen registers and trap and trace devices to gather foreign intelligence information and sets out the procedures and circumstances under which each of these investigative tools may be used.[118] In the event of a declaration of war, FISA authorizes the use of each of these investigative tools to gather foreign intelligence for up to 15 days without a court order. For electronic surveillance subsequent to a declaration of war, FISA provides, at 50 U.S.C.A. Section 1811, that:

> Notwithstanding any other law, the President, through the Attorney General, may authorize electronic surveillance without a court order under this subchapter to acquire

> foreign intelligence information for a period not to exceed fifteen calendar days following a declaration of war by the Congress.

In the context of physical searches, 50 U.S.C.A. Section 1829 includes language similar to that in Section 1811:

> Notwithstanding any other provision of law, the President, through the Attorney General, may authorize physical searches without a court order under this subchapter to acquire foreign intelligence information for a period not to exceed 15 calendar days following a declaration of war by the Congress.

For pen registers and trap and trace devices, 50 U.S.C.A. Section 1844 provides that:

> Notwithstanding any other provision of law, the President, through the Attorney General, may authorize the use of a pen register or trap and trace device without a court order under this subchapter to acquire foreign intelligence information for a period not to exceed 15 calendar days following a declaration of war by Congress.

None of these provisions appears to be triggered by an authorization for the use of force or the existence of a state of war under any authority other than a congressional declaration of war.[119]

In addition to the foregoing provisions, FISA has been amended to authorize the use of these investigative tools without a court order for foreign intelligence purposes in "emergency" circumstances as determined by the Attorney General. To do so the Attorney General must (1) find that an emergency exists, (2) determine that the factual basis for the issuance of an order to approve such surveillance, physical search, or pen register or trap and trace device also exists, (3) advise a judge of the U.S. Foreign Intelligence Surveillance Court (FISC) that a decision to use the emergency authority has been made, and (4) apply to the FISC judge so notified for a court order as soon as practicable (but no later than within 72 hours in the case of an electronic surveillance or physical search or 48 hours in the case of a pen register or trap and trace device).[120] These provisions do not expressly address the question of whether such emergency procedures might be triggered either by an authorization for the use of force or by a congressional declaration of war. However, depending upon the circumstances involved, these emergency powers, or other provisions within FISA,[121] might be utilized.

Assassination

As noted in the foregoing discussion of criminal law, 18 U.S.C.A. Section 1116 makes it a crime to kill or attempt to kill a "foreign official, official guest, or internationally protected person." The term "foreign official" includes, among others, a Chief of State or the political equivalent thereof while he or she is in the United States. "Internationally protected person" covers, among others, a Chief of State or the political equivalent thereof, whenever such person is in a country other than his or her own. This criminal provision does not apply to the killing or attempted killing of an internationally protected person in his or her own country. The United States courts may exercise jurisdiction over the killing or attempted killing of internationally protected persons in violation of 18 U.S.C. Section 1116 committed outside the United States where the victim is a representative, officer, employee or agent of the United States; where a perpetrator is a U.S. national; or where an offender is later found in the United States.

In addition, Part 2.11 of Executive Order 12333 forbids any person employed by or acting on behalf of the United States Government from engaging in, or conspiring to engage in, assassination. Part 2.12 of that executive order further prohibits any agency of the Intelligence Community from participating in or requesting any person to undertake activities forbidden by the order. The executive order does not define "assassination," nor does either the criminal statute or the executive order specifically address the applicability of the prohibition to an armed conflict in which the U.S. is engaged. However, in times of war, the targeting of an enemy's command and control structures may be regarded as strategically important, is lawful under international law, likely is not intended to be barred by E.O. 12333, and does not appear to be covered by 18 U.S.C. Section 1116. Hence, a declaration of war, because it creates a state of war regardless of whether actual hostilities have occurred, arguably creates a situation where such an act is not prohibited by domestic law. Less clear is the effect of an authorization for the use of force. Once a state of war comes into existence following such an authorization, then the legal situation appears to be the same as with a declaration. But prior to that development, the legal effect of an authorization for the use of force on the assassination ban appears somewhat ambiguous.

An executive order may be revoked by the President through another executive order. To the extent that an executive order is issued pursuant to authority granted by statute, Congress may repeal it or terminate the underlying statutory authority upon which it rests. The assassination ban is part of an executive order issued by President Reagan in 1981 under both statutory and constitutional authority. The order does not indicate the nature of the authority underlying the assassination ban in particular. If one were to argue that a statutory basis for the ban exists, then one might contend that an authorization for a use of force would, by implication, modify the ban or repeal it with respect to the context in which the use of force was authorized.

The Defense Production Act of 1950

Conversely, declarations of war or authorizations for the use of force do not appear to have any particular consequences for the broad authorities conferred by the Defense Production Act of 1950 (DPA), as amended.[122] The DPA was first enacted in 1950 to mobilize the nation's productive capacity after the outbreak of the Korean War. It currently plays a key role in enabling the United States to maintain a national defense/military readiness capability that will support a rapid and effective response to any threat to U.S. national security, including "an attack on the United States." The DPA has been reauthorized and amended a number of times, most recently in 2009. The original 1950 act contained seven titles, four of which were rescinded in 1953.[123] Currently, three titles of the DPA are in effect, and they are due to expire on September 30, 2014, unless renewed.[124] The authorities contained in the act are not triggered by any particular event but are continuously available "to ensure the national defense preparedness, which is essential to national security...."[125]

Title I (Priorities and Allocations)

This title[126] provides the President with the authority to require the priority performance of defense contracts and to allocate scarce critical and strategic materials essential to the national defense. This authority may also be extended to support the military requirements of allied nations when such extension is in the U.S. national defense interest. Priority contract performance, especially as implemented with respect to industrial resources, is intended to ensure sources of supply and timely delivery of required items for defense purposes.[127]

The post-Cold War use of this authority includes the 1990-1991 operations in the Persian Gulf (Desert Shield/Storm). During this operation, such items as computer and communications equipment, Global Positioning System receivers, chemical warfare protective clothing, and medical supplies were urgently required by both U.S. and Allied nation forces. More recently, DPA authority has been used to ensure timely delivery of critically needed items to support the deployment of U.S. and NATO troops in Bosnia and nearby areas and the availability of natural gas in California's energy crisis in December, 2000, and January, 2001.

Title I contains a section that prohibits the President from exercising his priorities and allocations authority unless he makes certain findings supporting the need for such action. Additional sections provide the President with authority relating to the hoarding of designated materials, penalties for the violation of any provision of Title I, small business preferences, etc.

Title III (Expansion of Productive Capacity and Supply)

This title[128] is used only in cases where domestic sources are required and domestic firms cannot, or will not, act on their own to meet a national defense production need. Because private firms may be reluctant to invest in production capabilities for a new material unless a near-term demand for the material is relatively certain, Title III authorizes the use of financial incentives to expand defense-related productive capacity of critical components, critical technology items, and industrial resources "essential to the national defense." These financial incentives include loan guarantees, direct federal loans, purchases, purchase guarantees, and installation of equipment in contractor facilities. The authorities conferred in this title become broader in times of a national emergency declared by the President or Congress.

Title VII (General Provisions)

This title[129] includes various provisions with relevance to defense industrial preparedness. Examples include (a) Section 708, which authorizes the President to provide antitrust defenses to private firms participating in voluntary agreements aimed at solving production and distribution problems involving national defense preparedness; (b) Section 710, which establishes a National Defense Executive Reserve (NDER) composed of recognized experts from various segments of the private sector and government (except full-time federal) employees for training for possible employment in the federal government in the event of an emergency; and (c) Section 721, a provision popularly known as the "Exon-Florio Amendment," which authorizes the President to suspend or prohibit the acquisition, merger, or takeover of a domestic firm by a foreign firm if such action would threaten to impair national security.[130]

Insurance Contracts

Another domestic legal issue implicated by declarations of war and authorizations for the use of force is their effect, if any, on insurance contracts, particularly with respect to clauses that exclude coverage for "acts of war." The overwhelming characterization of the events of September 11, 2001, as an "act of war" by public officials, sovereigns, international organizations, and the media, for instance, caused concern that insurance companies and the courts would interpret so called "war risk" exclusion clauses in the pertinent insurance contracts to deny claims related to the attacks. However, even a declaration of war by Congress does not appear to have an authoritative effect upon the construction of material terms contained in private contracts.[131] The intent of the parties, not the description of Congress, is what is most relevant to understanding whether the events of September 11 or any future terrorist attacks constitute "acts of war" within the meaning of private contracts,[132] and it is not uncommon for such exclusion clauses in insurance contracts to be given narrow constructions in order to allow recovery to the insured.[133]

In the leading case in this area, *Pan American World Airways, Incorporated v. Aetna Casualty and Surety Company,*[134] a jet was hijacked and destroyed by political dissidents in the Middle East. "Notwithstanding the obvious political overtones of the event," the court ruled that "the hijacking was too contained to come under the war or insurrection exclusion."[135] A rule of causation and a rule of identity informed this conclusion. According to the *Pan Am* decision, when a court interprets an insurance policy excluding from coverage any injuries "caused by" a certain class of conditions, "the causation inquiry stops at the efficient physical cause of the loss; it does not trace events back to their metaphysical beginnings."[136] In the *Pan Am* case, the court examined contract language excluding from coverage losses caused by a "military or usurped power" and stated that an act causing such a loss "must be at least that of a de facto government."[137] On the facts of the case, the court then found that the terrorist organization that highjacked the Pan Am airplane "was not a de facto government in the sky over London when the 747 was taken"[138] and held that the exclusion clause, therefore, did not apply.

This issue will not likely arise with respect to any future acts of terrorism on U.S. territory. In the aftermath of September 11, 2001, Congress enacted the Terrorism Risk Insurance Act to ensure the availability of commercial insurance coverage for losses due to acts of terrorism.[139]

Military Personnel

A number of provisions of the *U.S. Code* concern crimes under the Uniform Code of Military Justice, the activation of the reserves, the role of the Coast Guard, tax benefits for military personnel, and disability and death as the result of combat duty. None appear necessarily to require a declaration of war to be applicable, but a declaration can trigger their application.

Crimes under the UCMJ

Various crimes defined under the Uniform Code of Military Justice ("UCMJ," 10 U.S.C.A. §§801 et seq.) occur either primarily or exclusively in the context of states of hostilities (e.g., "misbehavior before the enemy" under Section 899; "subordinate compelling surrender" under Section 900; "improper use of countersign" under Section 901; "forcing a safeguard" under Section 902; "aiding the enemy" under Section 904; "misconduct as prisoner" under Section 905; and rules concerning "spies" under Section 906). Several of these crimes either only occur or occur in aggravated form "in time of war."

The Manual for Courts Martial sets out Rules for Court Martial. Rule 103(19) defines the expression "time of war," as follows:

> For purpose [*sic*] of ... implementing the applicable paragraphs of Parts IV and V of this Manual only, "time of war" means a period of war declared by Congress or the factual determination by the President that the existence of hostilities warrants a finding that a "time of war" exists for purposes of ... Parts IV and V of this manual.[140]

Thus, a congressional declaration is not indispensable to prosecutions of these crimes but can trigger their application. They do not appear to be triggered by an authorization for the use of force unless a state of war develops. In the absence of a presidential or congressional declaration, military courts have applied a variety of pragmatic tests to determine whether a "time of war" existed in connection with specific offenses.[141]

For some offenses, the statutes of limitations may be tolled in "time of war."[142] When the United States is "at war," the statute of limitations on offenses involving fraud against the United States or offenses committed in connection with U.S. property or procurement of contracts related to the prosecution of the war is suspended until three years after the termination of hostilities (10 U.S.C.A. Section 843(f)).[143] These provisions have been held to apply during hostilities that were initiated without a declaration of war or congressional authorization to use force.[144]

The jurisdiction of the military expands during time of war. Prior to 2006, the UCMJ permitted trial by court-martial of "persons serving with or accompanying an armed force in the field" in time of war (10 U.S.C.A. §802(a)(10)).When faced with the court-martial of civilians, courts interpreted the phrase "in time of war" to mean only during wars declared by Congress.[145] However, Congress amended 10 U.S.C.A. Section 802(a)(10) to extend military jurisdiction in "time of declared war or a contingency operation."[146] The provision has reportedly resulted in one conviction of a civilian contractor in Iraq,[147] a non-U.S. citizen whose Iraqi citizenship precluded jurisdiction under the Military Extraterritorial Jurisdiction Act.[148]

In time of war or conditions of martial law, military commissions may provide a special venue for trying persons not otherwise subject to the UCMJ.[149] Military jurisdiction expands during war to cover civilians accused of violating Sections 904 or 906 (aiding the enemy and spying), as well as other "offenders or offenses that by ... the law of war may be tried by military commissions, provost courts, or other military tribunals" (§821), at least insofar as the Constitution permits.[150]

The Military Commissions Act of 2009, chapter 47A of Title 10, U.S. Code, permits the trial by military commission of "alien unprivileged enemy belligerents" suspected of committing violations against the law of war or "other offenses triable by military commission."[151] The commissions may try such persons for offenses committed "before, on, or after September 11, 2001,"[152] without any requirement for the authorization for the use of force in response to the terrorist attacks of that date to have been in effect at the time the offense was committed. The definition of "unprivileged enemy belligerent" is restricted to those who engaged in or substantially supported hostilities against the United States or its coalition partners, except that those who were members of Al Qaeda at the time of the offense need not have such a connection to hostilities.[153] Thus, offenses defined by or under the jurisdiction of the Military Commissions Act do not depend on a declaration of war or authorization to use force.

Activation of Reserves

Chapter 1209 of title 10 of the *United States Code* (10 U.S.C.A. §§12301 *et seq.*) relates generally to activation of reserve forces. The Ready Reserve forces include members of the Army National Guard and the Air National Guard (see 10 U.S.C.A. §10145(b)). The authority conferred under Sections 12302 through 12304 can be exercised without a congressional declaration of war or national emergency; but those sections only allow reserve forces to be called to active duty for fixed statutory periods (i.e., up to 24 consecutive months under Sections 12302 and 12303 and up to 270 days under Section 12304). By contrast, the authority conferred under Section 12301 can be exercised "[i]n time of war or of national emergency declared by Congress" and allows reserve forces to be called to active duty "for the duration of the war or national emergency and for six months thereafter." The Standby Reserve (as distinguished from the Ready Reserve and Selected Reserve forces) can only be called to active service under the authority conferred by section 12301 (see Section 12306). While the Retired Reserve can be called to active service for up to 12 months under 10 U.S.C.A. Section 688, it can be called to service "for the duration" under the authority conferred by Section 12301 (see Section 12307). So-called "stop loss" authority is conferred under Section 12305. This authority allows the President, whenever persons are called to active service under Sections 12301, 12302, or 12304, to "suspend any provision of law relating to promotion, retirement, or separation" with respect to any member of the armed forces who the President determines is essential to the national security of the United States. This means that, when persons have been called to active service under the authority conferred by Section 12301 "for the duration" of a war or national emergency declared by Congress, otherwise applicable rules concerning promotions, retirements, and separations may not apply. Moreover, under Section 671a, the "period of active service" of any servicemember is extended to six months beyond the duration of any war in which the United States is engaged, unless the Secretary concerned terminates the period at an earlier date. Thus, for all of these sections, a declaration of war is not a necessary predicate, but it can trigger the application of Section 12301 and related provisions. Reemployment rights for reservists called to active duty available under the Uniformed Services Employment and Reemployment Rights Act (USERRA, 38 U.S.C.A. §§4301 *et seq.*) and benefits available through the Servicemembers Civil Relief Act (50 U.S.C.A. App. §§501—596) do not require a declaration of war, but depend generally on the authority under which the call to active duty was made, and may vary according to whether service was rendered during a period of war.

Coast Guard

Section 3 of title 14 of the *United States Code* specifies that "[u]pon the declaration of war if Congress so directs in the declaration or when the President directs, the Coast Guard shall operate as a service in the Navy...."[154] Thus, a congressional declaration of war is not indispensable to bring the Coast Guard under the control of the Navy, but it would have that effect.

Tax Provisions

There are several provisions of the Internal Revenue Code which apply to taxpayers involved directly or indirectly with war. A congressional declaration of war is not needed to render any of these provisions applicable.

Perhaps the most significant relevant provision of the Internal Revenue Code is Section 112 under which some or all of the pay received by members of the uniformed services for active service in a combat zone is excluded from gross income (i.e., is received tax-free). The same exemption applies to military pay received by service members hospitalized due to injuries sustained while serving in a combat zone, subject to a two-year limitation. The term "combat zone" is specially defined for purposes of this rule and means an area so designated by the President of the United States in an Executive Order, and such an Executive Order must be issued to make the tax exemption apply. No reference is made in this provision to any declaration by Congress of the existence of a state of war and, by its express terms, it applied to service in the Korean and Vietnam conflicts.

The pay of POWs and those listed as "missing in action" is also exempt (see (IRC §112(d)). In addition, pay received tax-free because of IRC Section 112 is exempt from federal income-tax withholding under IRC Section 3401(a)(1). Qualified military benefits are exempt from tax under IRC Section 134, and these include bonus payments made by a state or its political subdivision to a current or former member of the Armed Forces, or to his or her dependents, by reason of service in a combat zone designated under Section 112. Due dates for filing returns and for paying taxes, according to IRC Section 7508, are deferred for members of the uniformed services serving in a combat zone designated by the President for purposes of IRC Section 112. Telephone calls originating from combat zones designated under IRC Section 112 are exempt from the federal excise tax that would otherwise apply (see IRC §4253(d)). The so-called "additional estate tax" does not apply in the case of the estate of a member of the Armed Forces who is killed in action in a combat zone designated under IRC Section 112 or who dies as a result of wounds, disease, or injury suffered in such a combat zone (see IRC §2201).

An exemption from federal income tax for the current taxable year and any prior taxable year ending on or after the first day of service in a combat zone and the preceding taxable year is allowed under IRC Section 692 for a member of the Armed Forces who dies in a combat zone designated under IRC Section 112 or who dies as a result of wounds, disease, or injury suffered in such a combat zone. In addition, any unpaid taxes owed at the time of death will be forgiven. A similar exemption is also allowed in the case of a civilian federal employee killed in any military action involving the United States (see IRC §692).

Special rules for spouses of persons who become missing in action also appear in the Code (see IRC §§2(a)(3) and 6013).

Disability and Death

Subchapter II of chapter 11 of title 38 of the *United States Code* (38 U.S.C. §§1110 *et seq.*) relates to "wartime disability compensation." Relevant disability must result from personal injury suffered or disease contracted in the line of duty in active military, naval, or air service "during a period of war."[155] Thus, there is no explicit requirement of a congressional declaration of war. On the other hand, such a declaration would obviously assure that the particular period of hostilities in question is indeed a period of war. Some other veterans' benefits depend on whether the person seeking benefits served during a period of war.

Chapter 13 of title 38 of the *United States Code* (38 U.S.C.A. §§1301 *et seq.*) relates to service- connected deaths. Compensation in connection with such deaths is accorded without regard to whether or not they occurred during or as a result of a war declared by Congress.

Rules under 38 U.S.C.A. Section 2402 relating to the eligibility of members of the Armed Forces who die while on active duty to be buried in national cemeteries (including Arlington National Cemetery) and other rules concerning burial benefits are not contingent on a congressional declaration of war.

ITEMIZATION OF STANDBY STATUTORY AUTHORITIES

Under ordinary circumstances the President exercises the powers conferred on him by the Constitution and by statutes enacted by Congress. As noted in the preceding section, in extraordinary circumstances a number of additional statutory powers may become available; and his Constitutional powers are likely to be given a generous interpretation by the courts. The standby statutory authorities potentially available to the President and the executive branch number in the hundreds. Some are triggered by a declaration of war, some by the existence of a state of war (and, thus, also by a declaration of war), and some pursuant to a declaration or the existence of national emergency. Most can be triggered by one or more of the foregoing circumstances. None of these special authorities appears to be triggered by an authorization for the use of force (unless and until it leads to a state of war). With respect to those statutes that are triggered by the existence of a national emergency or of a state or time of war, the determination of whether such a condition exists would be made in the first instance by the executive branch, unless the statute provides otherwise.

Those authorities that require a declaration of national emergency as a predicate for coming into effect are not automatically activated by such a declaration. National emergency powers can be exercised only pursuant to the strictures of the National Emergencies Act.[156] In addition to requiring that the President publicly declare a national emergency, that act requires that he specify the emergency statutory authorities that he intends to use prior to their use and that he publish that information in the Federal Register and report it to Congress.[157] (On September 14, 2001, President Bush, for example, took this step by issuing a "Declaration of National Emergency by Reason of Certain Terrorist Attacks" and specifying 10 statutory authorities that he intended to use.[158]) Moreover, the act provides that Congress can terminate a declared emergency at any time by joint resolution and that, in any event, the emergency declaration and any statutory powers activated pursuant to it expire after one year unless the President specifically renews the declaration.[159]

The following subsections identify the standby authorities that become available to the President and the executive branch upon (1) a declaration of war, (2) the existence of a state of war, and (3) pursuant to a declaration of national emergency.[160] It is important to emphasize that a declaration of war activates not only the statutes listed in the first subsection but also—because a declaration of war automatically creates a state of war—those listed in the second section. The latter statutes are listed separately because they can come into effect even if a declaration of war is never adopted.

Within each subsection, the statutes are listed generally in the order in which they appear in the U.S. Code. The lists exclude the statutes detailed above concerning criminal law and taxes as well as the disaster relief authorities contained in the "Robert T. Stafford Disaster Relief and Emergency Assistance Act."[161]

(1) Statutory Authorities Triggered by a Declaration of War

Many of following provisions can be triggered by circumstances other than a declaration of war. But all would come into effect upon enactment of a declaration of war:

Congressional Budget Act

2 U.S.C.A. Section 198(b)—provides that the rule mandating that Congress adjourn sine die by July 31 of each year unless each House adopts a concurrent resolution, "shall not be applicable in any year if on July 31 of such year a state of war exists pursuant to a declaration of war by the Congress."

2 U.S.C.A. Section 641—provides that the requirement that amendments to a reconciliation bill not increase budget outlays or decrease budget outlay reductions, revenues, or revenue increases unless they include offsetting budget outlay reductions or revenue increases does not apply "if a declaration of war by the Congress is in effect."

2 U.S.C.A. Section 642(a)—provides that the requirement making bills, amendments, motions, and conference reports which provide new budget authority that would exceed what Congress has set forth in the concurrent resolution on the budget for that fiscal year or that would reduce revenues below what has been set forth in that concurrent resolution out of order in the House does not apply "when a declaration of war by the Congress is in effect."

2 U.S.C.A. Section 643(b)(2)—provides that the requirement making any bill, amendment, motion, or conference report that exceeds the discretionary spending limits set forth in 2 U.S.C.A. App. 901(c) out of order in the Senate does not apply "if a declaration of war by the Congress is in effect or a joint resolution pursuant to section 258 of the Balanced Budget and Emergency Deficit Control Act of 1985 [2 U.S.C.A. §907a] has been enacted."

2 U.S.C.A. Section 907a(b-c)—states that sequestration reports and orders and certain other requirements of the Budget Act are precluded or suspended "upon the enactment of a declaration of war" but that the sequestration procedures are restored "effective with the first fiscal year that begins in the session after the state of war is concluded by Senate ratification of the necessary treaties...."

Agricultural Exports

7 U.S.C.A. Section 5712(c)—allows the President to prohibit or curtail the export of any agricultural commodity "during a period for which the President has declared a national emergency or for which the Congress has declared war."

Armed Forces

10 U.S.C.A. Section 123b—provides that the President may waive the statutory ceiling placed on the number of members of the armed forces who may be stationed abroad in any fiscal year "if the President declares an emergency" and that the ceiling "does not apply in the event of a declaration of war or an armed attack on any member nation of the North Atlantic Treaty Organization, Japan, the Republic of Korea, or any other ally of the United States."

10 U.S.C.A. Section 802(a)—subjects "persons serving with or accompanying an armed force in the field ... in time of declared war or a contingency operation" to the Uniform Code of Military Justice.

10 U.S.C.A. Section 2350j(e)(3)(A)—allows the Secretary of Defense to carry out a military construction project financed by contributions from designated countries or regional organizations without prior explanation and justification to Congress if the project is necessary to support the armed forces "by reason of a declaration of war, or a declaration by the President of a national emergency pursuant to the National Emergencies Act that is in force at the time of the commencement of the project."

10 U.S.C.A. Section 2662(g)—provides that the congressional notice and wait provisions governing certain real property transactions by the Secretary of a military department and by the GSA for the Department of Defense do not apply, *inter alia*, if the transaction results from "a declaration of war ... or a declaration of a national emergency by the President pursuant to the National Emergencies Act."

10 U.S.C.A. Section 2808(a)—provides that the Secretary of Defense and the Secretaries of the military departments, with his authorization, may "without regard to any other provision of law" undertake military construction projects "not otherwise authorized by law" if necessary to support the use of the armed forces "in the event of a declaration of war or the declaration by the President of a national emergency under the National Emergencies Act that requires use of the armed forces."

10 U.S.C.A. Section 12311—provision for the Secretaries of the military departments to permit a member of a reserve component to serve on active duty for a period of five years does not apply "in time of war declared by Congress."

10 U.S.C.A. Section 12521—provides that the Ready Reserve Mobilization Income Insurance Program includes in "covered service" any period of more than 30days on active duty in support of forces activated "during a period of war declared by Congress or a period of national emergency declared by the President or Congress."

Coast Guard

14 U.S.C.A. Section 3—provides that the Coast Guard shall operate as a service in the Navy "upon the declaration of war if Congress so directs in the declaration or when the President directs...."

14 U.S.C.A. Section 661—provides that the President may, if there is in effect a declaration of war or national emergency at the end of any fiscal year, suspend any end-strength limitation prescribed by law for any military or civilian component of the Coast Guard for a period not to exceed 6 months after the end of the war or national emergency.

14 U.S.C.A. Section 724—provides that the President may, if there is in effect a declaration of war or national emergency at the end of any fiscal year, suspend any end-strength limitation prescribed by law for the number of officers in the Coast Guard Reserve for a period not to exceed 6 months after the end of the war or national emergency.

Small Business Administration

15 U.S.C.A. Section 636(n)—provides for the deferral of the repayment of interest and principal on direct loans by the SBA to a member of a reserve component who is ordered to active duty during a "period of military conflict," defined to mean "a period of war declared by Congress [or] a period of national emergency declared by the Congress or the President...."

Unilateral Trade Sanctions

22 U.S.C.A. Section 7203—provides that the prohibition in the "Trade Sanctions Reform and Export Enhancement Act of 2000" barring the President from imposing new unilateral agricultural or medical sanctions without the approval of Congress does not apply with respect to the imposition of such a sanction against a foreign country or entity "(A) pursuant to a declaration of war against the country or entity; (B) pursuant to specific statutory authorization for the use of the Armed Forces of the United States against the country or entity; (C) against which the Armed Forces of the United States are involved in hostilities; or (D) where imminent involvement by the Armed Forces of the United States in hostilities against the country or entity is clearly indicated by the circumstances...."

Armed Forces Retirement Home

24 U.S.C.A. Section 412—provides that "persons who ... served in a war theater during a time of war declared by Congress" are eligible to become residents of an Armed Forces Retirement Home.

Statutes of Limitation

28 U.S.C.A. Section 2416(d)—provides that, for the purpose of computing the time limitation periods for commencing court actions brought by the United States, "there shall be excluded all periods during which... the United States is in a state of war declared pursuant to Article I, Section 8, of the Constitution of the United States."

Tort Claims against the Federal Government

28 U.S.C.A. Section 2680(j)—exempts claims against the United States "arising out of the combatant activities of the military or naval forces, or the Coast Guard, during time of war" from the jurisdiction of courts.

Deferral of Civil Works Projects

33 U.S.C.A. Section 2293—authorizes the Secretary of the Army, "in the event of a declaration of war or a declaration by the President of a national emergency in accordance with the National Emergencies Act that requires or may require use of the Armed Forces," to terminate or defer Army civil works projects that he determines are not essential to the national defense and to apply the resources to projects that are essential.

Nuclear Regulatory Commission

42 U.S.C.A. Section 2138—authorizes the Nuclear Regulatory Commission to suspend any licenses it has granted relating to the production or use of special nuclear material, to order the recapture of any such material, and to order the operation of any such facility, "if the Commission finds it necessary to the common defense and security ... whenever the Congress declares that a state of war or national emergency exists."

Alien Enemy Act

50 U.S.C.A. Section 21—authorizes the President to "apprehend, restrain, secure, and remove" alien enemies ... whenever there is a declared war between the United States and any foreign nation or government, or any invasion or predatory incursion is perpetrated, attempted, or threatened against the territory of the United States by any foreign nation or government, and the President makes public proclamation of the event."

National Defense Stockpile

50 U.S.C.A. Section 98f(a)(2)—authorizes any person designated by the President, "(1) at any time the President determines the release of such materials is required for purposes of the national defense or (2) in time of war declared by the Congress or during a national emergency," to use, sell, or otherwise dispose of materials in the National Defense Stockpile that the designee determines are "required for purposes of the national defense."162

National Security Agency (NSA) Personnel Security

50 U.S.C.A. Section 832—authorizes the Secretary of Defense, "[d]uring any period of war declared by the Congress, or during any period when the Secretary determines that a national disaster exists, or in [other] exceptional cases ...," may authorize the employment, assignment or detail of personnel to the Agency and grant them temporary access to classified information pending the completion of a full field investigation, if he determines that "such action is clearly consistent with the national security."

Chemical and Biological Warfare Agents

50 U.S.C.A. Section 1515—authorizes the President to suspend the provisions of law governing the production, transportation, location, testing, and disposal of lethal chemical and biological warfare agents "during the period of any war declared by Congress and during the period of any national emergency declared by Congress or by the President."

National Emergencies Act

50 U.S.C.A. Section 1641—requires the President, "when the President declares a national emergency, or Congress declares war," to maintain a file and index of all significant orders issued during such emergency or war, to transmit such orders to the Congress, and to report to Congress each six months on the total expenditures during that period that are attributable to the exercise of emergency authorities conferred by such declaration.

Foreign Intelligence Surveillance Act (FISA)

50 U.S.C.A. Section 1811—provides that notwithstanding any other law, the President may authorize electronic surveillance without a court order under FISA "to acquire foreign intelligence information for a period not to exceed fifteen calendar days following a declaration of war by the Congress."

50 U.S.C.A. Section 1829—provides that notwithstanding any other law, the President may authorize physical searches without a court order under FISA "to acquire foreign

intelligence information for a period not to exceed 15 calendar days following a declaration of war by the Congress."

50 U.S.C.A. Section 1844—provides that notwithstanding any other provision of law, the President may authorize the use of a pen register or trap and trace device without a court order under FISA "to acquire foreign intelligence information for a period not to exceed 15 calendar days following a declaration of war by Congress."

Selective Service Act

50 U.S.C.A. App. Section 454(a)—provides that the President can vary the specified standards for physical and mental fitness of inductees into the armed forces "except in time of war or national emergency declared by the Congress"; that those who voluntarily enlist cannot have their enlistment extended without their consent "until after a declaration of war or national emergency by the Congress"; and that various exceptions from requirements of service in the reserves or from orders to active duty without consent do not apply "in time of war or national emergency declared by Congress."

50 U.S.C.A. App. Section 456—provides that various exceptions to liability for induction into the armed forces for veterans of World War II and members of the Reserves and the National Guard do not apply "after a declaration of war or national emergency made by the Congress" and that the exception for those who have had a close relative killed in the line of duty does not apply "during the period of a war or a national emergency declared by Congress."

(2) Statutory Authorities Triggered by the Existence of a State of War (and Thus Also by a Declaration of War)

In addition to the statutes that are explicitly triggered by a declaration of war, a number come into the effect if a state of war, or period of war, or simply "war" exists. Because a declaration of war automatically creates a state of war, these authorities also are triggered by the enactment of a declaration of war. But they can come into effect even if no declaration of war is adopted. As is the case with respect to many of the statutes in the foregoing subsection, many of these statutes can also be triggered pursuant to a declaration of national emergency, and at least one comes into play if Congress has enacted a specific authorization for the use of the Armed Forces. The statutes are set forth in the order in which they appear in the *U.S. Code*:

Administrative Procedure

5 U.S.C.A. Section 551(1)—excludes "military authority exercised in the field in time of war or in occupied territory" from the definition of "agency" for purposes of general administrative procedure.

5 U.S.C.A. Section 701(b)—excludes "military authority exercised in the field in time of war or in occupied territory" from the definition of "agency" for purposes of judicial review of administrative procedure.

Federal Employees

5 U.S.C.A. Section 5335(b)—requires that step increases mandated for federal civil service employees be preserved for those employees whose civilian service is interrupted by "service with the armed forces or by service in essential non-Government civilian employment during a period of war or national emergency."

5 U.S.C.A. Section 5343(e)(3)—requires that step increases mandated for federal prevailing rate employees be preserved for those employees whose civilian service is interrupted by "service with the armed forces or by service in essential non-Government civilian employment during a period of war or national emergency."

5 U.S.C.A. Section 8114(e)(3)—prohibits accounting for "bonus or pay for particularly hazardous service in time of war" when computing pay to compensate government employees for work injuries.

5 U.S.C.A. Section 8332(g)—provides that a civil service employee who leaves his civilian position to serve in the military "during the period of a war, or of a national emergency as proclaimed by the President or declared by Congress" is deemed not to be separated from his civil service position for purposes of determining his or her creditable service for retirement purposes, unless the military service extends beyond 5 years.

Aliens

8 U.S.C.A. Section 1182(a)(8)—provides that any person "who has departed from or who has remained outside the United States to avoid or evade training or service in the armed forces in time of war or a period declared by the President to be a national emergency" is ineligible to receive a visa and inadmissible into the United States, and is thus ineligible for citizenship.

8 U.S.C.A. Section 1231(b)(2)—provides that when the Attorney General decides that it is "impracticable, inadvisable, inconvenient, or impossible" to remove an alien to the country where the alien is a citizen or subject because the "United States is at war," the alien may be removed to the "country that is host to a government in exile of the country of which the alien is a citizen or subject" or to "a country... that is very near to the country that is host to a government in exile of the country of which the alien is a citizen or subject" or to "a country ... that is very near to the country of which the alien is a citizen or subject."

8 U.S.C.A. Section 1425—makes any person who deserted or shall desert the armed forces or left the United States with the intent to avoid the draft at "any time during which the United States has been or shall be at war" ineligible to become a naturalized citizen of the United States.

8 U.S.C.A. Section 1438—authorizes the Attorney General to naturalize former United States citizens who lost citizenship by serving "in the military, air, or naval forces of any

country at war with a country with which the United States was at war after December 7, 1941, and before September 2, 1945."

8 U.S.C.A. Section 1442(a)—authorizes the Attorney General to naturalize an alien from a country with which the United States is at war after the alien's loyalty to the United States is established if the alien's application for naturalization was "pending at the beginning of the state of war and the applicant is otherwise entitled to admission to citizenship."

8 U.S.C.A. Section 1455(d)—prohibits the Attorney General from charging or collecting a naturalization fee "during the time when the United States is at war" from an alien in the military, air, or naval service of the United States for filing an application for naturalization or issuing a certificate of naturalization upon admission to citizenship.

8 U.S.C.A. Section 1481(a)(3) and (6)—provides that a person who is a national of the United States whether by birth or naturalization shall lose his nationality by serving in the armed forces of a foreign state "if such armed forces are engaged in hostilities against the United States" and by voluntarily making "a formal written renunciation of nationality ... whenever the United States shall be in a state of war" and the Attorney General approves such renunciation as "not contrary to the interests of national defense."

Armed Forces

10 U.S.C.A. Section 123—authorizes the President to "suspend the operation of any provision of law relating to the promotion, involuntary retirement, or separation of commissioned officers of the Army, Navy, Air Force, Marine Corps, or Coast Guard Reserve ... in time of war, or of a national emergency declared by Congress or the President" until one year after the war or national emergency terminates.

10 U.S.C.A. Section 123a—authorizes the President to defer any end-strength limitation prescribed by law for any military or civilian component of the armed forces if "there is in effect a war or national emergency" until six months after the war or national emergency terminates.

10 U.S.C.A. Section 152(a)—provides that "in time of war there is no limit on the number of reappointments" the President may make of the same person to the two-year position of Chairman of the Joint Chiefs of Staff.

10 U.S.C.A. Section 154(a)—provides that "in time of war there is no limit on the number of reappointments" the President may make of the same person to the two-year position of Vice Chairman of the Joint Chiefs of Staff.

10 U.S.C.A. Section 155(f)(4)—lifts the four-year limitation on the tours of duty of officers assigned or detailed to duty on the Joint Staff of the Joint Chiefs of Staff "in time of war; or during a national emergency declared by the President or Congress."

10 U.S.C.A. Section 194(e)—lifts the caps on the number of armed forces and civilian employees that can be assigned or detailed to permanent duty in management headquarters activities or otherwise in the Defense Agencies and DOD Field Activities "in time of war; or during a national emergency declared by the President or Congress."

10 U.S.C.A. Section 351—authorizes the President to "arm, have armed, or allow to be armed" any watercraft or aircraft used as a means of transportation "on, over, or under water" during a "war and at any other time when the President determines that the security of the United States is threatened by the application, or the imminent danger of application, of

physical force by any foreign government or agency against the United States, its citizens, the property of its citizens, or their commercial interests."

10 U.S.C.A. Section 519—provides that "in time of war or of national emergency declared by Congress" enlistments in the armed forces shall be for the duration of the war or emergency plus six months.

10 U.S.C.A. Section 527—allows the President to suspend the limitations placed on the number of general officers in the Army, Air Force, and Marines and of flag officers in the Navy, and the number of such officers who may be designated in various ranks, "in time of war, or of national emergency declared by Congress or the President" until up to one year after the war or national emergency terminates.

10 U.S.C.A. Section 603—allows the President to appoint "any qualified person" to any officer grade in the Army, Navy, Air Force, and Marines up to major general or rear admiral "in time of war, or of national emergency declared by the Congress or the President" for up to 2 years or 6 months after the war or national emergency has terminated, whichever occurs first.

10 U.S.C.A. Section 620(d)—allows the Secretary of a military department to exclude a reserve officer ordered to active duty "during a war or national emergency" from the active duty roster of officers.

10 U.S.C.A. Section 671—provides that "in time of war or a national emergency declared by Congress or the President" basic training may not be less than 12 weeks (except for certain health care professionals).

10 U.S.C.A. Section 688(f)—waives the 12-month limitation on the period for which retired members of the armed forces can be recalled to active duty and the prohibition on recalling certain categories of retired officers to active duty "in time of war or of national emergency declared by Congress or the President."

10 U.S.C.A. Section 690(c)—waives the limitation on the number of retired general officers and flag officers who may be on active duty at any one time "in time of war or of national emergency declared by Congress or the President."

10 U.S.C.A. Section 708(d)—allows the Secretary of a military department to cancel a leave of absence granted for educational purposes "in time of war, or of national emergency declared by Congress or the President."

10 U.S.C.A. Section 712—allows the President to detail members of the armed forces to any foreign country he deems advisable to assist in military matters "during a war or a declared national emergency."

10 U.S.C.A. Section 772(e)—authorizes a person not on active duty who served honorably "in time of war" in the Army, Navy, Air Force, or Marine Corps to bear the title, and, "when authorized by regulations prescribed by the President," wear the uniform, of the "highest grade held by him during that war."

10 U.S.C.A. Section 843—provides that a person charged with "absence without leave or missing movement in time of war," or with murder or rape, or any offense punishable by death, may be tried and punished at any time without limitation and that a person charged with an "offense the trial of which in time of war is certified to the President by the Secretary concerned to be detrimental to the prosecution of the war or inimical to the national security" may be tried and punished up to "six months after the termination of hostilities as proclaimed by the President or by a joint resolution of Congress."

10 U.S.C.A. Section 843(f)—when the United States is "at war," suspends the statute of limitations until three years after the termination of hostilities for offenses under the UCMJ that involve fraud against the United States, as well as those committed "in connection the acquisition, care, handling, custody, control, or disposition of any [U.S.] real or personal property," or committed "in connection with the negotiation, procurement, award, performance, payment, interim financing, cancellation, or other termination or settlement, of any contract, subcontract, or purchase order which is connected with or related to the prosecution of the war, or with any disposition of termination inventory by any war contractor or Government agency."

10 U.S.C.A. Section 871(b)—allows the Secretary of a military department to commute a court-martial sentence of dismissal to a reduction in grade "in time of war or national emergency."

10 U.S.C.A. Section 885(c)—provides that any person found guilty of desertion or attempt to desert the armed forces shall be punished, "if the offense is committed in time of war," by death or "such other punishment as a court-martial may direct."

10 U.S.C.A. Section 890—provides that any member of the armed forces who "willfully disobeys a lawful command of his superior commissioned officer" shall be punished, "if the offense is committed in time of war," by death or "such other punishment as a court-martial may direct."

10 U.S.C.A. Section 901—provides that any person subject to the UCMJ who "in time of war discloses the parole or countersign to any person not entitled to receive it" or who gives to another who is entitled to receive and use the parole or countersign a "different parole or countersign from that which, to his knowledge, he was authorized and required to give," shall be punished by death or such other punishment as a court-martial may direct.

10 U.S.C.A. Section 905—provides that any person subject to the UCMJ who, "while in the hands of the enemy in time of war," acts to the detriment of other prisoners to receive favorable treatment or maltreats his fellow prisoners without justifiable cause shall be punished as a court-martial may direct.

10 U.S.C.A. Section 906—provides that "any person who in time of war is found lurking as a spy or acting as a spy" with respect to the armed forces or defense entities shall be tried by a court-martial and, if convicted, be punished by death.

10 U.S.C.A. Section 913—provides that any sentinel or look-out who is found drunk or sleeping at his post, or who leaves it before he is relieved, shall be punished by death if the offense is committed "in time of war" and by such other punishment as a court-martial may direct at other times.

10 U.S.C.A. Section 978(e)—allows the President to suspend the requirement that persons seeking to enlist in the armed forces be tested for drug and alcohol use and dependency "in time of war, or time of emergency declared by Congress or the President."

10 U.S.C.A. Section 1104(d)—provides that members of the armed forces on active duty "during and immediately following a period of war, or during and immediately following a national emergency involving the use of the armed forces in armed conflict" may receive health-care services from the Department of Veterans Affairs.

10 U.S.C.A. Section 1161(a)—provides that no commissioned officer may be dismissed from any armed force except by sentence of a general court-martial, in commutation of a sentence of a general court-martial, or "in time of war, by order of the President."

10 U.S.C.A. Sections1201(b) and 1203(b)—provides that the Secretary of a military department may allow a member of his armed force to retire on disability even though the disability is less than 30 percent under the standard schedule of rating disabilities used by the Department of Veterans Affairs if the member has at least 20 years of service and the disability was incurred "in line of duty in time of war or national emergency."

10 U.S.C.A. Section 1491(e)—allows the Secretary of Defense to waive the requirement that a funeral honors detail be provided for the funeral of any veteran if "necessary ... to meet the requirements of war, national emergency, or a contingency operation or other military requirements."

10 U.S.C.A. Section 1580—allows the Secretary of Defense or of the military department concerned to designate any employee of DOD as an emergency essential employee if they provide immediate support to combat operations in a combat zone "in connection with a war, a national emergency declared by Congress or the President, or the commencement of combat operations of the armed forces in the zone."

10 U.S.C.A. Section 2208—allows the Secretary of Defense to waive the requirement that Congress be given written notification of the advance billing of a customer of a working-capital fund "during a period of war or national emergency."

10 U.S.C.A. Section 2366(c)—authorizes the President to suspend the operation of any provision related to the survivability testing and lethality testing required before full-scale production of any major systems and munitions programs "in time of war or mobilization."

10 U.S.C.A. Section 2457(b)—states as policy the dispersal of manufacturing facilities and standardization of equipment among North Atlantic Treaty Organization members to "minimize potential economic hardship to parties to the agreements and increase the survivability, in time of war."

10 U.S.C.A. Section 2461(e)—provides that the conditions and prerequisites to the privatization of a DOD commercial or industrial type function do "not apply during war or during a period of national emergency declared by the President or Congress."

10 U.S.C.A. Section 2538—authorizes the President, through the head of any department, to seize any plant that is "equipped to manufacture, or that in the opinion of the head of that department is capable of being readily transformed into a plant for manufacturing, arms or ammunition, parts thereof, or necessary supplies for the armed forces" and to manufacture products at such plant "in time of war or when war is imminent," if the head of the plant refuses to cooperate with an order for arms or supplies.

10 U.S.C.A. Section 2539—provides that the Secretary of Defense may maintain a list of privately owned plants in the United States that have a capacity "sufficient to warrant conversion into ammunition plants in time of war or when war is imminent," and may obtain complete information as to the equipment of each of those plants.

10 U.S.C.A. Section 2552—provides that the Secretary of a military department may lend equipment under the jurisdiction of that department that is on hand, and that can be temporarily spared, to "any organization formed by the American National Red Cross that needs it for instruction and practice for the purpose of aiding the Army, Navy, or Air Force in time of war."

10 U.S.C.A. Section 2632—allows the Secretary of a military department to provide transportation for employees working in a private plant that is manufacturing material for that department "during a war or a national emergency declared by Congress or the President."

10 U.S.C.A. Section 2644—authorizes the Secretary of Defense in "time of war" to take possession and assume control of all or part of any system of transportation to transport troops, war material, and equipment, or "for other purposes related to the emergency."

10 U.S.C.A. Section 2663(b)—provides that, "in time of war or when war is imminent," the United States may, immediately upon the filing of a petition for condemnation, acquire any interest in land, including temporary use, needed for the site, construction, or operation of fortifications, coast defenses, or military training camps, the construction and operation of plants for the production of nitrate and other compounds and the manufacture of explosives or other munitions of war, or the development and transmission of power for the operation of these production plants.

10 U.S.C.A. Section 2733(b)—extends the time that a claim brought against the United States for damage to or loss of real property, damage to or loss of personal property, or personal injury or death caused by an officer, employee, or a member of the Army, Navy, Air Force, Marine Corps, or Coast Guard that arose in "time of war or armed conflict, or if such a war or conflict intervened," from two years after it accrues to two years after the war or armed conflict is terminated.

10 U.S.C.A. Section 2734(b)—limits claims "in the case of a national of a country at war with the United States, or of any ally of that country," to those in which the claims commission or local military commander determines the claimant is friendly to the United States.

10 U.S.C.A. Section 3014(f)(4)—provides that the ceilings on the number of members of the armed forces, civilians, officers, and general officers that may be assigned or detailed for duty in the Office of the Secretary of the Army and on the Army Staff "do not apply in time of war or during a national emergency declared by the President or Congress."

10 U.S.C.A. Section 3033(a)(1)—allows the President to reappoint a Chief of Staff of the Army for an additional term of four years "in time of war or during a national emergency declared by Congress."

10 U.S.C.A. Section 3063(b)—allows the Secretary of the Army to discontinue or consolidate the basic branches of the Army designated by statute "for the duration of any war, or of any national emergency declared by Congress."

10 U.S.C.A. Section 3691—provides that officers of the Army who have aeronautical ratings as observers may be rated as flying officers in "time of war."

10 U.S.C.A. Section 4780(a)—authorizes the Secretary of the Army to acquire by lease any building, or part of a building, in the District of Columbia that may be needed for military purposes in "time of war or when war is imminent."

10 U.S.C.A. Section 5014(f)(4)—provides that the ceilings on the number of members of the armed forces, civilians, officers, and general and flag officers that may be assigned or detailed for duty in the Office of the Secretary of the Navy, the Office of the Chief of Naval Operations, and the Headquarters Marine Corps "do not apply in time of war or during a national emergency declared by the President or Congress."

10 U.S.C.A. Section 5033—allows the President to reappoint a Chief of Naval Operations for an additional term of four years "in time of war or during a national emergency declared by Congress."

10 U.S.C.A. Section 5043—allows the President to reappoint a Commandant of the Marine Corps for an additional term of four years "in time of war or national emergency declared by Congress."

10 U.S.C.A. Section 5133(c)—provides that "except in time of war, any officer of a staff corps who has served as a chief of bureau for a full term is exempt from sea duty."

10 U.S.C.A. Section 5450—provides that the limitation to ten on the number of retired flag officers who may be on active duty at any one time in the Regular Navy does not apply "in time of war or national emergency." 10 U.S.C.A. Section 5451—authorizes the President to suspend any provision of the "preceding sections" during a war or national emergency. (The only relevant preceding section that has not been repealed has its own exception for war or national emergency.)

10 U.S.C.A. Section 5540(b)—provides that, "except in time of war," each member of the Navy and Marine Corps who is serving on a naval vessel, whose term of enlistment has expired, and who desires to return to the United States but is retained by a senior officer "as essential to the public interest," is entitled to an increase in basic pay of 25 percent.

10 U.S.C.A. Section 6408—provides that "No officer who holds the grade of warrant officer, W–1, may be dismissed from the Navy or the Marine Corps except in time of war, by order of the President."

10 U.S.C.A. Section 6485—provides that members of the Fleet Reserve and Fleet Marine

Corps Reserve may be ordered to active duty "in time of war or national emergency declared by Congress, for the duration of the war or national emergency and for six months thereafter, (and) in time of national emergency declared by the President...."

10 U.S.C.A. Section 6486—provides that the Secretary of the Navy may not release a member of the Fleet Reserve or the Fleet Marine Corps Reserve from active duty "in time of war or national emergency declared by Congress or by the President" unless certain conditions are met.

10 U.S.C.A. Section 6911(b)—provides that "except in time of war or emergency declared by Congress," 20 percent of the aviation cadets procured in each fiscal year shall be procured from qualified enlisted members of the Regular Navy and the Regular Marine Corps.

10 U.S.C.A. Section 6972—provides that the crypt and window spaces of the Naval Academy Chapel may be used only for memorials to officers of the Navy who have successfully commanded a fleet or squadron in battle or who have "received the thanks of Congress for conspicuously distinguished services in time of war."

10 U.S.C.A. Section 7224—authorizes the Secretary of the Navy to designate persons who can be transported and subsisted on naval vessels at government expense "in time of war or during a national emergency declared by the President."

10 U.S.C.A. Section 7225—provides that the Secretary of the Navy shall prescribe a suitable flag to be known as the Navy Reserve flag to be flown by a seagoing merchant vessel designated by the Secretary as "suitable for service as a naval auxiliary in time of war."

10 U.S.C.A. Section 7226—provides that the Secretary of the Navy shall prescribe a suitable pennant to be known as the Naval Reserve yacht pennant to be flown by a yacht or similar vessel if "the vessel has been designated by the Secretary, under such regulations as he prescribes, as suitable for service as a naval auxiliary in time of war."

10 U.S.C.A. Section 7722—provides that "whenever in time of war" the Secretary of the Navy certifies to a court, or to a judge of a court, that the prosecution of a suit would tend to endanger the security of naval operations in the war, or would tend to interfere with those operations, all further proceedings in the suit shall be stayed.

10 U.S.C.A. Section 7724—provides that, "if in time of war, with respect to any claim against the United States on which a suit would lie," the Secretary of the Navy certifies to the court in which proceedings are pending for the taking of certain depositions, that the proceedings would tend to endanger or interfere with the security of the United States, "then the proceedings may not be started or, if they have been started, they shall, when the certificate is filed, be stayed." The Secretary may extend or shorten such a stay by filing a new certificate. 10 U.S.C.A. Section 7725.

10 U.S.C.A. Section 8014(f)(4)—provides that the ceilings on the number of members of the armed forces, civilians, officers, and general officers that can be assigned or detailed for duty in the Office of the Secretary of the Air Force do not apply "in time of war or during a national emergency declared by the President or Congress."

10 U.S.C.A. Section 8033(a)(1)—allows the President to reappoint the Chief of Staff of the Air Force for an additional term of four years "in time of war or during a national emergency declared by Congress."

10 U.S.C.A. Section 8257(d)—provides that, "except in time of war or of emergency declared by Congress," at least 20 percent of the aviation cadets designated in each fiscal year shall be selected from members of the Regular Air Force or the Regular Army who are eligible and qualified.

10 U.S.C.A. Section 8691—provides that officers of the Air Force who have aeronautical ratings as observers may be rated as flying officers in "time of war."

10 U.S.C.A. Section 9773(c)—provides that in selecting sites for air bases and depots and in determining the alteration or enlargement of existing air bases or depots, the Secretary of the Air Force shall consider the need "to permit, in time of peace, training and effective planning in each strategic area for the use and expansion of commercial, municipal, and private flying installations in time of war."

10 U.S.C.A. Section 9780(a)—authorizes the Secretary of the Army to acquire by lease any building, or part of a building, in the District of Columbia that may be needed for military purposes in "time of war or when war is imminent."

Reserves

10 U.S.C.A. Section 10102—states the purpose of the reserves to be "to provide trained units and qualified persons available for active duty in the armed forces, in time of war or national emergency, and at such other times as the national security may require."

10 U.S.C.A. Section 12006—allows the President, "in time of war, or of national emergency," to suspend the statutory ceilings placed on the number of reserve commissioned officers, reserve general officers, and rear admirals in the Army, Navy, Air Force, and Marine Corps reserves for up to one year beyond the end of the war or national emergency, notwithstanding the earlier termination date prescribed by the National Emergencies Act.

10 U.S.C.A. Section 12103—extends enlistments in the reserves that are in effect "at the beginning of a war or of a national emergency declared by Congress," or that are entered into during such a war or emergency, and that would otherwise expire, until six months after the war or emergency has ended, unless earlier terminated by the Secretary concerned.

10 U.S.C.A. Section 12243—allows the President to suspend any law relating to the promotion or mandatory retirement or separation of permanent reserve warrant officers "in time of war, or of emergency declared after May 29, 1954, by Congress or the President."

10 U.S.C.A. Section 12301—allows the Secretary of a military department, "in time of war or of national emergency declared by Congress, or when otherwise authorized by law," to order any reserve unit or member to active duty without their consent for the duration of the war or emergency and up to six months thereafter, and allows reserves on inactive or retired status to be called up if those on active status or in the inactive National Guard are insufficient.

10 U.S.C.A. Section 12311—provides that if an agreement between the Secretary and a member of the reserves specifying a set term of active duty expires "during a war or during a national emergency declared by Congress or the President," the Reserve may be kept on active duty without his consent.

10 U.S.C.A. Section 12313—limits the discretion of the Secretary concerned to release a Reserve from active duty "in time of war or of national emergency declared by Congress or the President...."

10 U.S.C.A. Section 12316—provides that a Reserve who is called up "for a period of more than 30 days in time of war or national emergency" and who is otherwise entitled to a pension, retired or retainer pay, or disability compensation shall receive either that compensation, if it is greater, or the pay and allowances prescribed for the duty he is performing.

10 U.S.C.A. Section 14317—provides that reserve officers not on the active-duty list when ordered to active duty "in time of war or national emergency" may be considered for promotion by a mandatory or special selection board; or in the case of an officer who "is serving on active duty in support of a contingency operation, by a vacancy promotion board."

10 U.S.C.A. Section 16163—provides educational assistance to reservists who "served on active duty in support of a contingency operation for 90 consecutive days or more" after September 11, 2001, and to members of the National Guard who "performed full time National Guard duty under section 502 (f) of title 32 for 90 consecutive days or more when authorized by the President or Secretary of Defense for the purpose of responding to a national emergency declared by the President and supported by Federal funds."

10 U.S.C.A. Section 16201—provides that the Secretary of each military department may provide financial assistance to persons in training for degrees in medicine or dentistry or other health professions specialties "critically needed in wartime" in exchange for a commitment to subsequent service in the Ready Reserve, including the possibility of being ordered to active duty "in time of war or national emergency."

10 U.S.C.A. Section 18235—bars the Secretary of Defense from disposing or allowing the use of facilities for the reserves in any manner that would interfere with their use "in time of war or national emergency, by other units of the armed forces or by the United States for any other purpose."

10 U.S.C.A. Section 18236—bars a state from disposing or allowing the use of facilities constructed for the reserves with the help of a federal grant in any manner that would interfere with their use "in time of war or national emergency, by other units of the armed forces or by the United States for any other purpose." 19 U.S.C.A. Section 2293(i) (temporarily added by P.L. 111-5, extended to January 21, 2014, by P.L. 112-40)—authorizes waivers of requirements for receiving trade readjustment allowances and related benefits for adversely

affected workers who are reservists and were called to active duty under 32 U.S.C.A. Section 502(f).

Trading with the Enemy Act

12 U.S.C.A. Section 95a—authorizes the President, "during the time of war ... through any agency that he may designate," to investigate, regulate, or prohibit, any transactions in foreign exchange, or transactions "involving any property in which any foreign country or a national thereof has any interest."

Coast Guard

14 U.S.C.A. Section 2—provides that the Coast Guard "shall maintain a state of readiness to function as a specialized service in the Navy in time of war, including the fulfillment of Maritime Defense Zone responsibilities."

14 U.S.C.A. Section 275—allows the President, "in time of war, or of national emergency declared by the President or Congress," to suspend any section of this chapter with respect to the selection, promotion, or involuntary separation of Coast Guard officers and to promote to the next higher grade any officer serving on active duty in the grade of ensign or above and any warrant officer serving on active duty in a grade below chief warrant officer, until up to six months after the end of the war or national emergency.

14 U.S.C.A. Section 331—allows the Secretary to order any regular officer of the Coast Guard on the retired list to active duty "in time of war or national emergency."

14 U.S.C.A. Section 359—allows the Commandant to order any enlisted member of the Coast Guard on the retired list to active duty "in times of war or national emergency."

14 U.S.C.A. Section 367—allows an enlisted member of the Coast Guard to be detained beyond the term of his enlistment "during a period of war or national emergency as proclaimed by the President, and, in the interest of national defense," for up to six months after the end of the war or emergency.

14 U.S.C.A. Section 371—requires that at least 20 percent of the aviation cadets procured in each fiscal year be qualified enlisted members of the Coast Guard, "except in time of war or national emergency."

14 U.S.C.A. Section 508—provides that any "person who is convicted by court martial for desertion from the Coast Guard in time of war" and is consequently dismissed or dishonorably discharged, shall afterwards not be enlisted, appointed or commissioned in any military or naval service under the United States "unless he is restored to duty in time of war."

14 U.S.C.A. Section 636—allows commissioned and warrant officers of the Coast Guard to perform all of the functions of a notary public "in time of war or national emergency."

14 U.S.C.A. Section 652—provides that legal changes lifting restrictions on the Navy "for the duration of a war or national emergency proclaimed by the President," including those regarding procurement and personnel, shall automatically apply to the Coast Guard.

14 U.S.C.A. Section 660(a)—allows the Secretary to provide transportation to and from work for persons employed by a private plant manufacturing material for the Coast Guard "during a war or during a national emergency declared by Congress or the President."

14 U.S.C.A. Section 722—allows the President to suspend any part of the subchapter concerning commissioned officers in the Coast Guard Reserve "in time of war or national emergency declared by Congress."

Federal Energy Regulatory Commission

16 U.S.C.A. Section 824a(c)—allows the Federal Energy Regulatory Commission to order the temporary connection of electric energy facilities and such generation, delivery, interchange, or transmission of electric energy as in its judgment will best meet the emergency and serve the public interest "during the continuance of any war in which the United States is engaged, or whenever the Commission determines that an emergency exists by reason of a sudden increase in the demand for electric energy, or a shortage of electric energy, or of fuel or water for generating facilities, or other causes."

Tennessee Valley Authority

16 U.S.C.A. Section 831d(g)—directs the Tennessee Valley Authority to maintain a plant "for the production of explosives in the event of war or a national emergency" unless Congress releases it from the obligation.

16 U.S.C.A. Section 831s—reserves to the government the right, "in case of war or national emergency," to take control of the TVA "for the purpose of manufacturing explosives or for other war purposes."

Criminal Prosecutions

18 U.S.C. Section 3287—whenever the United States is at war or Congress has authorized the use of force, suspends the statute of limitations with respect to prosecution of fraud against the United States or certain crimes related to U.S. real or personal property, as well as offenses committed in relation to contracts or purchase orders related to the use of the U.S. armed forces, until five years after the end of hostilities as proclaimed by the President or Congress by concurrent resolution.

Imports

19 U.S.C.A. Section 1318—allows the Secretary of the Treasury, "whenever the President shall by proclamation declare an emergency to exist by reason of a state of war, or otherwise," to have additional time to perform any act prescribed by the Tariff Act of 1930, as amended, and to permit the import of food, clothing, and medical supplies for use in emergency relief work free of duty. (This function was transferred to the Secretary of Commerce, to be exercised in consultation with the Secretary of the Treasury, under

Reorganization Plan No. 3 of 1979, 19 U.S.C.A. §2171 note, and therefore does not appear to be subject to delegation to the Secretary of Homeland Security pursuant to 6 U.S.C.A. §212.)

Student Financial Aid

20 U.S.C.A. Section 1098bb authorizes the Secretary of Education to waive or modify statutory and regulatory provisions applicable to student financial aid programs as he deems necessary "in connection with a war or other military operation or national emergency" for the relief of an "affected individual" as defined in 20 U.S.C.A. Section 1098ee(2) to mean one who is "serving on active duty during a war or other military operation or national emergency [declared by the President]" or "is performing qualifying National Guard duty during a war or other military operation or national emergency," among other things.

Neutrality

22 U.S.C.A. Section 441—provides that when the President finds that there exists "a state of war between foreign states," the President shall issue a proclamation naming the states involved and shall revoke such proclamation when the "state of war ... shall have ceased." As a result of such a proclamation, it becomes illegal for persons within the United States to conduct financial transactions with the warring parties, unless the United States is "at war." 22 U.S.C.A. Section 447.

Miscellaneous

22 U.S.C.A. Section 1623—provides that a commission authorized to settle international claims "shall have jurisdiction to receive, examine, adjudicate, and render a final decision" with respect to claims between the United States government and a foreign government "exclusive of governments against which the United States declared the existence of a state of war during World War II."

22 U.S.C.A. Section 1974—provisions protecting U.S. vessels from seizure by a foreign country do not apply with respect to a "seizure made by a country at war with the United States."

22 U.S.C.A. Section 4056(f)—deems that a member of the Foreign Service who has left the Service to enter military service "during a period of war, or national emergency proclaimed by the President or declared by the Congress" has not, for retirement benefit purposes, left the Service unless more than 5 years expire.

Accounting and Contracts

31 U.S.C.A. Section 3522(b)(3)—extends the time for the armed forces to submit accounts to the Comptroller General from the usual 60 days to 90 days "during a war or national emergency and for 18 months after the war or emergency ends."

Contracts

31 U.S.C.A. Section 3726—excludes a "time of war" from the three-year deadline for federal agencies to file claims with the Administrator of General Services related to transportation or freight forwarding or to deduct from amounts subsequently owed to carriers or freight forwarders the amount paid on a bill in excess of the allowable rates.

31 U.S.C.A. Section 3727—allows a contract with DOD, the General Services Administration, and the Department of Energy to provide, or to be changed without consideration to provide, that a future payment under a contract to an assignee is not subject to reduction or setoff "during a war or national emergency proclaimed by the President or declared by law and ended by proclamation or law."

National Guard

32 U.S.C.A. Section 104—authorizes the President, in time of peace, to detail a commissioned officer of the Regular Army to perform the duties of chief of staff for each fully organized division of the Army National Guard in order "to insure prompt mobilization of the National Guard in time of war or other emergency."

32 U.S.C.A. Section 111—permits the President to suspend various statutory provisions relating to federal recognition of promotions in the Army and Air National Guard "in time of war, or of emergency declared by Congress."

Armed Forces

32 U.S.C.A. Section 703(b)—provides that "in time of actual or threatened war, the United States may requisition for military use" supplies and military publications bought by a state or territory "for cash, at cost plus transportation" from the Army or Air Force.

32 U.S.C.A. Section 715(b)—provides that "in time of war or armed conflict or if such a war or armed conflict intervenes within two years after it accrues, and if good cause is shown," the time within which a claim against the United States for property loss, personal injury or death caused by the National Guard must be filed is extended from two years from the time the claim accrued to "two years after the war or armed conflict is terminated."

National Oceanic and Atmospheric Administration

33 U.S.C.A. Section 854a-1—provides that the laws that pertain to the temporary appointment or advancement of commissioned officers "in time of war or national emergency" in the Navy shall also apply to personnel in National Oceanic and Atmospheric Administration (NOAA)., subject to a few limitations.

33 U.S.C.A. Section 3030—provides that the laws that pertain to the temporary appointment or advancement of commissioned officers "in time of war or national emergency" in the Navy shall also apply to officers of the NOAA, subject to a few limitations.

33 U.S.C.A. Section 3033—allows the President, "in time of emergency declared by the President or by the Congress, and in time of war," to suspend all or any part of the laws pertaining to the promotion of commissioned officers in the NOAA.

33 U.S.C.A. Section 3063—provides that the Secretaries of Defense and Commerce shall prescribe regulations governing the duties to be performed by NOAA "in time of war" and providing for the cooperation of NOAA with the military departments "in time of peace in preparation for its duties in time of war."

Ocean Dumping

33 U.S.C.A. Section 1902—states that provisions applying pollution control standards derived from the MARPOL Protocol to warships, naval auxiliaries, and vessels owned by the United States, other than submersibles, shall not apply "during time of war or a declared national emergency."

33 U.S.C.A. Section 2503—lifts the prohibition on the ocean dumping of potentially infectious medical waste by public vessels "during time of war or a declared national emergency."

Patents

35 U.S.C.A. Section 181—provides that an order by the Commissioner of Patents that a patent or patent application be kept secret for national security reasons, which otherwise must be renewed each year, shall remain in effect "during a time when the United States is at war" and for one year following the cessation of hostilities and "during a national emergency declared by the President" and for six months thereafter.

Armed Forces

37 U.S.C.A. Section 202—entitles an officer in the Coast Guard who holds a permanent appointment as rear admiral (lower half) on the retired list, and who "in time of war or

national emergency has served satisfactorily on active duty for two years in that grade or in a higher grade," to the pay of a rear admiral when on active duty.

37 U.S.C.A. Section 301(d)—provides that "in time of war, the President may suspend the payment of incentive pay" to members of a uniformed service for certain hazardous duties.

37 U.S.C.A. Section 301a(c)—provides that "in time of war, the President may suspend the payment of aviation career incentive pay" to members of a uniformed service.

37 U.S.C.A. Section 304(e)—provides that "in time of war, the President may suspend the payment of diving duty pay" to members of a uniformed service.

37 U.S.C.A. Section 477(d)—provides that the exceptions to the prohibition on members of the uniformed services receiving more than one dislocation allowance a year "does not apply in time of national emergency or in time of war."

37 U.S.C.A. Section 901—provides that "in time of war, an officer of an armed force who is serving with troops operating against an enemy and who exercises, under assignment in orders issued by competent authority, a command above that pertaining to his grade," is entitled to the pay and allowances "appropriate to the command so exercised."

37 U.S.C.A. Section 909—authorizes the continuation of special pay or incentive pay for members of the armed forces who are involuntarily retained on duty under Sections123 or 12305 of Title 10 unless "in time of war" the President suspends the authority under which the special pay or incentive pay was given.

Veterans' Care

38 U.S.C.A. Section 8111A—authorizes the Secretary of the Department of Veterans Affairs to provide hospital care, nursing home care, and medical services to members of the Armed Forces on active duty "during and immediately following a period of war, or a period of national emergency declared by the President or the Congress that involves the use of the Armed Forces in armed conflict."

Reemployment Rights

38 U.S.C.A. Section 4303(16))—includes within the definition of "uniformed services" for purposes of entitlement to the reemployment and other rights protected by the statute "the Armed Forces, the Army National Guard and the Air National Guard ..., the commissioned corps of the Public Health Service, and any other category of persons designated by the President in time of war or national emergency."

38 U.S.C.A. Section 4312(c))—limits the reemployment rights of those absent from their jobs because of service in the uniformed service to five years unless a longer absence is because the individual, *inter alia*, was "ordered to or retained on active duty (other than for training) under any provision of law because of a war or national emergency declared by the President or Congress, as determined by the Secretary concerned."

Sale of War Supplies to Foreign States

40 U.S.C.A. Section 1310—authorizes the President to sell war supplies, materials, and equipment, and the buildings, plants, and equipment necessary for their production, "to any foreign State or Government, engaged in war against any Government with which the United States is at war."

Defense Structures in the District of Columbia

40 U.S.C.A. Section 8722(b)(2)—excludes from the consultation procedures mandated for federal and D.C. agencies with the National Capital Planning Commission for construction projects in D.C. "structures erected by the Department of Defense during wartime or national emergency within existing military, naval, or Air Force reservations, except that the appropriate defense agency shall consult with the Commission as to any developments which materially affect traffic or require coordinated planning of the surrounding area."

Public Contracts

41 U.S.C.A. Section 1710(e)—provides that requirement for public-private competition prior to the conversion of an agency function to contractor performance do not apply "during war or during a period of national emergency declared by the President or Congress."

Public Health Service

42 U.S.C.A. Section 211(k)—allows commissioned officers in the Regular Corps of the Public Health Service to be recommended for promotion to any higher grade in their category, including the director grade, whether or not a vacancy exists in such grade, "in time of war or of national emergency proclaimed by the President."

42 U.S.C.A. Section 213—provides that commissioned officers of the Public Health Service and their surviving beneficiaries shall, "with respect to active service performed by such officers ... in time of war" be entitled to all rights, privileges, immunities, and benefits now or hereafter provided "under any law of the United States in the case of commissioned officers of the Army or their surviving beneficiaries on account of active military service, except retired pay and uniform allowances."

42 U.S.C.A. Section 217—authorizes the President to use the Public Health Service, "in time of war, or of emergency proclaimed by the President ... in such manner as shall in his judgment promote the public interest" and, "in time of war, or of emergency involving the national defense proclaimed by the President," to declare the commissioned corps of the Service to be a military service constituting a branch of the land and naval forces of the United States subject to the Uniform Code of Military Justice.

Infectious Diseases

42 U.S.C.A. Section 266—authorizes the Surgeon General, on recommendation of the National Advisory Health Council, to "provide by regulations for the apprehension and examination, in time of war," of any individual reasonably believed to be infected with a disease that is the "probable source of infection to members of the armed forces of the United States or to individuals engaged in the production or transportation of arms, munitions, ships, food, clothing, or other supplies for the armed forces."

Nuclear Energy

42 U.S.C.A. Section 2165—authorizes the commission that controls information on atomic energy development in the United States "during the state of war or period of national disaster due to enemy attack to employ individuals and to permit individuals access to Restricted Data prior to completion of a security investigation report ... "

Public Lands

43 U.S.C.A. Section 155—states that the provisions of the Engle Act governing the use of the public lands of the United States by the Department of Defense for defense purposes shall not apply "in time of war or national emergency hereafter declared by the President or Congress."

Natural Resources

43 U.S.C.A. Section 1314 (b)—gives the United States, "in time of war or when necessary for national defense," the right of first refusal to purchase any portion of lands and natural resources which are "specifically recognized, confirmed, established, and vested in and assigned to the respective States and others."

43 U.S.C.A. Section 1341(b)—provides that, "in time of war," the United States shall have the right of first refusal to purchase at the market price all or any portion of "any mineral produced from the outer Continental Shelf."

43 U.S.C.A. Section 1341(c)—allows the Secretary of the Interior to suspend leases on the outer Continental Shelf, on the recommendation of the Secretary of Defense, "during a state of war or national emergency declared by the Congress or the President of the United States after August 7, 1953."

43 U.S.C.A. Section 1353 (f)—clarifies that "nothing in this section" related to the federal purchase and disposition of oil and gas shall prohibit the right of the United States to purchase any oil or gas produced on the outer Continental Shelf "in time of war."

Destruction of Records

44 U.S.C.A. Section 3311—provides that "during a state of war between the United States and another nation, or when hostile action by a foreign power appears imminent," the head of an agency may authorize the destruction of records in his legal custody "situated in a military or naval establishment, ship, or other depository outside the territorial limits of continental United States."

Shipping

46 U.S.C.A. Section 5116—provides that a person causing or allowing the alteration, concealment, or removal of an official mark placed on a vessel by the government, "except to make a lawful change or to escape enemy capture in time of war," commits a class A misdemeanor.

46 U.S.C.A. Section 7113—provides that a licensed master, mate, pilot, or engineer of a vessel propelled by machinery or carrying hazardous liquid cargoes in bulk is not "liable to draft in time of war, except for performing duties authorized by the license."

46 U.S.C.A. Section 52101—provides reemployment rights for certain merchant seamen subject to certification by the Secretary of Transportation, *inter alia*, that the individual was employed on a vessel "that is owned, chartered, or controlled by the United States and used by the United States for a war, armed conflict, national emergency, or maritime mobilization need...."

46 U.S.C.A. Section 53107—requires the Secretary of Transportation to include in each operating agreement with merchant security fleet contractors an Emergency Preparedness Agreement providing that, "upon a request by the Secretary of Defense during time of war or national emergency, or whenever determined by the Secretary of Defense to be necessary for national security or contingency operation ..., a contractor for a vessel covered by an operating agreement under this chapter shall make available commercial transportation resources (including services)."

46 U.S.C.A. Section 53902—provides that government war risk insurance may be provided to vessels only on the condition that the vessel will be available to the government "in time of war or national emergency."

46 U.S.C.A. App. Section 56102—prohibits, "when the United States is at war or during any national emergency, the existence of which is declared by proclamation of the President," the transfer of any vessel or shipyard to non-citizens without the approval of the Secretary of Transportation.

46 U.S.C.A. Section 60311—exempts hospital ships in the ports of the United States "in time of war," from all tonnage taxes, light money, and pilotage charges in the ports of the United States" if the vessel is covered by a certain treaty.

Communications

47 U.S.C.A. Section 308—allows the Federal Communications Commission to waive the requirement of a formal written application for construction permits and station licenses, and

modifications and renewals thereof, "during a national emergency proclaimed by the President or declared by Congress and during the continuance of any war in which the United States is engaged and when such action is necessary for the national defense or security or otherwise in furtherance of the war effort."

47 U.S.C.A. Section 606—authorizes the President, "during the continuance of a war in which the United States is engaged," to direct that communications carriers give preference or priority to "such communications as in his judgment may be essential to the national defense and security"; to use the armed forces to prevent any obstruction of interstate or foreign communication by radio or wire "during any war in which the United States is engaged"; to suspend or amend all rules and regulations governing wire communications; to close any facility or station for wire communication; and to authorize the use or control of any such facility by the government "upon proclamation ... that there exists a state or threat of war involving the United States."

Railroads

49 U.S.C.A. Section 11124(a)—authorizes the President, "during time of war or threatened war," to direct the Transportation Board to "give preference or priority to the movement of certain traffic" and to direct all rail carriers within the Board's jurisdiction to "adopt every means within their control to facilitate and expedite" military traffic.

Procurement of Ships and Material during War

50 U.S.C.A. Section 82—authorizes the President, in time of war, to place orders for ships, modify or cancel existing contracts, require the owner or occupier of a ship or material manufacturing factory to supply specified articles, and to take over for use or operation by the government any factory, regardless of the existence of contract or agreement.

Protection of Ships and Harbors

50 U.S.C.A. Section 191—authorizes the Secretary of Transportation, "whenever the President by proclamation or Executive order declares a national emergency to exist by reason of actual or threatened war, insurrection, invasion, or disturbance or threatened disturbance of the international relations of the United States," to adopt rules and regulations governing the anchorage and movement of all vessels, foreign and domestic, in the territorial waters of the United States and, if necessary, to take possession of such vessels; and also authorizes the President, "whenever the President finds that the security of the United States is endangered by reason of actual or threatened war, or invasion, or insurrection or subversive activity, or of disturbances or threatened disturbances of the international relations of the United States," to take steps to safeguard all vessels, harbors, ports, and waterfront facilities in the United States against destruction, loss, or injury.

Federal Emergency Management Agency

50 U.S.C.A. Section 404(b)—provides that one function of the Director of the Federal Emergency Management Agency is to advise the President about programs for the "effective use in time of war of the Nation's natural and industrial resources for military and civilian needs, for the maintenance and stabilization of the civilian economy in time of war, and for the adjustment of such economy to war needs and conditions, policies for unifying, in time of war, the activities of Federal agencies and departments engaged in or concerned with production, procurement, distribution, or transportation of military or civilian supplies, materials, and products, and the relationship between potential supplies of, and potential requirements for, manpower, resources, and productive facilities in time of war."

Central Intelligence Agency (CIA) Retirement Plan

50 U.S.C.A. Section 2083—provides that a participant in the CIA retirement plan who, "during the period of any war or of any national emergency as proclaimed by the President or declared by the Congress," leaves to enter military service shall not be deemed as separated from the agency for purposes of the retirement plan unless the military service extends beyond five years.

International Emergency Economic Powers

50 U.S.C.A. Section 1702—authorizes the President, "when the United States is engaged in armed hostilities or has been attacked by a foreign country or foreign nationals, [to] confiscate any property, subject to the jurisdiction of the United States."

Trading with the Enemy Act

50 U.S.C.A. App. Section 2—defines "the beginning of the war ," for purposes of the "Trading with the Enemy Act of 1917," as "midnight ending the day on which Congress has declared, or shall declare war or the existence of a state of war."

50 U.S.C.A. App. Section 5(b)—provides extensive authority to the President, "during the time of war ... through any agency that he may designate," to regulate economic transactions with foreign countries and nationals, including the power to block any enemy property within the jurisdiction of the United States and to vest title to that property in the United States.

50 U.S.C.A. App. Section 9—authorizes the President, "in time of war or during any national emergency declared by the President," to sell foreign assets frozen under TWEA notwithstanding the existence of a suit by a person claiming that the property was improperly frozen or that he is otherwise legally entitled to the property if "the interest and welfare of the United States require the sale...."

50 U.S.C.A. App. Section 10—provides that any citizen or corporation of the United States or corporation desiring to "manufacture, or cause to be manufactured, a machine, manufacture, composition of matter, or design, or to carry on, or to use any trade-mark, print, label or cause to be carried on, a process under any patent or copyrighted matter owned or controlled by an enemy or ally of enemy at any time during the existence of a state of war" may apply to the President for a license.

50 U.S.C.A. App. Section 38—provides that any person in the United States may legally donate and deliver any article intended to be used solely to relieve human suffering to persons in a country with which the United States was at war "at any time after the date of cessation of hostilities."

Selective Service Act

50 U.S.C.A. App. Section 460(e)—provides that the statutory ceiling on the number of armed forces personnel who may be assigned to the Selective Service System does not apply "during a time of war or a national emergency declared by Congress or the President" and mandates that the System be maintained as an active standby organization capable of immediate operation "in the event of a national emergency."

(3) Statutory Authorities Triggered by Declaration or Existence of National Emergency

As noted, many of the statutes in the previous two subsections can also be triggered not only by a declaration of war or the existence of a state of war but also by a declaration of national emergency. There are, in addition, a number of statutes that can be triggered only upon a declaration of national emergency or the existence of such an emergency. These standby authorities do not automatically come into effect upon the issuance of a declaration of national emergency but only in conformity with the procedures set forth in the National Emergencies Act. The statutes, listed generally in the order in which they appear in the U.S. Code Annotated, include the following:

Federal Employees

5 U.S.C.A. Section 3326—allows retired members of the armed forces to be appointed to civil service positions in the Department of Defense for 180 days after their retirement if "a state of national emergency exists."

5 U.S.C.A. Section 5303—allows the President, "because of national emergency or serious economic conditions affecting the general welfare," to alter the annual adjustment in pay schedules that would otherwise be effective.

5 U.S.C.A. Section 5304a—allows the President, "because of national emergency or serious economic conditions affecting the general welfare," to alter the locality-based comparability pay increases that would otherwise be effective.

Agriculture

7 U.S.C.A. Section 1332(c)—requires the Secretary of Agriculture to increase or terminate a national marketing quota for wheat in case of "a national emergency or ... a material increase in the demand for wheat." (Note: This authority was suspended from 1996 to 2002., 7 U.S.C.A. Section 7301(a), and from 2002 to 2007, 7 U.S.C.A. Section 7992(a)(1).For earlier suspensions, see note to 7 U.S.C.A. §1332.)

7 U.S.C.A. Section 1371(b)—requires the Secretary of Agriculture to increase or terminate a national marketing quota or acreage allotment for cotton or rice, if necessary to meet "a national emergency or ... a material increase in export demand."

7 U.S.C.A. Section 1444(e)(4)—allows the Secretary of Agriculture to require a set-aside of cropland if he determines that the "total supply of agricultural commodities will, in the absence of such a set-aside, be excessive taking into account the need for an adequate carryover to maintain reasonable and stable supplies and prices and to meet a national emergency."

7 U.S.C.A. Section 1444(h)(5)(A)(i)—allows the Secretary of Agriculture to limit the acreage planted to extra long staple cotton if he determines that the "total supply of extra long staple cotton, in the absence of such limitation, will be excessive taking into account the need for an adequate carryover to maintain reasonable and stable prices and to meet a national emergency."

7 U.S.C.A. Section 1736y(3)—declares it to be the policy of the United States that the export of agricultural commodities and products should not be prohibited or limited except "in time of a national emergency declared by the President under the Export Administration Act (50 App. U.S.C.A. §§2401 *et seq.*).

7 U.S.C.A. Section 1743(a)(6)—allows the Commodity Credit Corporation to dispose of commodity set-asides "in accordance with the directions of the President ... to meet any national emergency declared by the President."

7 U.S.C. Section 1982—provides relief from certain agricultural loan obligations for reservists mobilized under any "provision of law during a war or during a national emergency declared by the President or Congress."

7 U.S.C.A. Section 4208(b)—provides that the policies stated in the "Farmland Protection Policy Act (7 U.S.C.A. §§4201-4208) do not apply "to the acquisition or use of farmland for national defense purposes during a national emergency."

Armed Services

10 U.S.C.A. Section 1064—authorizes members of the National Guard called to duty during a federally declared disaster or "a national emergency declared by the President or Congress" to use commissary stores and MWR retail facilities.

10 U.S.C.A. Section 1076a—permits the Secretary of Defense, during a "national emergency declared by the President or Congress," to waive the charges otherwise payable by a member of the Selected Reserve of the Ready Reserve or a member of the Individual Ready Reserve for dental insurance coverage if necessary to ensure readiness for deployment.

10 U.S.C.A. Section 2304—allows the Secretaries of the military departments and the Department of Transportation as well as the Administrator of NASA to exclude a particular

source from a competitive procurement procedure or to solicit bids only from particular sources when it would be in the interest of national defense in having a facility, producer, manufacturer, or other supplier "available for furnishing the property or service in case of a national emergency or industrial mobilization."

10 U.S.C.A. Section 4025—prescribes that "during a national emergency declared by the President" the regular working hours of laborers producing military supplies or munitions for the Army are 8 hours a day and 40 hours a week, but allows these limits to be exceeded under regulations prescribed by the Secretary of the Army.

10 U.S.C.A. Section 9025—provides that "during a national emergency declared by the President" the working hours of laborers and mechanics employed by the Department of the Air Force are 8 hours a day and 40 hours a week but allows the Secretary of the Air Force to alter these hours by regulation.

10 U.S.C.A. Section 12302—allows the Secretary of a military department, "in time of national emergency declared by the President after January 1, 1953, or when otherwise authorized by law," to order any member or unit of the Ready Reserve to active duty without their consent for up to 24 months.

Fort McHenry

16 U.S.C.A. Section 440—allows Fort McHenry to be closed "in case of a national emergency" and to be used for military purposes "during the period of the emergency."

Customs Service

19 U.S.C.A. Section 1318(b)—authorizes the Secretary of the Treasury, "when necessary to respond to a national emergency declared under the National Emergencies Act," to temporarily eliminate, consolidate, or relocate any office of the Customs Service, modify its hours of service or services rendered, and "take any other action necessary to respond directly to the national emergency...." (This authority may be delegated to the Secretary of Homeland Security pursuant to 6 U.S.C.A. §212.)

Barro Colorado Island

20 U.S.C.A. Section 79—directs that Barro Colorado Island in Gatun Lake in the Canal Zone be left in its natural state for scientific observation and investigation "except in the event of declared national emergency."

Foreign Relations[163]

22 U.S.C.A. Section 2318(a)—authorizes the President, if "an unforeseen emergency exists which requires immediate military assistance to a foreign country or international

organization" to provide up to $100 million in defense articles and services apart from the authority of the Arms Export Control Act but only upon notice to Congress.

22 U.S.C.A. Section 4103(c)—allows the President to suspend any statutory provision relating to labor-management relations in the Foreign Service "if the President determines in writing that the suspension is necessary in the interest of national security because of an emergency."

Federal Highways

23 U.S.C.A. Section 127(h)—permits the Secretary of Transportation to waive vehicle weight limits on the portion of Interstate Route 95 in Maine between Augusta and Bangor for the purpose of making bulk shipments of jet fuel to the air National Guard Base at the Bangor International Airport "during a period of national emergency."

National Oceanographic and Atmospheric Administration

33 U.S.C.A. Section 3061—authorizes the President, "whenever in his judgment a sufficient national emergency exists," to transfer such vessels, equipment, stations, and commissioned officers of NOAA to a military department "as he may deem in the best interests of the country."

Basic Pay of the Uniformed Services

37 U.S.C.A. Section 1009(e)—permits the President to provide for alternative pay adjustments if he considers the formula otherwise required by law to be inappropriate because of "national emergency or serious economic conditions affecting the general welfare," provided a plan for such alternative adjustment is submitted to Congress by September 1 of the preceding year.

Veterans Affairs

38 U.S.C.A. Section 1721—authorizes the Secretary of the Department of Veterans Affairs to prescribe rules for good conduct by those receiving services in Department facilities "during a period of national emergency (other than a period of war or an emergency described in section 8111A of [title 38])."

Davis-Bacon Act

40 U.S.C.A. Section 3147—allows the President to suspend the requirements of the Davis- Bacon Act mandating that laborers and mechanics on federal and D.C. construction and public works projects be paid prevailing wages "in the event of a national emergency."

Real Property and Contracts

40 U.S.C.A. Section 545—allows GSA to negotiate disposal and contracts for disposal of surplus property without first seeking public bids "but subject to obtaining such competition as is feasible under the circumstances, if necessary in the public interest during the period of a national emergency declared by the President or the Congress...."

40 U.S.C.A. Section 905—allows GSA to waive the procedures otherwise applicable to the disposal or acquisition of real property in urban areas "during any period of national emergency proclaimed by the President."

41 U.S.C.A. Section 3304)—authorizes executive agencies to use noncompetitive procurement procedures if "it is necessary to award the contract to a particular source or sources in order (A) to maintain a facility, producer, manufacturer, or other supplier available for furnishing property or services in case of a national emergency or to achieve industrial mobilization...."

Public Health

42 U.S.C.A. Section 204—establishes in the Public Health Service a Reserve Corps "for the purpose of securing a reserve for duty in the Service in time of national emergency," which is to "be available and ready for involuntary calls to active duty during national emergencies and public health crises, similar to the uniformed service reserve personnel."[164]

42 U.S.C.A. Section 1320b-5—authorizes the Secretary of Health and Human Services to waive or modify certain requirements of Medicare, Medicaid, State Children's Health Insurance programs, and the Health Insurance Portability and Accountability Act, related to certification or licensing of health care providers, sanctions related to physician referrals, deadlines and other penalties, in response to an emergency declared by the President pursuant to the National Emergencies Act.

Ryan White Comprehensive AIDS Resources Emergency Act of 1990

42 U.S.C.A. Section 300ff-83—authorizes the Secretary of Health and Human Services to waive requirements with respect to certain Human Immunodeficiency Virus programs during an emergency or disaster declared by the President pursuant to the National Emergencies Act, among other authorities.

Prohibition of Compensation

42 U.S.C.A. Section 1712—bars employees of contractors of the U.S. providing services outside of the U.S. who suffer injury or death from a war hazard from receiving compensation if they have been "convicted in a court of competent jurisdiction of any subversive act against the United States or any of its allies, committed after the declaration by the President on May 27, 1941, of the national emergency ..."

Relocation

42 U.S.C.A. Section 4625(c)(3)—waives the requirement in the Uniform Relocation Assistance Act that a person displaced from their dwelling by a project of a federal agency or one undertaken with federal financial assistance not be required to move until afforded a reasonable opportunity to relocate to a comparable dwelling in the case of "a national emergency declared by the President."

Resources

42 U.S.C.A. Section 6393(a)(2)(A)—waives the requirement that a minimum of 30 days be allowed for comment on proposed rules and regulations to implement the domestic supply availability and standby energy authorities of the Energy Policy and Conservation Act "if the President finds that such waiver is necessary to act expeditiously during an emergency affecting the national security of the United States."

Merchant Marine

46 U.S.C.A. Section 7507—permits the Secretary of the department in which the Coast Guard is operating to extend a license of certificate of registry for not more than one year in response to a national emergency or natural disaster.

46 U.S.C.A. Section 8103(h)(1)—allows the President to suspend the citizenship requirements that otherwise apply to the officers and seamen on documented vessels of the U.S. "during a proclaimed national emergency."

46 U.S.C.A. Section 8301(d)—allows the Secretary of the Department in which the Coast Guard is operating to suspend the requirements relating to the number of licensed individuals that vessels subject to inspection must have "during a national emergency proclaimed by the President."

46 U.S.C.A. Section 57521—permits the Secretary of Transportation to terminate any charter of DOT vessels "whenever the President shall proclaim that the security of the national defense makes it advisable, or during any national emergency declared by proclamation of the President."

46 U.S.C.A. Section 56301—authorizes the Secretary of Transportation to requisition or purchase any vessel or other watercraft owned by citizens of the United States "whenever the

President shall proclaim that the security of the national defense makes it advisable or during any national emergency declared by proclamation of the President" and to transfer the possession or control of any such vessel or watercraft to any other department or agency of the government.

Airports

49 U.S.C.A. Section 114—gives the Under Secretary of Transportation responsible for the Transportation Security Administration the authority "during a national emergency" to coordinate all domestic transportation and oversee the transportation-related responsibilities of other non-military federal departments and agencies but states that this authority "shall not supersede" the authority of other federal departments and agencies related to transportation.

49 U.S.C.A. Section 40101 note, as added by P.L. 107-71, Section 127 (November 19, 2001)—authorizes the Secretary of Transportation "during a national emergency affecting air transportation or intrastate air transportation" to grant complete or partial waivers from restrictions that would otherwise apply regarding the carriage by aircraft of freight, mail, emergency medical supplies, personnel, or patients.

49 U.S.C.A. Section 47152(5)—provides that the United States, "during a national emergency declared by the President or Congress," is entitled to use, control, or possess any part of a public airport that is on surplus property donated by the government.

50 U.S.C.A. Section 196—provides that at any time vessels can be requisitioned under 46 U.S.C.A. Section 1242, *supra*, which can come into effect "whenever the President shall proclaim that the security of the national defense makes it advisable or during any national emergency declared by proclamation of the President," the President may also purchase or requisition merchant vessels not owned by U.S. citizens and lying idle in U.S. waters "which the President finds necessary to the national defense."

Modification of Defense Contracts

50 U.S.C.A. Section 1435—provides that the President's authority to modify defense contracts in order to "facilitate the national defense" without regard to other provisions of law regarding the making, performance, amendment, or modification of contracts is effective "only during a national emergency declared by Congress or the President" and for six months after the termination thereof.

National Emergencies Act

50 U.S.C.A. Section 1631—requires the President, whenever he "declares a national emergency," to specify in the declaration or by subsequent executive orders published in the *Federal Register* and transmitted to Congress which emergency statutory authorities he or other officers will exercise, prior to their exercise.

International Economic Emergency Powers Act

50 U.S.C.A. Section 1701—authorizes the President to exercise the extensive powers with respect to the property of, and economic transactions with, a foreign country or entity granted by the International Emergency Economic Powers Act (IEEPA) "to deal with any unusual and extraordinary threat, which has its source in whole or substantial part outside the United States, to the national security, foreign policy, or economy of the United States, if the President declares a national emergency with respect to such threat."

50 U.S.C.A. Section 1702—exempts from any economic embargo imposed under IEEPA donations of articles such as food, clothing, and medicine intended to relieve human suffering unless the President determines, *inter alia*, that such donations "would seriously impair his ability to deal with any national emergency declared under section 1701 of this title."

50 U.S.C.A. Section 1706—provides that foreign assets frozen pursuant to IEEPA may remain frozen beyond the date of the termination of the national emergency if necessary "on account of claims involving such country or its nationals."

Defense Production Act

50 U.S.C.A. App. Section 2091(a)(2)—provides that certain conditions that are prerequisite to the President's exercise of the authority under Title III to provide guarantees for the financing of contracts or other operations deemed necessary for the "procurement of materials or performance of services for the national defense" do not apply "during periods of national emergency declared by Congress or the President."

50 U.S.C.A. App. Section 2091(d)(1)(B)—provides that the aggregate ceiling of $50 million on the total amount of financing guarantees that can be outstanding under Title III and certain other conditions may be waived "during a period of national emergency declared by the Congress or the President."

50 U.S.C.A. App. Section 2092—provides that certain Presidential determinations that are prerequisite to the making of direct federal loans under Title III for the expansion of productive capacity and supply for the national defense do not apply and that the aggregate ceiling of $50 million on such loans and certain other procedural requirements may be waived "during periods of national emergency declared by the Congress or the President."

50 U.S.C.A. App. Section 2093—provides that a number of conditions and prerequisites to the exercise of the authority under Title III to expand the productive capacity and supply of private industry for national defense purposes by means of purchase and resale of an industrial resource, a critical technology item, or a critical and strategic raw material may be waived "during periods of national emergency declared by the Congress or the President."

CONGRESSIONAL PROCEDURES FOR DECLARING WAR OR AUTHORIZING THE USE OF FORCE

The following section discusses how Congress would act on a joint resolution or bill to declare war or authorize the use of force if the House and Senate were to consider that measure under the regular procedures of each house. It also describes how a measure declaring war or authorizing the use of force would be considered under the procedures contained in the War Powers Resolution of 1973.[165]

Regular Procedures

The Senate's published precedents do not suggest that a measure proposing to declare war or authorize the use of force, if considered outside the framework of the War Powers Resolution, would be immune from the potentially laborious process to which other bills and joint resolutions are subject (except those that benefit from special expedited procedures under rule-making statutes). For example, a joint resolution declaring war or authorizing the use of force presumably would not be eligible for immediate floor consideration at the time it is introduced, and it presumably would be subject to possible delays resulting from the Senators' exercise of their right to debate at length.

Similarly, the precedents of the House apparently do not grant privilege to a joint resolution declaring war or authorizing the use of force either under the "leave to report" authority that House rules and precedents give to certain House committees or as a question of the privileges of the House. Concerning the latter, former House Parliamentarian Wm. Holmes Brown has observed that "Rule IX [on questions of privilege] is concerned not with the privileges of the Congress as a legislative branch, but only with the privileges of the House itself." Thus, neither the enumeration of legislative powers in Article I, sec. 8 of the Constitution nor the prohibition of that article against any withdrawal from the Treasury except by enactment of an appropriation renders a measure purporting to exercise or limit those powers a question of the privileges of the House.[166]

Because a joint resolution declaring war or authorizing the use of force proposes to exercise a constitutional power of "the Congress as a legislative branch," not of the House alone, it would seem, therefore, not to qualify as a question of privilege. If so, the House would consider the joint resolution according to its established procedures for dealing with other legislative measures,[167] unless the proposed declaration or authorization were to be considered under the terms of the War Powers Resolution.

Congress has adopted eight declarations of war during the 20th century—two at the outset of U.S. involvement in World War I and six in the course of World War II. House and Senate consideration of the initial declarations in each of these wars is illustrative of the process that Congress followed. On both occasions, the House and Senate acted to declare war in response to urgent presidential requests made personally before joint sessions of Congress. In light of the importance that most Members attached to these requests, it is not surprising that, in both cases, the two houses acted on the joint resolutions quickly and without following all their regular legislative procedures.

By way of illustration, the following is a brief summary of how the House and Senate considered the initial joint resolutions to declare war in 1917 and 1941.

World War I

Congress convened on April 2, 1917, and on that evening, President Wilson addressed both houses to request that Congress declare war against Germany. Immediately after the President's address, Senator Martin introduced S.J.Res. 1, to declare war, which was referred to the Committee on Foreign Relations. Also on April 2, Representative Flood introduced a companion resolution, H.J.Res 24, which was referred to the Committee on Foreign Affairs.

The Senate committee reported S.J.Res. 1 with an amendment on the following day. Senator LaFollette objected to a unanimous consent request that the Senate consider the measure immediately. Consequently, the joint resolution had to lie over for a day, pursuant to paragraph 4(a) of Senate Rule XVII. On April 4, the Senate agreed by unanimous consent to consider the joint resolution, agreed to the committee amendment, and, after considerable debate, passed the joint resolution by a roll call vote of 82-6.

The House committee reported H.J.Res. 24 on April 4, and the House then agreed, by unanimous consent, to consider the measure on the following day "under the general rules of the House." Because the joint resolution, once reported, was placed on the Union Calendar, "the general rules of the House" required that it be considered in Committee of the Whole. Consequently, when the House convened on April 5, Representative Flood moved that the House resolve into Committee of the Whole to consider H.J.Res. 24. Before the House agreed to his motion, however, it also agreed to Representative Flood's unanimous consent request that the House instead consider S.J.Res. 1, which the Senate already had passed. After much debate, and after rejecting two amendments in Committee of the Whole and a motion to recommit with instructions in the House, the House passed S.J. Res. 1 by a roll call vote of 373-50.

World War II

On December 8, 1941, President Franklin D. Roosevelt addressed a joint session of Congress and asked for a declaration of war against Japan. Immediately after the joint session ended, the Senate reconvened and, following a live quorum call, Senator Connolly introduced a joint resolution declaring war. At Senator Connolly's request, and by unanimous consent, the Senate agreed to consider the joint resolution immediately, without committee consideration. Within minutes, and after brief statements by Senators Connolly and Vandenberg, the Senate passed the joint resolution by a roll call vote of 82-0.

Also immediately after the President's address, the House acted by considering and agreeing to Representative McCormack's motion to suspend the rules and pass H.J.Res. 254, which Representative McCormack introduced at that time. December 8 being a Monday, suspension motions were in order on that day. Immediately after the House passed H.J.Res. 254 by a roll call vote of 388-1, the House received a message from the Senate that it already had passed its joint resolution, now numbered S.J. Res. 116. The House then agreed to Representative McCormack's unanimous consent request that the House take the Senate joint resolution from the Speaker's table and agree to it. This action was necessary in order for both houses to pass the same measure, making it eligible to be presented to the President for his signature.

Congressional Procedures under the War Powers Resolution

Enactment of the War Powers Resolution in November 1973 created special expedited procedures by which the House and Senate can act on joint resolutions or bills to declare war or authorize the use of force, if those measures are considered in accordance with the other, related provisions of that law.[168]

These expedited procedures were enacted into law as part of the War Powers Resolution as an exercise of the constitutional rule-making powers of the House and Senate. Article I of the Constitution empowers each house to set its own rules. When Congress enacts into law provisions that affect only the internal operations of the House or Senate, or both, those provisions are known as rule-making provisions of law that are enacted pursuant to this grant of power under Article I. Such rule-making provisions have exactly the same force and effect as provisions contained in the Standing Rules of the House and Senate.[169] Consequently, the house to which certain rule-making provisions apply may enforce, ignore, waive, suspend, supplement, or amend them by its own unilateral action, as it sees fit. For example, the House could adopt a special rule, or the Senate could agree to a unanimous consent request, that would supersede some or all of the procedures described here.

Section 4(a) of the War Powers Resolution directs the President to submit a report to Congress within 48 hours after U.S. armed forces are introduced "into hostilities or into situations where imminent involvement in hostilities is clearly indicated by the circumstances."[170] Section 5(a) provides for the receipt and for the referral to committee of any such presidential report. Under Section 5(b), the President is required to terminate use of the armed forces within 60 calendar days (90 days in some circumstances) after submitting his report unless Congress takes any one of several actions. One of these actions is to declare war; another is to "enact a specific authorization for such use of United States Armed Forces" as an alternative to declaring war. Under another section of the War Powers Resolution, Congress can also adopt a bill or joint resolution at any time requiring the President to remove the armed forces unless a declaration of war or statutory authorization has been enacted.[171]

Section 6 of the War Powers Resolution contains the expedited, or "fast-track," procedures that were included in the law to enable the House and Senate to act within the 60 calendar-day period on a bill or joint resolution contemplated by Section 5(b).[172]

If, under Section 6(a), such a measure is introduced at least 30 calendar days before the end of the 60-day period, the measure is referred to the House Foreign Affairs Committee or the Senate Foreign Relations Committee, as the case may be. That committee is required to report one such measure, with its recommendations, not later than 24 calendar days before the end of the 60-day period. This provision suggests that the committee can report the measure with the committee's proposed amendments, if any. The subsection also provides that its provisions are to govern "unless such House shall otherwise determine by the yeas and nays." In other words, the House or Senate can, by a rollcall vote decided by a simple majority, release its committee from the obligation to report a measure proposing to declare war or to take some other action enumerated in Section 5(b).

If the House or Senate committee does report, it is not required to report the measure favorably. Instead, it may report it unfavorably or without recommendation. But what if either the Senate or House committee fails to report a covered bill or joint resolution within the time permitted? The Senate Parliamentarian has stated that the Senate Foreign Relations Committee would be automatically discharged if it failed to report as required by this subsection. The House Parliamentarian has stated that, should the House Foreign Affairs Committee fail to report in a timely manner, a privileged motion to discharge that committee would be in order on the House floor.

Section 6(b) governs initial House and Senate floor consideration of a joint resolution reported from committee pursuant to Section 6(a). Under Section 6(b), the bill or joint \resolution, once reported (or once the committee is discharged), "shall become the pending business" of the House or Senate, as the case may be. By making a covered measure the pending business on the House or Senate floor, the War Powers Resolution evidently makes the measure privileged for floor consideration in the House (without the need for the Rules Committee to report a special rule for that purpose), or obviates the need for a motion (that usually is debatable) to proceed to the measure's consideration in the Senate. Because Section 6(b) contains no provisions to the contrary, the measure presumably would be amendable on the floor of either house to the same extent as any other bill or joint resolution that house considers, or could be tabled.

Section 6(b) goes on to require that the House or Senate vote on final passage of the measure within three calendar days after having become the pending business, "unless such House shall otherwise determine by yeas and nays." The effect of this subsection probably is more significant for the Senate than the House, because it is designed to preclude a filibuster on the Senate floor. In addition, the last provision of the subsection evidently gives either house options to adjust the timing and length of floor consideration by adopting any of several conceivable motions by rollcall vote. For example, either house might agree by motion to postpone consideration of the measure to a date certain. Alternatively, either house might dispose of the measure by a rollcall vote in favor of a motion to table or recommit it or to postpone its consideration indefinitely. Under the same authority, the House or Senate also might be able to shorten the debate to less than three calendar days or to extend the time for debate.

Sections 6(c) and 6(d) address the process for the House and Senate to reach agreement when each has passed a measure covered by Section 5(b). In summary, Section 6(c) provides for expedited committee and floor action in one house on a covered measure that the other house already has passed. Finally, Section 6(d) states that if a conference is necessary to reach a compromise between House and Senate versions of a covered measure, the conferees are to be appointed "promptly," the conferees are to report in either agreement or disagreement within specified time periods, and the two houses are to act on the conference report before the end of the 60-day period.

These last two subsections raise the problem that no rules or rule-making statute can compel the House and Senate to reach agreement. All that expedited procedures can do is to require that the conferees report, and that the House and Senate act on their report, by a time certain. The War Powers Resolution cannot ensure that both houses will agree on the same position by the end of the 60-day period. If the two houses were unable to agree by the end of the 60 days, that situation presumably would be reflected in (1) votes by one or both houses to reject a conference report in agreement, or (2) votes by both houses to agree to a conference report in disagreement (in other words, votes in each house to accept the report of the conferees that they were unable to reach agreement within the time allotted them). In either case, there is nothing in the statute that would preclude the two houses from appointing a new conference committee that might present a new conference report in agreement at some later date. However, a conference report filed in the Senate after the expiration of the 60-day period might well be subject to extended debate because, presumably, consideration of the report no longer would be governed by Section 6. Instead, the report would be considered under the Senate's regular procedures.

APPENDIX A. TEXTS OF FORMAL DECLARATIONS OF WAR BY THE UNITED STATES

War with Great Britain 1812

(Act of June 18, 1812, ch. 102, 2 Stat 755)

CHAP. CII.—*An Act declaring War between the United Kingdom of Great Britain and Ireland and the dependencies thereof, and the United States of America and their territories.*

Be it enacted by the Senate and House of Representatives of the United States of America in Congress assembled, That war be and the same is hereby declared to exist between the United Kingdom of Great Britain and Ireland and the dependencies thereof, and the United States of America and their territories; and that the President of the United States is hereby authorized to use the whole land and naval force of the United States to carry the same into effect, and to issue to private armed vessels of the United States commissions or letters of marque and general reprisal, in such form as he shall think proper, and under the seal of the United States, against the vessels, goods, and effects of the government of the said United Kingdom of Great Britain and Ireland, and the subjects thereof.

APPROVED, June 18, 1812.

[Terminated by Treaty of Ghent, entered into force Feb. 17, 1815. 8 Stat. 218, Treaty Series 109.]

War with Mexico 1846

(Act of May 13, 1846, ch. 16, 9 Stat. 9)

CHAP. XVI.—*An Act providing for the Prosecution of the existing War between the United States and the Republic of Mexico.*

Whereas, by the act of the Republic of Mexico, a state of war exists between that Government and the United States:

Be it enacted by the Senate and House of Representatives of the United States of America in Congress assembled, That, for the purpose of enabling the government of the United States to prosecute said war to a speedy and successful termination, the President be, and he is hereby, authorized to employ the militia, naval, and military forces of the United States, and to call for and accept the services of any number of volunteers, not exceeding fifty thousand, who may offer their services, either as cavalry, artillery, infantry, or riflemen, to serve twelve months after they shall have arrived at the place of rendezvous, or to the end of the war, unless sooner discharged, according to the time for which they shall have been mustered into service; and that the sum of ten millions of dollars, out of any moneys in the treasury, or to come into the treasury, not otherwise appropriated, be, and the same is hereby, appropriated for the purpose of carrying the provisions of this act into effect.

SEC. 2. *And be it further enacted*, That the militia, when called into the service of the United States by virtue of this act, or any other act, may, if in the opinion of the President of the United States the public interest requires it, be compelled to serve for a term not exceeding six months after their arrival at the place of rendezvous, in any one year, unless sooner discharged.

SEC. 3. *And be it further enacted,* That the said volunteers shall furnish their own clothes, and if cavalry, their own horses and horse equipments; and when mustered into service shall be armed at the expense of the United States.

SEC. 4. *And be it further enacted,* That said volunteers shall, when called into actual service, and while remaining therein, be subject to the rules and articles of war, and shall be, in all respects except as to clothing and pay, placed on the same footing with similar corps of the United States army; and in lieu of clothing every non-commissioned officer and private in any company, who may thus offer himself, shall be entitled, when called into actual service, to receive in money a sum equal to the cost of clothing of a non-commissioned officer or private (as the case may be) in the regular troops of the United States.

SEC 5. *And be it further enacted,* That the said volunteers so offering their services shall be accepted by the President in companies, battalions, squadrons, and regiments, whose officers shall be appointed in the manner prescribed by law in the several States and Territories to which such companies, battalions, squadrons, and regiments, shall respectively belong.

SEC. 6. *And be it further enacted,* That the President of the United States be, and he is hereby, authorized to organize companies so tendering their service into battalions or squadrons, battalions and squadrons into regiments, regiments into brigades, and brigades into divisions, as soon as the number of volunteers shall render such organization, in his judgment, expedient; and the President shall, if necessary, apportion the staff, field, and general officers among the respective States and Territories from which the volunteers shall tender their services as he may deem proper.

SEC 7. *And be it further enacted,* That the volunteers who may be received into the service of thc United States by virtue of the provisions of this act, and who shall be wounded or otherwise disabled in the service, shall be entitled to all the benefit which may be conferred on persons wounded in the service of the United States.

SEC 8. *And be it further enacted,* That the President of the United States be, and he is hereby, authorized forthwith to complete all the public armed vessels now authorized by law, and to purchase or charter, arm, equip, and man, such merchant vessels and steam boats as, upon examination, may be found fit, or easily converted into armed vessels fit for the public service, and in such number as he may deem necessary for the protection of the seaboard, lake coast, and the general defense of the country.

SEC. 9. *And be it further enacted,* That whenever the militia or volunteers are called and received into the service of the United States, under the provisions of this act, they shall have the organization of the army of the United States, and shall have the same pay and allowances; and all mounted privates, non-commissioned officers, musicians, and artificers, shall be allowed 40 cents per day for the use and risk of their horses, except of horses actually killed in action; and if any mounted volunteer, private, non-commissioned officer, musician, or artificer, shall not keep himself provided with a serviceable horse, the said volunteer shall serve on foot.

APPROVED, May 13, 1846.

[Terminated by Treaty of Guadalupe Hidalgo, entered into force May 30, 1848. 9 Stat. 922, Treaty Series 207.]

War with Spain 1898

(Act of April 25, 1898, ch. 189, 30 Stat. 364)

CHAP. 189.—An Act Declaring that war exists between the United States of America and the Kingdom of Spain.

Be it enacted by the Senate and House of Representatives of the United States of America in Congress assembled, First. That war be, and the same is hereby, declared to exist, and that war has existed since the twenty-first day of April, anno Domini eighteen hundred and ninety-eight, including said day, between the United States of America and the Kingdom of Spain.

Second. That the President of the United States be, and he hereby is, directed and empowered to use the entire land and naval forces of the United States, and to call into the actual service of the United States the militia of the several States, to such extent as may be necessary to carry this Act into effect.

APPROVED, April 25, 1898.

[Terminated by Treaty of Paris, entered into force April 11, 1899. 30 Stat. 1754, Treaty Series 343.]

War with Germany 1917

(Act of April 6, 1917, ch. 1, 40 Stat. 1)

CHAP. 1.—Joint Resolution Declaring that a state of war exists between the Imperial German Government and the Government and the people of the United States and making provision to prosecute the same.

Whereas the Imperial German Government has committed repeated acts of war against the Government and the people of the United States of America: Therefore be it

Resolved by the Senate and House of Representatives of the United States of America in Congress assembled, That the state of war between the United States and the Imperial German Government which has thus been thrust upon the United States is hereby formally declared; and that the President be, and he is hereby, authorized and directed to employ the entire naval and military forces of the United States and the resources of the Government to carry on war against the Imperial German Government; and to bring the conflict to a successful termination all of the resources of the country are hereby pledged by the Congress of the United States.

APPROVED, April 6, 1917.

[Terminated by Act of July 2, 1921, [S.J.Res. 16] ch. 40, 42 Stat. 105 which declared the state of war between the U.S. and Germany to be at an end. Recognized by Treaty on Establishment of Friendly Relations, entered into force November 11, 1921. 42 Stat. 1939, Treaty Series 658.]

War with Austria-Hungary 1917

(Act of December 7, 1917, ch. 1, 40 Stat. 429)

CHAP. 1—*Joint Resolution Declaring that a state of war exists between the Imperial and Royal Austro-Hungarian Government and the Government and the people of the United States, and making provision to prosecute the same.*

Whereas the Imperial and Royal Austro-Hungarian Government has committed repeated acts of war against the Government and the people of the United States of America: Therefore be it

Resolved by the Senate and House of Representatives of the United States of America in Congress assembled, That a state of war is hereby declared to exist between the United States of America and the Imperial and Royal Austro-Hungarian Government; and that the President be, and he is hereby, authorized and directed to employ the entire naval and military forces of the United States and the resources of the Government to carry on war against the Imperial and Royal Austro- Hungarian Government; and to bring the conflict to a successful termination all the resources of the country are hereby pledged by the Congress of the United States.

APPROVED, December 7, 1917.

[Terminated by Act of July 2, 1921, [S.J. Res. 16] ch. 40, 42 Stat. 105 which declared the state of war between the U.S. and Austria, a successor state and government to the Austro-Hungarian monarchy, to be at an end. 42 Stat. 105. This was recognized by a Treaty on Establishment of Friendly Relations, entered into force November 8, 1921. 42 Stat. 1939, Treaty Series 658. The Act of July 2, 1921, also declared the state of war between the U.S. and Hungary, a successor state and government to the Austro-Hungarian monarchy, to be at an end. This was recognized by a Treaty on Establishing Friendly Relations, entered into force December 17, 1921. 42 Stat. 1951, Treaty Series 660.]

War with Japan 1941

(Act of December 8, 1941, ch. 561, 55 Stat. 795) [Chapter 561]

JOINT RESOLUTION

Declaring that a state of war exists between the Imperial Government of Japan and the Government and the people of the United States and making provisions to prosecute the same.

Whereas the Imperial Government of Japan has committed unprovoked acts of war against the Government and the people of the United States of America: Therefore be it

Resolved by the Senate and House of Representatives of the United States of America in Congress assembled, That the state of war between the United States and the Imperial Government of Japan which has thus been thrust upon the United States is hereby formally declared; and the President is hereby authorized and directed to employ the entire naval and military forces of the United States and the resources of the Government to carry on war against the Imperial Government of Japan; and, to bring the conflict to a successful termination, all of the resources of the country are hereby pledged by the Congress of the United States.

APPROVED, December 8, 1941, 4:10 p.m., E.S.T.

[Terminated by Treaty of Peace with Japan, entered into force April 28, 1952. 3 UST 3169, TIAS 2490.]

War with Germany 1941

(Act of December 11, 1941, ch. 564, 55 Stat. 796)
[CHAPTER 564]
JOINT RESOLUTION

Declaring that a state of war exists between the Government of Germany and the Government and the people of the United States and making provision to prosecute the same.

Whereas the Government of Germany has formally declared war against the Government and the people of the United States of America: Therefore be it

Resolved by the Senate and House of Representatives of the United States of America in Congress assembled, That the state of war between the United States and the Government of Germany which has thus been thrust upon the United States is hereby formally declared; and the President is hereby authorized and directed to employ the entire naval and military forces of the United States and the resources of the Government to carry on war against the Government of Germany; and, to bring the conflict to a successful termination, all of the resources of the country are hereby pledged by the Congress of the United States.

APPROVED, December 11, 1941, 3:05 p.m., E.S.T.

[Terminated by [H.J.Res. 289] Act of October 19, 1951, ch. 519, 65 Stat. 541]

War with Italy 1941

(Act of December 11, 1941, ch. 565, 55 Stat. 797)
[CHAPTER 565]
JOINT RESOLUTION

Declaring that a state of war exists between the Government of Italy and the Government and the people of the United States and making provision to prosecute the same.

Whereas the Government of Italy has formally declared war against the Government and the people of the United States of America: Therefore be it

Resolved by the Senate and House of Representatives of the United States of America in Congress assembled, That the state of war between the United States and the Government of Italy which has thus been thrust upon the United States is hereby formally declared; and the President is hereby authorized and directed to employ the entire naval and military forces of the United States and the resources of the Government to carry on war against the Government of Italy; and, to bring the conflict to a successful termination, all of the resources of the country are hereby pledged by the Congress of the United States.

APPROVED, December 11, 1941, 3:06 p.m., E.S.T.

[Terminated by Treaty of Peace with Italy, entered into force September 15, 1947. 4 UST 311, 61 Stat. 1245.]

War with Bulgaria 1942

(Act of June 5, 1942, ch. 323, 56 Stat. 307)
[CHAPTER 323]
JOINT RESOLUTION

Declaring that a state of war exists between the Government of Bulgaria and the Government and the people of the United States and making provisions to prosecute the same.

Whereas the Government of Bulgaria has formally declared war against the Government and the people of the United States of America: Therefore be it

Resolved by the Senate and House of Representatives of the United States of America in Congress assembled, That the state of war between the United States and the Government of Bulgaria which has thus been thrust upon the United States is hereby formally declared; and the President is hereby authorized and directed to employ the entire naval and military forces of the United States and the resources of the Government to carry on war against the Government of Bulgaria; and, to bring the conflict to a successful termination, all of the resources of the country are hereby pledged by the Congress of the United States.

APPROVED, June 5, 1942.

[Terminated by Treaty of Peace with Bulgaria, entered into force September 15, 1947. 4 UST 429, 61 Stat. 1915.]

War with Hungary 1942

(Act of June 5, 1942, ch. 324, 56 Stat. 307) [CHAPTER 324]

JOINT RESOLUTION

Declaring that a state of war exists between the Government of Hungary and the Government and the people of the United States and making provisions to prosecute the same.

Whereas the Government of Hungary has formally declared war against the Government and the people of the United States of America: Therefore be it

Resolved by the Senate and House of Representatives of the United States of America in Congress assembled, That the state of war between the United States and the Government of Hungary which has thus been thrust upon the United States is hereby formally declared; and the President is hereby authorized and directed to employ the entire naval and military forces of the United States and the resources of the Government to carry on war against the Government of Hungary; and, to bring the conflict to a successful termination all of the resources of the country are hereby pledged by the Congress of the United States.

APPROVED, June 5, 1942.

[Terminated by Treaty of Peace with Hungary, entered into force September 15, 1947. 4 UST 453, 61 Stat. 2065.]

War with Rumania 1942

(Act of June 5, 1942, ch. 325, 56 Stat. 307) [CHAPTER 325]

JOINT RESOLUTION

Declaring that a state of war exists between the Government of Rumania and the Government and the people of the United States and making provisions to prosecute the same.

Whereas the Government of Rumania has formally declared war against the Government and the people of the United States of America: Therefore be it

Resolved by the Senate and House of Representatives of the United States of America in Congress assembled, That the state of war between the United States and the Government of Rumania which has thus been thrust upon the United States is hereby formally declared; and the President is hereby authorized and directed to employ the entire naval and military forces of the United States and the resources of the Government to carry on war against the Government of Rumania; and, to bring the conflict to a successful termination, all of the resources of the country are hereby pledged by the Congress of the United States.

APPROVED, June 5, 1942.

[Terminated by Treaty of Peace with Rumania, entered into force September 15, 1947. 4 UST 403, 61 Stat. 1757.]

APPENDIX B. TEXTS OF KEY AUTHORIZATIONS OF USE OF FORCE

Protection of the Commerce and Coasts of the United States

(Act of May 28, 1798, ch. 48, 1 Stat. 561)

CHAP. XLVIII.—*An Act more effectually to protect the Commerce and Coasts of the United States.*

Whereas armed vessels sailing under authority or pretence [sic] of authority from the Republic of France, have committed depredations on the commerce of the United States, and have recently captured the vessels and property of citizens thereof, on and near the coasts, in violation of the law of nations, and treaties between the United States and the French nation. Therefore:

Be it enacted by the Senate and House of Representatives of the United States of America in Congress assembled, That it shall be lawful for the President of the United States, and he is hereby authorized to instruct and direct the commanders of the armed vessels belonging to the United States to seize, take and bring into any port of the United States, to be proceeded against according to the laws of nations, any such armed vessel which shall have committed or which shall be found hovering on the coasts of the United States, for the purpose of committing depredations on the vessels belonging to citizens thereof;—and also to retake any ship or vessel, of any citizen or citizens of the United States which may have been captured by any such armed vessel.

APPROVED, May 28, 1798.

Protection of the Commerce of the United States

(Act of July 9, 1798, ch. 68, 1 Stat. 578)

CHAP. LXVIII.—An Act further to protect the Commerce of the United States.

SEC. 1. *Be it enacted by the Senate and House of Representatives of the United States of America in Congress assembled,* That the President of the United States shall be, and he is hereby authorized to instruct the commanders of the public armed vessels which are, or which shall be employed in the service of the United States, to subdue, seize and take any armed French vessel, which shall be found within the jurisdictional limits of the United States, or elsewhere, on the high seas, and such captured vessel, with her apparel, guns and appurtenances, and the goods or effects which shall be found on board the same, being French property, shall be brought within some port of the United States, and shall be duly proceeded against and condemned as forfeited; and shall accrue and be distributed, as by law is or shall be provided respecting the captures which shall be made by the public armed vessels of the United States.

SEC. 2. *And be it further enacted*, That the President of the United States shall be, and he is hereby authorized to grant to the owners of private armed ships and vessels of the United States, who shall make application thereof, special commissions in the form which he shall direct, and under the seal of the United States; and such private armed vessels, when duly commissioned, as aforesaid, shall have the same license and authority for the subduing, seizing and capturing any armed French vessel, and for the recapture of the vessels, goods and effects of the people of the United States, as the public armed vessels of the United States may by law have; and shall be, in like manner, subject to such instructions as shall be ordered by the President of the United States, for the regulation of their conduct. And the commissions which shall be granted, as aforesaid, shall be revocable at the pleasure of the President of the United States.

SEC. 3. *Provided, and be it further enacted*, That every person intending to set forth and employ an armed vessel, and applying for a commission, as aforesaid, shall produce in writing the name, and a suitable description of the tonnage and force of the vessel, and the name and place of residence of each owner concerned therein, the number of the crew and the name of the commander, and the two officers next in rank appointed for such vessel; which writing shall be signed by the person or persons making such application, and filed with the Secretary of State, or shall be delivered to any other officer or person who shall be employed to deliver out such commissions, to be by him transmitted to the Secretary of State.

SEC. 4. *And provided, and be it further enacted*, That before any commission, as aforesaid, shall be issued, the owner or owners of the ship or vessel for which the same shall be requested, and the commander thereof, for the time being, shall give bond to the United States, with at least two responsible sureties, not interested in such vessel, in the penal sum of seven thousand dollars; or if such vessel be provided with more than one hundred and fifty men, then in the penal sum of fourteen thousand dollars; with condition that the owners, and officers, and crews who shall be employed on board of such commissioned vessel, shall and will observe the treaties and laws of the United States and the instructions which shall be given them for the regulation of their conduct: And will satisfy all damages and injuries which shall be done or committed contrary to the tenor thereof, by such vessel, during her commission, and to deliver up the same when revoked by the President of the United States.

SEC. 5. *And be it further enacted,* That all armed French vessels, together with their apparel, guns and appurtenances, and any goods or effects which shall be found on board the same, being French property, and which shall be captured by any private armed vessel or vessels of the United States, duly commissioned, as aforesaid, shall be forfeited, and shall accrue to the owners thereof, and the officers and crews by whom such captures shall be made; and on due condemnation had, shall be distributed according to any agreement which shall be between them; or in failure of such agreement, then by the discretion of the court before whom such condemnation shall be.

SEC. 6. *And be it further enacted,* That all vessels, goods and effects, the property of any citizen of the United States, or person resident therein, which shall be recaptured, as aforesaid, shall be restored to the lawful owners, upon payment by them, respectively, of a just and reasonable salvage, to be determined by the mutual agreement of the parties concerned, or by the decree of any court of the United States having maritime jurisdiction according to the nature of each case: Provided, that such allowance shall not be less than one eighth, or exceeding one half of the full value of such recapture, without any deduction. And such salvage shall be distributed to and among the owners, officers and crews of the private armed vessel or vessels entitled thereto, according to any agreement which shall be between them; or in case of no agreement, then by the decree of the court who shall determine upon such salvage.

SEC. 7. *And be it further enacted,* That before breaking bulk of any vessel which shall be captured, as aforesaid, or other disposal or conversion thereof, or of any articles which shall be found on board the same, such capture shall be brought into some port of the United States, and shall be libelled and proceeded against before the district court of the same district; and if after a due course of proceedings, such capture shall be decreed as forfeited in the district court, or in the circuit court of the same district, in the case of any appeal duly allowed, the same shall be delivered to the owners and captors concerned therein, or shall be publicly sold by the marshal of the same court, as shall be finally decreed and ordered by the court. And the same court, who shall have final jurisdiction of any libel or complaint of any capture, as aforesaid, shall and may decree restitution, in whole or in part, when the capture and restraint shall have been made without just cause, as aforesaid; and if made without probable cause, or otherwise unreasonably, may order and decree damages and costs to the party injured, and for which the owners, officers and crews of the private armed vessel or vessels by which such unjust capture shall have been made, and also such vessel or vessels shall be answerable and liable.

SEC. 8. *And be it further enacted,* That all French persons and others, who shall be found acting on board any French armed vessel, which shall be captured, or on board of any vessel of the United States, which shall be captured, or on board of any vessel of the United States, which shall be recaptured, as aforesaid, shall be reported to the collector of the port in which they shall first arrive, and shall be delivered to the custody of the marshal, or of some civil or military officer of the United States, or of any state in or near such port; who shall take charge for their safe keeping and support, at the expense of the United States.

APPROVED, July 9, 1798.

Protection of the Commerce and Seamen of the United States against the Tripolitan Cruisers

(Act of February 6, 1802, ch. 4, 2 Stat.129)

CHAP. IV.—*An Act for the protection of the Commerce and Seamen of the United States, against the Tripolitan Cruisers.*

Whereas the regency of Tripoli, on the coast of Barbary, has commenced a predatory warfare against the United States:

Be it enacted by the Senate and House of Representatives of the United States of America in Congress assembled, That it shall be lawful fully to equip, officer, man, and employ such of the armed vessels of the United States as may be judged requisite by the President of the United States, for protecting effectually the commerce and seamen thereof on the Atlantic ocean, the Mediterranean and adjoining seas.

SEC. 2. *And be it further enacted*, That it shall be lawful for the President of the United States to instruct the commanders of the respective public vessels aforesaid, to subdue, seize and make prize of all vessels, goods, and effects, belonging to the Bey of Tripoli, or to his subjects, and to bring or send the same into port, to be proceeded against, and distributed according to the law; and also to cause to be done all such other acts of precaution or hostility as the state of war will justify, and may, in his opinion, require.

SEC. 3. *And be it further enacted*, That on the application of, the owners of private armed vessels of the United States, the President of the United States may grant to them special commissions, in the form which he shall direct, under the seal of the United States; and such private armed vessels, when so commissioned, shall have the like authority for subduing, seizing, taking, and bringing into port, any Tripolitan vessel, goods or effects, as the before-mentioned public armed vessels may by law have; and shall therein be subject to the instruction which may be given by the President of the United States for the regulation of their conduct; and their commissions shall be revocable at his pleasure. Provided, that before any commission shall be granted, as aforesaid, the owner or owners of the vessel for which the same may be requested, and the commander thereof, for the time being, shall give bond to the United States, with at least two responsible sureties, not interested in such vessel, in the penal sum of seven thousand dollars; or, if such vessel be provided with more than one hundred and fifty men, in the penal sum of fourteen thousand dollars, with condition for observing the treaties and laws of the United States, and the instructions which may be given, as aforesaid; and also, for satisfying all damages and injuries which shall be done, contrary to the tenor thereof, by such commissioned vessel; and for delivering up the commission, when revoked by the President of the United States.

SEC. 4. *And be if further enacted*, That any Tripolitan vessel, goods or effects, which shall be so captured and brought into port, by any private armed vessel of the United States, duly commissioned, as aforesaid, may be adjudged good prize, and thereupon shall accrue to the owners and officers, and men of the capturing vessel, and shall be distributed according to the agreement which shall have been made between them, or, in failure of such agreement, according to the discretion of the court having cognizance of the capture.

SEC. 5. And be it further enacted, That the seamen may be engaged to serve in the navy of the United States for a period not exceeding two years; but the President may discharge the same sooner, if in his judgment, their services may be dispensed with.

APPROVED, February 6, 1802.

[Repealed by P.L. 1028, 84th Congress, 2d Sess (August 10, 1956); 70A Stat. 644, sec. 53(b)]

Protection of the Commerce and Seamen of the United States against the Algerine Cruisers

(Act of March 3, 1815, ch. 90, 3 Stat. 230)

CHAP. XC.—*An Act for the protection of the commerce of the United States against the Algerine cruisers.*

Whereas the Dey of Algiers, on the coast of Barbary, has commenced a predatory warfare against the United States—

Be it enacted by the Senate and House of Representatives of the United States of America, in Congress assembled, That it shall be lawful fully to equip, officer, man and employ such of the armed vessels of the United States as may be judged requisite by the President of the United States for protecting effectually the commerce and seamen thereof on the Atlantic Ocean, the Mediterranean and adjoining seas.

SEC. 2. *And be it further enacted*, That it shall be lawful for the President of the United States to instruct the commanders of the respective public vessels aforesaid, to subdue, seize, and make prize of all vessels, goods and effects of or belonging to the Dey of Algiers, or to his subjects, and to bring or send the same into port, to be proceeded against and distributed according to law; and, also, to cause to be done all such other acts of precaution or hostility, as the state of war will justify, and may in his opinion require.

SEC. 3. *And be it further enacted*, That on the application of the owners of private armed vessels of the United States, the President of the United States may grant them special commissions in the form which he shall direct under the seal of the United States; and such private armed vessels, when so commissioned, shall have the like authority for subduing, seizing, taking and bringing into port any Algerine vessel, goods or effects, as the before-mentioned public armed vessels may by law have; and shall therein be subject to the instructions which may be given by the President of the United States for the regulation of their conduct; and their commissions shall be revokable at his pleasure. *Provided*, That before any commission shall be granted as aforesaid, the owner or owners of the vessels of which the same may be requested, and the commander thereof for the time being shall give bond to the United States, with at least two responsible sureties, not interested in such vessel, in the penal sum of seven thousand dollars, or if such vessel be provided with more than one hundred and fifty men, in the penal sum of fourteen thousand dollars, with condition for observing the treaties and laws of the United States, and the instructions which may be given as aforesaid, and also for satisfying all damages and injuries which shall be done contrary to the tenor thereof by such commissioned vessel, and for delivering up the commission when revoked by the President of the United States.

SEC. 4. *And be if further enacted*, That any Algerine vessel, goods, or effects which may be so captured and brought into port, by any private armed vessel, of the United States, duly commissioned as aforesaid, may be adjudged good prize, and thereupon shall accrue to the owners, and officers, and men of the capturing vessel, and shall be distributed according to the agreement which shall have been made between them, or, in failure of such agreement, according to the discretion [of] the court having cognisance of the capture.

APPROVED, March 3, 1815.

[Repealed by P.L. 1028, 84th Congress, 2d Sess (August 10, 1956); 70A Stat. 644, sec. 53(b)]

Suppression of Piracy

(33 U.S.C. §§381-387. R.S.§§4293-4299. R.S.§4293, 4294, and 4295 are derived from the Acts of March 3, 1819, ch. 77, 3 Stat. 510 and 512; January 30, 1823, 3 Stat. 513, ch. 7, 3 Stat. 721. R.S.§4296 is derived from the Acts of March 3, 1819, ch. 77, 3 Stat. 513; January

30, 1823, ch. 7, 3 Stat. 721; August 5, 1861, ch. 48, 12 Stat. 314. R.S.§§4297, 4298, and 4299 are derived from the Act of August 5, 1861, ch. 48, 12 Stat. 315.)

TITLE 33. CHAPTER 7.

Section 381. Use of public vessels to suppress piracy

The President is authorized to employ so many of the public armed vessels as in his judgement the service may require, with suitable instructions to the commanders thereof, in protecting the merchant vessels of the United States and their crews from piratical aggressions and depredations.

Section 382. Seizure of piratical vessels generally

The President is authorized to instruct the commanders of the public armed vessels of the United States to subdue, seize, take, and send into any port of the United States, any armed vessel or boat, or any vessel or boat, the crew whereof shall be armed, and which shall have attempted or committed any piratical aggression, search, restraint, depredation, or seizure, upon any vessel of the United States, or of the citizens thereof, or upon any other vessel; and also to retake any vessel of the United States, or its citizens, which may have been unlawfully captured upon the high seas.

Section 383. Resistance of pirates by merchant vessels

The commander and crew of any merchant vessel of the United States, owned wholly, or in part, by a citizen thereof, may oppose and defend against any aggression, search, restraint, depredation, or seizure, which shall be attempted upon such vessel, or upon any other vessel so owned, by the commander or crew of any armed vessel whatsoever, not being a public armed vessel of some nation in amity with the United States, and may subdue and capture the same; and may also retake any vessel so owned which may have been captured by the commander or crew of any such armed vessel, and send the same into any port of the United States.

Section 384. Condemnation of piratical vessels

Whenever any vessel, which shall have been built, purchased, fitted out in whole or in part, or held for the purpose of being employed in the commission of any piratical aggression, search, restraint, depredation, or seizure, or in the commission of any other act of piracy as defined by the law of nations, or from which any piratical aggression, search, restraint, depredation, or seizure shall have been first attempted or made, is captured and brought into or captured in any port of the United States, the same shall be adjudged and condemned to their use, and that of the captors after due process and trial in any court having admiralty jurisdiction, and which shall be holden for the district into which such captured vessel shall be brought; and the same court shall thereupon order a sale and distribution thereof accordingly, and at its discretion.

Section 385. Seizure and condemnation of vessels fitted out for piracy

Any vessel built, purchased, fitted out in whole or in part, or held for the purpose of being employed in the commission of any piratical aggression, search, restraint, depredation, or seizure, or in the commission of any other act of piracy, as defined by the law of nations, shall be liable to be captured and brought into any port of the United States if found upon the high seas, or to be seized if found in any port or place within the United States, whether the same shall have actually sailed upon any piratical expedition or not, and whether any act of piracy shall have been committed or attempted upon or from such vessel or not; and any such vessel may be adjudged and condemned, if captured by a vessel authorized as hereinafter mentioned [33 USCS §386] to the use of the United States, and to that of the captors, and if seized by a collector [the Secretary of the Treasury], surveyor or marshal, then to the use of the United States.

Section 386. Commissioning private vessels for seizure of piratical vessels

The President is authorized to instruct the commanders of the public armed vessels of the United States, and to authorize the commanders of any other armed vessels sailing under the authority of any letters of marque and reprisal granted by Congress, or the commanders of any other suitable vessels, to subdue, seize, take, and, if on the high seas, to send into any port of the United States, any vessel or boat built, purchased, fitted out, or held as mentioned in the preceding section [33 USCS §385].

Section 387. Duties of officers of customs and marshals as to seizure

The collectors of the several ports of entry [the Secretary of the Treasury] the surveyors of the several ports of delivery [the Secretary of the Treasury] and the marshals of the several judicial districts within the United States, shall seize any vessel or boat built, purchased, fitted out, or held as mentioned in section forty-two hundred and ninety-seven [33 USCS §385], which may be found within their respective ports or districts, and to cause the same to be proceeded against and disposed of as provided by that section.

Authorization for the President to Employ the Armed Forces of the United States for Protecting the Security of Formosa, the Pescadores, and Related Positions and Territories of That Area

(Act of January 29, 1955, ch.4, 69 Stat. 7. [H.J.Res. 159, P.L. 84-4])

P.L. 4, CHAPTER 4—Joint Resolution authorizing the President to employ the Armed Forces of the United States for protecting the security of Formosa, the Pescadores and related positions and territories of that area.

Whereas the primary purpose of the United States, in its relations with all other nations, is to develop and sustain a just and enduring peace for all; and

Whereas certain territories in the West Pacific under the jurisdiction of the Republic of China are now under armed attack, and threats and declarations have been and are being made by the Chinese Communists that such armed attack is in aid of and in preparation for armed attack on Formosa and the Pescadores,

Whereas such armed attack if continued would gravely endanger the peace and security of the West Pacific Area and particularly of Formosa and the Pescadores; and

Whereas the secure possession by friendly governments of the Western Pacific Island chain, of which Formosa is a part, is essential to the vital interests of the United States and all friendly nations in or bordering upon the Pacific Ocean; and

Whereas the President of the United States on January 6, 1955, submitted to the Senate for its advice and consent to ratification a Mutual Defense Treaty between the United States of America and the Republic of China, which recognizes that an armed attack in the West Pacific area directed against territories, therein described, in the region of Formosa and the Pescadores, would be dangerous to the peace and safety of the parties to the treaty: Therefore be it

Resolved by the Senate and House of Representatives of the United States of America in Congress assembled, That the President of the United States be and he hereby is authorized to employ the Armed Forces of the United States as he deems necessary for the specific purpose of securing and protecting Formosa, and the Pescadores against armed attack, this authority to include the securing and protection of such related positions and territories of that area now in friendly hands and the taking of such other measures as he judges to be required or appropriate in assuring the defense of Formosa and the Pescadores.

This resolution shall expire when the President shall determine that the peace and security of the area is reasonably assured by international conditions created by action of the United States or otherwise, and shall so report to the Congress.

APPROVED, January 29, 1955, 8:42 a.m.

[Repealed by P.L. 93-475 [S. 3473] October 26, 1975. 88 Stat. 1439]

Promotion of Peace and Stability in the Middle East

(P.L. 85-7, 71 Stat. 5, March 9, 1957 [H.J.Res. 117])

P.L. 85-7—Joint Resolution, To promote peace and stability in the Middle East.

Resolved by the Senate and House of Representatives of the United States of America in Congress assembled, That the President be and hereby is authorized to cooperate with and assist any nation or group of nations in the general area of the Middle East desiring such assistance in the development of economic strength dedicated to the maintenance of national independence.

SEC. 2. The President is authorized to undertake, in the general area of the Middle East, military assistance programs with any nation or group of nations of that area desiring such assistance. Furthermore, the United States regards as vital to the national interest and world peace the preservation of the independence and integrity of the nations of the Middle East. To this end, if the President determines the necessity thereof, the United States is prepared to use armed forces to assist any such nation or group of such nations requesting assistance against armed aggression from any country controlled by international communism: *Provided*, That such employment shall be consonant with the treaty obligations of the United States and with the Constitution of the United States.

SEC. 3. The President is hereby authorized to use during the balance of fiscal year 1957 for economic and military assistance under this joint resolution not to exceed $200,000,000 from any appropriation now available for carrying out the provisions for the Mutual Security Act of 1954, as amended, in accord with the provisions of such Act: *Provided*, That, whenever the President determines it to be important to the security of the United States, such use may be under the authority of section 401 (a) of the Mutual Security Act of 1954, as amended (except that the provisions of section 105 (a) thereof shall not be waived), and without regard to the provisions of section 105 of the Mutual Security Appropriation Act, 1957: *Provided further*, That obligations incurred in carrying out the purposes of the first sentence of section 2 of this joint resolution shall be paid only out of appropriations for military assistance, and obligations incurred in carrying out the purposes of the first section of this joint resolution shall be paid only out of appropriations other than those for military assistance. This authorization is in addition to other existing authorizations with respect to the use of such appropriations. None of the additional authorization contained in this section shall be used until fifteen days after the Committee on Foreign Relations of the Senate, the Committee on Foreign Affairs of the House of Representatives, the Committees on Appropriations of the Senate and the House of Representatives and, when military assistance is involved, the Committees on Armed Services of the Senate and the House of Representatives have been furnished a report showing the object of the proposed use, the country for the benefit of which such use is intended, and the particular appropriation or appropriations for carrying out the provisions of the Mutual Security Act of 1954, as amended, from which the funds are proposed to be derived: Provided, That funds available under this section during the balance of fiscal year 1957 shall, in the case of any such report submitted during the last fifteen days of the fiscal year, remain available for use under this section for the purposes stated in such report for a period of twenty days following the date of submission of such report. Nothing contained in this joint resolution shall be construed as itself authorizing the appropriation of additional funds for the purpose of carrying out the provisions of the first section or of the first sentence of section 2 of this joint resolution.

SEC. 4. The President should continue to furnish facilities and military assistance, within the provisions of applicable law and established policies, to the United Nations Emergency Force in the Middle East, with a view to maintaining the truce in that region.

SEC. 5. The President shall within the months of January and July of each year report to the Congress his action hereunder.

SEC. 6. This joint resolution shall expire when the President shall determine that the peace and security of the nations in the general area of the Middle East are reasonably assured by international conditions created by action of the United Nations or otherwise except that it may be terminated earlier by a concurrent resolution of the two Houses of Congress.

APPROVED, March 9, 1957.

Maintenance of International Peace and Security in Southeast Asia

(P.L. 88-408, 78 Stat. 384, August 10, 1964 [H.J.Res. 11450])

P.L. 88-408, 78 Stat.—Joint Resolution, To promote the maintenance of international peace and security in southeast Asia.

Whereas naval units of the Communist regime in Vietnam, in violation of the principles of the Charter of the United Nations and of international law, have deliberately and repeatedly attacked the United States naval vessels lawfully present in international waters, and have thereby created a serious threat to international peace; and

Whereas these attacks are part of a deliberate and systematic campaign of aggression that the Communist regime in North Vietnam has been waging against its neighbors and the nations joined with them in the collective defense of their freedom; and

Whereas the United States is assisting the peoples of southeast Asia to protect their freedom and has no territorial, military or political ambitions in that area, but desires only that these peoples should be left in peace to work out their own destinies in their own way: Now, therefore, be it

Resolved by the Senate and House of Representatives of the United States of America in Congress assembled, That the Congress approves and supports the determination of the President, as Commander in Chief, to take all necessary measures to repel any armed attack against the forces of the United States and to prevent further aggression.

SEC. 2. The United States regards as vital to its national interest and to world peace the maintenance of international peace and security in southeast Asia. Consonant with the Constitution of the United States and the Charter of the United Nations and in accordance with its obligations under the Southeast Asia Collective Defense Treaty, the United States is, therefore, prepared, as the President determines, to take all necessary steps, including the use of armed force, to assist any member or protocol state of the Southeast Asia Collective Defense Treaty requesting assistance in defense of its freedom.

SEC. 3. This resolution shall expire when the President shall determine that the peace and security of the area is reasonably assured by international conditions created by action of the United Nations or otherwise, except that it may be terminated earlier by concurrent resolution of the Congress.

APPROVED, August 10, 1964

[Repealed by P.L. 91-672 [H.R. 15628] January 12, 1971. 84 Stat. 2053]

Multinational Force in Lebanon

(P.L. 98-119, 97 Stat. 805, October 12, 1983 [S.J.Res. 159])

P.L. 98-119, 97 Stat. 805—*Joint Resolution providing statutory authorization under the War Powers Resolution for continued United States participation in the multinational peacekeeping force in Lebanon in order to obtain withdrawal of all foreign forces from Lebanon.*

Resolved by the Senate and House of Representatives of the United States of America in Congress assembled,

SHORT TITLE

SECTION 1. This joint resolution may be cited as the "Multinational Force in Lebanon Resolution."

FINDINGS AND PURPOSE SEC. 2.

(a) The Congress finds that—
   (1) the removal of all foreign forces from Lebanon is an essential United States foreign policy objective in the Middle East;
   (2) in order to restore full control by the Government of Lebanon over its own territory, the United States is currently participating in the multinational peacekeeping force (hereafter in this resolution referred to as the "Multinational Force in Lebanon") which was established in accordance with the exchange of letters between the Governments of the United States and Lebanon dated September 25, 1982;
   (3) the Multinational Force in Lebanon better enables the Government of Lebanon to establish its unity, independence, and territorial integrity;
   (4) progress toward national political reconciliation in Lebanon is necessary; and
   (5) United States Armed Forces participating in the Multinational Force in Lebanon are now in hostilities requiring authorization of their continued presence under the War Powers Resolution.
(b) The Congress determines that the requirements of section 4(a)(1) of the War Powers Resolution became operative on August 29, 1983. Consistent with section 5(b) of the War Powers Resolution, the purpose of this joint resolution is to authorize the

continued participation of the United States Armed forces in the Multinational Force in Lebanon.

(c) The Congress intends this joint resolution to constitute the necessary specific statutory authorization under the War Powers Resolution for continued participation by United States Armed Forces in the Multinational Force in Lebanon.

AUTHORIZATION FOR CONTINUED PARTICIPATION OF UNITED STATES ARMED FORCES IN THE MULTINATIONAL FORCE IN LEBANON

SEC. 3. The President is authorized, for purposes of section 5(b) of the War Powers Resolution, to continue participation by United States Armed Forces in the Multinational Force in Lebanon, subject to the provisions of section 6 of this joint resolution. Such participation shall be limited to performance of the functions, and shall be subject to the limitations, specified in the agreement establishing the Multinational Force in Lebanon as set forth in the exchange of letters between the Governments of the United States and Lebanon dated September 25, 1982, except that this shall not preclude such protective measures as may be necessary to ensure the safety of the Multinational Force in Lebanon.

REPORTS TO THE CONGRESS

SEC. 4. As required by section 4(c) of the War Powers Resolution, the President shall report periodically to the Congress with respect to the situation in Lebanon, but in no event shall he report less often than once every three months. In addition to providing the information required by that section on the status, scope, and duration of hostilities involving the Unites States Armed Forces, such reports shall describe in detail—

(1) the activities being performed by the Multinational Force in Lebanon;
(2) the present composition of the Multinational Force in Lebanon, including a description of the responsibilities and deployment of the armed forces of each participating country;
(3) the results of efforts to reduce and eventually eliminate the Multinational Force in Lebanon;
(4) how continued United States participation in the Multinational Force in Lebanon is advancing United States foreign policy interests in the Middle East; and
(5) what progress has occurred toward national political reconciliation among all Lebanese groups.

STATEMENTS OF POLICY

SEC. 5.

(a) The Congress declares that the participation of the armed forces of other countries in the Multinational Force in Lebanon is essential to maintain the international character of the peacekeeping function in Lebanon.
(b) The Congress believes that it should continue to be the policy of the United States to promote continuing discussions with Israel, Syria, and Lebanon with the objective of bringing about the withdrawal of all foreign troops from Lebanon and establishing an environment which will permit the Lebanese Armed Forces to carry out their responsibilities in the Beirut area.

(c) It is the sense of the Congress that, not later than one year after the date of enactment of this joint resolution and at least once a year thereafter, the United States should discuss with the other members of the Security Council of the United Nations the establishment of a United Nations peacekeeping force to assume the responsibilities of the Multinational Force in Lebanon. An analysis of the implications of the response to such discussions for the continuation of the Multinational Force in Lebanon shall be included in the reports required under paragraph (3) of section 4 of this resolution.

DURATION OF AUTHORIZATION FOR UNITED STATES PARTICIPATION IN THE MULTINATIONAL FORCE IN LEBANON

SEC. 6. The participation of United States Armed Forces in the Multinational Force in Lebanon shall be authorized for purposes of the War Powers Resolution until the end of the eighteen- month period beginning on the date of enactment of this resolution unless the Congress extends such authorization, except that such authorization shall terminate sooner upon the occurrence of any one of the following:

(1) the withdrawal of all foreign forces from Lebanon, unless the President determines and certifies to the Congress that continued United States Armed Forces participation in the Multinational Force in Lebanon is required after such withdrawal in order to accomplish the purposes specified in the September 25, 1982, exchange of letters providing for the establishment of the Multinational Force in Lebanon; or
(2) the assumption by the United Nations or the Government of Lebanon of the responsibilities of the Multinational Force in Lebanon; or
(3) the implementation of other effective security arrangements in the area; or
(4) the withdrawal of all other countries from participation in the Multinational Force in Lebanon.

INTERPRETATION OF THIS RESOLUTION

SEC. 7.

(a) Nothing in this joint resolution shall preclude the President from withdrawing United States Armed Forces participation in the Multinational Force in Lebanon if circumstances warrant, and nothing in this joint resolution shall preclude the Congress by joint resolution from directing such a withdrawal.
(b) Nothing in this joint resolution modifies, limits or supersedes any provision of the War Powers Resolution or the requirement of section 4(a) of the Lebanon Emergency Assistance Act of 1983, relating to congressional authorization for any substantial expansion in the number or role of United States Armed Forces in Lebanon.

CONGRESSIONAL PRIORITY PROCEDURES FOR AMENDMENTS

SEC. 8.

(a) Any joint resolution or bill introduced to amend or repeal this Act shall be referred to the Committee on Foreign Affairs of the House of Representatives or the Committee on Foreign Relations of the Senate, as the case may be. Such joint resolution or bill shall be considered by such committee within fifteen calendar days and may be reported out, together with its recommendations, unless such House shall otherwise determine pursuant to its rules.

(b) Any joint resolution or bill so reported shall become the pending business of the House in question (in the case of the Senate the time for debate shall be equally divided between the proponents and the opponents) and shall be voted on within three calendar days thereafter, unless such House shall otherwise determine by the yeas and nays.

(c) Such a joint resolution or bill passed by one House shall be referred to the committee of the other House named in subsection (a) and shall be reported out by such committee together with its recommendations within fifteen calendar days and shall thereupon become the pending business of such House and shall be voted upon within three calendar days, unless such House shall otherwise determine by the yeas and nays.

(d) In the case of any disagreement between the two Houses of Congress with respect to a joint resolution or bill passed by both Houses, conferees shall be promptly appointed and the committee of conference shall make and file a report with respect to such joint resolution within six calendar days after the legislation is referred to the committee of conference. Notwithstanding any rule in either House concerning the printing of conference reports in the Record or concerning any delay in the consideration of such reports, such report shall be acted on by both Houses not later than six calendar days after the conference report is filed. In the event the conferees are unable to agree within forty-eight hours, they shall report back to the respective Houses in disagreement.

APPROVED, October 12, 1983.

Authorization of the Use of U.S. Armed Forces Pursuant to U.N. Security Council Resolution 678 with Respect to Iraq

(P.L. 102-1, 105 Stat. 3, January 14, 1991 [H.J.Res. 77])

P.L. 102-1, 105 Stat. 3—*To authorize the use of United States Armed Forces pursuant to United Nations Security Council Resolution 678.*

Whereas the Government of Iraq without provocation invaded and occupied the territory of Kuwait on August 2, 1990;

Whereas both the House of Representatives (in H.J.Res. 658 of the 101st Congress) and the Senate (in S.Con.Res. 147 of the 101st Congress) have condemned Iraq's invasion of Kuwait and declared their support for international action to reverse Iraq's aggression;

Whereas, Iraq's conventional, chemical, biological, and nuclear weapons and ballistic missile programs and its demonstrated willingness to use weapons of mass destruction pose a grave threat to world peace;

Whereas the international community has demanded that Iraq withdraw unconditionally and immediately from Kuwait and that Kuwait's independence and legitimate government be restored;

Whereas the United Nations Security Council repeatedly affirmed the inherent right of individual or collective self-defense in response to the armed attack by Iraq against Kuwait in accordance with Article 51 of the United Nations Charter;

Whereas, in the absence of full compliance by Iraq with its resolutions, the United Nations Security Council in Resolution 678 has authorized member states of the United Nations to use all necessary means after January 15, 1991, to uphold and implement all relevant Security Council resolutions and to restore international peace and security to the area; and

Whereas Iraq has persisted in its illegal occupation of, and brutal aggression against Kuwait: Now, therefore, be it

Resolved by the Senate and House of Representatives of the United States of America in Congress assembled,

SECTION 1. SHORT TITLE.

This joint resolution may be cited as the "Authorization for Use of Military Force Against Iraq Resolution."

SEC. 2. AUTHORIZATION FOR USE OF UNITED STATES ARMED FORCES.

(a) AUTHORIZATION.—The President is authorized, subject to subsection (b), to use United States Armed Forces pursuant to United Nations Security Council Resolution 678 (1990) in order to achieve implementation of Security Council Resolutions 660, 661, 662, 664, 665, 666, 667, 669, 670, 674, and 677.

(b) REQUIREMENT FOR DETERMINATION THAT USE OF MILITARY FORCE IS NECESSARY.—Before exercising the authority granted in subsection (a), the President shall make available to the Speaker of the House of Representatives and the President pro tempore of the Senate his determination that—

  (1) the United States has used all appropriate diplomatic and other peaceful means to obtain compliance by Iraq with the United Nations Security Council resolution cited in subsection (a); and

  (2) that those efforts have not been and would not be successful in obtaining such compliance.

(c) WAR POWERS RESOLUTION REQUIREMENTS.—

  (1) SPECIFIC STATUTORY AUTHORIZATION.—Consistent with section 8(a)(1) of the War Powers Resolution, the Congress declares that this section is intended to constitute specific statutory authorization within the meaning of section 5(b) of the War Powers Resolution.

  (2) APPLICABILITY OF OTHER REQUIREMENTS.—Nothing in this resolution supersedes any requirement of the War Powers Resolution.

SEC. 3. REPORTS TO CONGRESS.

At least once every 60 days, the President shall submit to the Congress a summary on the status of efforts to obtain compliance by Iraq with the resolutions adopted by the United Nations Security Council in response to Iraq's aggression.

APPROVED, January 14, 1991.

Authorization of the Use of U.S. Armed Forces Against Those Responsible for the Recent Attacks Launched Against the United States

(P.L. 107-40, 115 Stat. 224, September 18, 2001 [S. J. Res. 23])

To authorize the use of United States Armed Forces against those responsible for the recent attacks launched against the United States.

Whereas, on September 11, 2001, acts of treacherous violence were committed against the United States and its citizens, and

Whereas, such acts render it both necessary and appropriate that the United States exercise its rights to self-defense and to protect United States citizens both at home and abroad, and

Whereas, in light of the threat to the national security and foreign policy of the United States posed by these grave acts of violence, and

Whereas, such acts continue to pose an unusual and extraordinary threat to the national security and foreign policy of the United States,

Whereas the President has authority under the Constitution to take action to deter and prevent acts of international terrorism against the United States.

Resolved by the Senate and the House of Representatives of the United States of America in Congress assembled.

SECTION 1. SHORT TITLE

This joint resolution may be cited as the "Authorization for Use of Military Force"

SECTION 2. AUTHORIZATION FOR USE OF UNITED STATES ARMED FORCES

(a) That the President is authorized to use all necessary and appropriate force against those nations, organizations, or persons he determines planned, authorized, committed, or aided the terrorist attacks that occurred on September 11, 2001, or harbored such organizations or persons, in order to prevent any future acts of international terrorism against the United States by such nations, organizations or persons.

(b) War Powers Resolution Requirements

   (1) SPECIFIC STATUTORY AUTHORIZATION - Consistent with section 8(a)(1) of the War Powers Resolution, the Congress declares that this section is intended to constitute specific statutory authorization within the meaning of section 5(b) of the War Powers Resolution.

   (2) APPLICABILITY OF OTHER REQUIREMENTS - Nothing in this resolution supercedes any requirement of the War Powers Resolution.

APPROVED, September 18, 2001.

Authorization of the Use of Force against Iraq Resolution of 2002

(P.L. 107-243, 116 Stat. 1498, October 16, 2002 [H.J.Res. 114])

To authorize the use of United States Armed Forces against Iraq.

Whereas in 1990 in response to Iraq's war of aggression against and illegal occupation of Kuwait, the United States forged a coalition of nations to liberate Kuwait and its people in order to defend the national security of the United States and enforce United Nations Security Council resolutions relating to Iraq;

Whereas after the liberation of Kuwait in 1991, Iraq entered into a United Nations sponsored cease-fire agreement pursuant to which Iraq unequivocally agreed, among other things, to eliminate its nuclear, biological, and chemical weapons programs and the means to deliver and develop them, and to end its support for international terrorism;

Whereas the efforts of international weapons inspectors, United States intelligence agencies, and Iraqi defectors led to the discovery that Iraq had large stockpiles of chemical weapons and a large scale biological weapons program, and that Iraq had an advanced nuclear weapons development program that was much closer to producing a nuclear weapon than intelligence reporting had previously indicated;

Whereas Iraq, in direct and flagrant violation of the cease-fire, attempted to thwart the efforts of weapons inspectors to identify and destroy Iraq's weapons of mass destruction stockpiles and development capabilities, which finally resulted in the withdrawal of inspectors from Iraq on October 31, 1998;

Whereas in P.L. 105-235 (August 14, 1998), Congress concluded that Iraq's continuing weapons of mass destruction programs threatened vital United States interests and international peace and security, declared Iraq to be in "material and unacceptable breach of its international obligations" and urged the President "to take appropriate action, in accordance with the Constitution and relevant laws of the United States, to bring Iraq into compliance with its international obligations";

Whereas Iraq both poses a continuing threat to the national security of the United States and international peace and security in the Persian Gulf region and remains in material and unacceptable breach of its international obligations by, among other things, continuing to possess and develop a significant chemical and biological weapons capability, actively seeking a nuclear weapons capability, and supporting and harboring terrorist organizations;

Whereas Iraq persists in violating resolution of the United Nations Security Council by continuing to engage in brutal repression of its civilian population thereby threatening international peace and security in the region, by refusing to release, repatriate, or account for non-Iraqi citizens wrongfully detained by Iraq, including an American serviceman, and by failing to return property wrongfully seized by Iraq from Kuwait;

Whereas the current Iraqi regime has demonstrated its capability and willingness to use weapons of mass destruction against other nations and its own people;

Whereas the current Iraqi regime has demonstrated its continuing hostility toward, and willingness to attack, the United States, including by attempting in 1993 to assassinate former President Bush and by firing on many thousands of occasions on United States and Coalition Armed Forces engaged in enforcing the resolutions of the United Nations Security Council;

Whereas members of al Qaida, an organization bearing responsibility for attacks on the United States, its citizens, and interests, including the attacks that occurred on September 11, 2001, are known to be in Iraq; Whereas Iraq continues to aid and harbor other international terrorist organizations, including organizations that threaten the lives and safety of United States citizens;

Whereas the attacks on the United States of September 11, 2001, underscored the gravity of the threat posed by the acquisition of weapons of mass destruction by international terrorist organizations;

Whereas Iraq's demonstrated capability and willingness to use weapons of mass destruction, the risk that the current Iraqi regime will either employ those weapons to launch a surprise attack against the United States or its Armed Forces or provide them to international terrorists who would do so, and the extreme magnitude of harm that would result to the

United States and its citizens from such an attack, combine to justify action by the United States to defend itself;

Whereas United Nations Security Council Resolution 678 (1990) authorizes the use of all necessary means to enforce United Nations Security Council Resolution 660 (1990) and subsequent relevant resolutions and to compel Iraq to cease certain activities that threaten international peace and security, including the development of weapons of mass destruction and refusal or obstruction of United Nations weapons inspections in violation of United Nations Security Council Resolution 687 (1991), repression of its civilian population in violation of United Nations Security Council Resolution 688 (1991), and threatening its neighbors or United Nations operations in Iraq in violation of United Nations Security Council Resolution 949 (1994);

Whereas in the Authorization for Use of Military Force Against Iraq Resolution (P.L. 102-1), Congress has authorized the President "to use United States Armed Forces pursuant to United Nations Security Council Resolution 678 (1990) in order to achieve implementation of Security Council Resolution 660, 661, 662, 664, 665, 666, 667, 669, 670, 674, and 677";

Whereas in December 1991, Congress expressed its sense that it "supports the use of all necessary means to achieve the goals of United Nations Security Council Resolution 687 as being consistent with the Authorization of Use of Military Force Against Iraq Resolution (P.L. 102-1)," that Iraq's repression of its civilian population violates United Nations Security Council Resolution 688 and "constitutes a continuing threat to the peace, security, and stability of the Persian Gulf region," and that Congress, "supports the use of all necessary means to achieve the goals of United Nations Security Council Resolution 688";

Whereas the Iraq Liberation Act of 1998 (P.L. 105-338) expressed the sense of Congress that it should be the policy of the United States to support efforts to remove from power the current Iraqi regime and promote the emergence of a democratic government to replace that regime;

Whereas on September 12, 2002, President Bush committed the United States to "work with the United Nations Security Council to meet our common challenge" posed by Iraq and to "work for the necessary resolutions," while also making clear that "the Security Council resolutions will be enforced, and the just demands of peace and security will be met, or action will be unavoidable";

Whereas the United States is determined to prosecute the war on terrorism and Iraq's ongoing support for international terrorist groups combined with its development of weapons of mass destruction in direct violation of its obligations under the 1991 cease-fire and other United Nations Security Council resolutions make clear that it is in the national security interests of the United States and in furtherance of the war on terrorism that all relevant United Nations Security Council resolutions be enforced, including through the use of force if necessary;

Whereas Congress has taken steps to pursue vigorously the war on terrorism through the provision of authorities and funding requested by the President to take the necessary actions against international terrorists and terrorist organizations, including those nations, organizations, or persons who planned, authorized, committed, or aided the terrorist attacks that occurred on September 11, 2001, or harbored such persons or organizations;

Whereas the President and Congress are determined to continue to take all appropriate actions against international terrorists and terrorist organizations, including those nations, organizations, or persons who planned, authorized, committed, or aided the terrorist attacks that occurred on September 11, 2001, or harbored such persons or organizations;

Whereas the President has authority under the Constitution to take action in order to deter and prevent acts of international terrorism against the United States, as Congress recognized in the joint resolution on Authorization for Use of Military Force (P.L. 107-40); and

Whereas it is in the national security interests of the United States to restore international peace and security to the Persian Gulf region: Now, therefore, be it

Resolved by the Senate and House of Representatives of the United States of America in Congress assembled,

SECTION 1. SHORT TITLE.

This joint resolution may be cited as the "Authorization for Use of Military Force Against Iraq Resolution of 2002."

SEC. 2. SUPPORT FOR UNITED STATES DIPLOMATIC EFFORTS.

The Congress of the United States supports the efforts by the President to—

(1) strictly enforce through the United Nations Security Council all relevant Security Council resolutions regarding Iraq and encourages him in those efforts; and
(2) obtain prompt and decisive action by the Security Council to ensure that Iraq abandons its strategy of delay, evasion and noncompliance and promptly and strictly complies with all relevant Security Council resolutions regarding Iraq.

SEC. 3. AUTHORIZATION FOR USE OF UNITED STATES ARMED FORCES.

(a) Authorization.—The President is authorized to use the Armed Forces of the United States as he determines to be necessary and appropriate in order to—
    (1) defend the national security of the United States against the continuing threat posed by Iraq; and
    (2) enforce all relevant United Nations Security Council resolutions regarding Iraq.
(b) Presidential Determination.—In connection with the exercise of the authority granted in subsection (a) to use force the President shall, prior to such exercise or as soon thereafter as may be feasible, but no later than 48 hours after exercising such authority, make available to the Speaker of the House of Representatives and the President pro tempore of the Senate his determination that—
    (1) reliance by the United States on further diplomatic or other peaceful means alone either (A) will not adequately protect the national security of the United States against the continuing threat posed by Iraq or (B) is not likely to lead to enforcement of all relevant United Nations Security Council resolutions regarding Iraq; and
    (2) acting pursuant to this joint resolution is consistent with the United States and other countries continuing to take the necessary actions against international terrorist and terrorist organizations, including those nations, organizations, or persons who planned, authorized, committed or aided the terrorist attacks that occurred on September 11, 2001.
(c) War Powers Resolution Requirements.—

(1) Specific statutory authorization.—Consistent with section 8(a)(1) of the War Powers Resolution, the Congress declares that this section is intended to constitute specific statutory authorization within the meaning of section 5(b) of the War Powers Resolution.
(2) Applicability of other requirements.—Nothing in this joint resolution supersedes any requirement of the War Powers Resolution.

SEC. 4. REPORTS TO CONGRESS.

(a) Reports.—The President shall, at least once every 60 days, submit to the Congress a report on matters relevant to this joint resolution, including actions taken pursuant to the exercise of authority granted in section 3 and the status of planning for efforts that are expected to be required after such actions are completed, including those actions described in section 7 of the Iraq Liberation Act of 1998 (P.L. 105-338).
(b) Single Consolidated Report.—To the extent that the submission of any report described in subsection (a) coincides with the submission of any other report on matters relevant to this joint resolution otherwise required to be submitted to Congress pursuant to the reporting requirements of the War Powers Resolution (P.L. 93-148), all such reports may be submitted as a single consolidated report to the Congress.
(c) Rule of Construction.—To the extent that the information required by section 3 of the Authorization for Use of Military Force Against Iraq Resolution (P.L. 102-1) is included in the report required by this section, such report shall be considered as meeting the requirements of section 3 of such resolution.

APPROVED, October 16, 2002.

End Notes

[1] See **Table 1** for presidential and congressional actions taken regarding all formal declarations of war by the United States. See **Appendix A** for the texts of these declarations.

[2] It is beyond the scope of this report to detail the often complex circumstances underlying the nature, motivations, and timing of presidential requests for war declarations. Those matters have been the subject of important debates among scholars. The texts of specific presidential messages requesting a declaration of war are found in Richardson, James D. (ed.) *A Compilation of the Messages and Papers of the Presidents* (20 vol., Washington, 1897-1917.) as follows: Madison: Vol. II, pp. 484-490.; Polk: Vol. V, pp. 2287-2293.; McKinley: Vol. XIII, pp. 6296-6297; Wilson: Vol. XVI, pp. 8226-8233 (for Germany) and Vol. XVI, pp. 8399-8406 (for Austria-Hungary); Rosenman, Samuel I. (comp.) The Public Papers and Addresses of Franklin D. Roosevelt, 1941. New York, Harper & Brothers, 1950), pp. 514-515 (for Japan) and pp. 532 (for Germany and Italy); Rosenman, Samuel I. (comp.) The Public Papers and Addresses of Franklin D. Roosevelt, 1942. New York, Harper & Brothers, 1950), pp. 257 (declarations for Bulgaria, Hungary and Rumania).

[3] Act of June 5, 1942, ch. 325, 56 Stat. 307.

[4] Richardson, Messages and Papers of the Presidents, Vol XIII, pp. 6296-6297. Act of April 25, 1898, ch. 189, 30 Stat. 364. Joint Resolution of April 20, 1898, [Res. 24] 30 Stat. 738. An earlier message by McKinley requesting authorization to use U.S. military force to resolve the Cuban-Spanish conflict was submitted to Congress on April 11, 1898. Richardson, Messages and Papers of the Presidents, Vol. XIII, pp. 6281-6292.

[5] Richardson, Messages and Papers of the Presidents, Vol. XVI, pp. 8226-8233. Act of April 6, 1917, ch.1, 40 Stat.1. [Germany]. Richardson, Messages and Papers of the Presidents, Vol. XVI, pp. 8399-8406. Act of December 7, 1917, ch. 1, 40 Stat. 429.[Austria-Hungary].

[6] Rosenman, *Public Papers of President Roosevelt, 1941*, pp. 514-515. Act of December 8, 1941, ch. 561, 55 Stat. 795.[Japan]; Rosenman, *Public Papers of President Roosevelt 1941*, p. 532. Act of December 11, 1941, ch. 564, 55 Stat. 796. [Germany].Act of December 11, 1941, ch. 565, 55 Stat. 797.[Italy].

[7] Rosenman, *Public Papers of President Roosevelt, 1942*, p. 257. Act of June 5, 1942, ch. 323, 56 Stat. 307. [Bulgaria]. Act of June 5, 1942, ch. 324, 56 Stat. 307.[Hungary]. Act of June 5, 1942, ch. 325, 56 Stat. 307.[Rumania].

[8] There have been numbers of scholarly works written that address, in depth, the circumstances surrounding most of the measures discussed herein. It is beyond the scope of this report to itemize fully the complex diplomatic, political and military motivations that led to their enactment. For general background see Bemis, Samuel Flagg , A Diplomatic History of the United States, New York, Holt, Rinehart and Winston, 5th ed. 1965; DeConde, Alexander, A History of American Foreign Policy, New York, Charles Scribner's Sons, 3rd ed., 2 vol. 1978; Bailey, Thomas A., A Diplomatic History of the American People, Englewood Cliffs, Prentice Hall, Inc., 10th ed. 1980.

[9] The text of President John Adams's messages to Congress are found in Richardson, James D. (ed.) *A Compilation of the Messages and Papers of the Presidents* (20 vol., Washington, 1897-1917), Vol. I, pp. 223-229, 254-255; also in Annals of the Congress of the United States, 5th Congress, 1st session, pp.54-59,1271-1272.

[10] Act of May 28, 1798, ch. 48, 2 Stat. 561.

[11] Act of July 9, 1798, ch. 68, 2 Stat. 578.

[12] The text of President Thomas Jefferson's message to Congress is found in Richardson, James D. (ed.) *A Compilation of the Messages and Papers of the Presidents* (20 vol., Washington, 1897-1917), Vol. I, pp. 314-320; Also in Annals of the Congress of the United States, 7th Congress, 1st session, pp. 12-16.

[13] Act of February 6, 1802, ch. 4, 1 Stat. 129.

[14] The text of President James Madison's message to Congress is found in Richardson, James D. (ed.) *A Compilation of the Messages and Papers of the Presidents* (20 vol., Washington, 1897-1917), Vol. II, p. 539; Also in Annals of the Congress of the United States, 13th Congress, 3rd session, p. 269.

[15] Act of March 3, 1815, Chap. 90, 3 Stat. 230.

[16] For a detailed treatment of the problem of piracy in the West Indies during the U.S. early national period see Francis B.C. Bradlee. Piracy in the West Indies and Its Suppression. Salem: The Essex Institute, 1923 [reprinted 1970 by MacDonald and Janes, London]. Also see chapter 12 in Craig L. Symonds. Navalists and Antinavalists. Newark: University of Delaware Press, 1980. For recent use of the piracy statute in connection with activity off the coast of Somalia, see CRS Report R40528, *Piracy off the Horn of Africa*, by Lauren Ploch Blanchard et al. For criminal prosecutions of accused pirates, see CRS Report R41455, *Piracy: A Legal Definition*, by R. Chuck Mason.

[17] Public Papers of the Presidents of the United States. Dwight D. Eisenhower. 1955, Washington. U.S. Government Printing Office, 1959, pp. 207-211.

[18] P.L. 84-4, 69 Stat. 7, January 29, 1955. The House passed H.J.Res. 159 by a vote of 410-3 on January 25, 1955; the Senate passed the joint resolution by a vote of 85-3 on January 28, 1955.

[19] P.L. 93-475, §3, 88 Stat. 1439, October 26, 1974.

[20] Public Papers of the Presidents of the United States. Dwight D. Eisenhower. 1957, Washington. U.S. Government Printing Office, 1958, pp. 6, 11-15.

[21] P.L. 85-7, 71 Stat. 5 March 9, 1957 [H.J.Res. 117]. The Senate Committees on Foreign Relations and Armed Services, in a joint report, noted that in considering the legislation various strongly held views had been "vigorously expressed" regarding the constitutional powers of the President and of the Congress, as well as the proper constitutional procedure to be followed in the situation contemplated by the legislation. The final legislative language adopted reflected this debate. This language had, the Senate committees said, "the virtue of remaining silent on the question of the relationship between the Congress and the President with respect to the use of the Armed Forces for the objectives stated in the resolution." The Senate committees also argued that although there was sharp division as to the "proper constitutional processes" to follow in support of the President's request, there was none regarding the substantive policy involved. They stated that "the clear statement of policy in section 2 of the resolution as reported is preferable to a blanket authorization to the President to use the Armed Forces in this area." U.S. Congress. Senate. Committees on Foreign Relations and Armed Services, 85th Congress, 1st session, S.Rept. 70, February 14, 1957 [to accompany S.J. Res. 19], pp. 1, 8-9. The text of the Senate bill was adopted by the Congress in lieu of that of the House bill. The Senate passed the joint resolution, H.J.Res. 117, as amended, by a vote of 72-19 on March 5, 1957; the House passed H.J.Res. 117 with the Senate amendments by a vote of 350-60 on March 7, 1957. The joint resolution was signed on March 9, 1957.

[22] The resolution is codified at 22 U.S.C.A. §§1961-65.

[23] Public Papers of the Presidents of the United States. Lyndon B. Johnson. 1963-64, Washington. U.S. Government Printing Office, 1965, pp. 927, 930-932.

[24] P.L. 88-408, 78 Stat. 384, August 10, 1964. The House passed H.J.Res. 1145 on August 7, 1964, by a vote of 414-0; the Senate passed it on August 7, 1964 by a vote of 88-2. This joint resolution was later repealed in 1971 by P.L. 91-672, §12, 84 Stat. 2053 (1971).

[25] P.L. 91-672, §12, 84 Stat. 2055, January 12, 1971.

[26] For an explanation of the requirements of the War Powers Resolution, *see infra* at 27-28.

[27] P.L. 98-43, 97 Stat. 214, June 27, 1983 [S. 639].

[28] P.L. 98-119, 97 Stat. 805, October 12, 1983 [S.J.Res. 159].

[29] Public Papers of the Presidents of the United States. Ronald Reagan. 1983, Washington. U.S. Government Printing Office, 1985, pp.1444-1445. Shortly afterward, on October 23, 1983, 241 U.S. Marines in Lebanon were killed by a suicide truck bombing, raising fresh questions in Congress and U.S. public opinion about U.S. participation in the Lebanon peacekeeping endeavor. On February 7, 1984, President Reagan announced the Marines would be redeployed and on March 30, 1984, reported to Congress that U.S. participation in the Multinational Force in Lebanon had ended.

[30] For an overview of congressional actions during the fall and winter of 1990 as well as the President's actions in response to the events in the Persian Gulf, see CRS Report R42699, *The War Powers Resolution: After Thirty-Eight Years*, pp. 24-26.

[31] Dellums v. Bush, 752 F. Supp. 1141 (D.D.C. 1990).

[32] Public Papers of the Presidents of the United States. George Bush 1991. Washington, U.S. Government Printing Office, 1992, pp. 13-14, 19-20.

[33] The House passed H.J.Res. 77 by a vote of 250 to 183. The Senate passed S.J.Res. 2 and then accepted the language in H.J.Res. 77. The Senate vote was 52 to 47. P.L. 102-1, 105 Stat. 3, January 14, 1991. On January 12, to emphasize the congressional power to declare war, the House also adopted by a vote of 302 to 131 H.Con.Res. 32 expressing the sense that Congress must approve any offensive military actions against Iraq; the Senate did not act on the measure.

[34] Public Papers of the Presidents of the United States. George Bush 1991. Washington, U.S. Government Printing Office, 1992, p. 40. Subsequently, on June 20,1992, President Bush reiterated his view of his constitutional authority during remarks to the Texas State Republican Convention in Dallas, Texas. On that occasion President Bush said: "Some people say, why can't you bring the same kind of purpose and success to the domestic scene as you did in Desert Shield and Desert Storm? And the answer is: I didn't have to get permission from some old goat in the United States Congress to kick Saddam Hussein out of Kuwait. That's the reason." Public Papers of the Presidents of the United States. George Bush 1992-93. Washington, U.S. Government Printing Office, 1993, p. 995.

[35] Public Papers of the Presidents of the United States. George Bush 1991. Washington, U.S. Government Printing Office, 1992, p. 42, 52. Emphasis added.

[36] Presidential statement of September 12, 2001. Office of the White House Press Secretary, available at http://georgewbush-whitehouse.archives.gov/news/releases/2001/09/20010912-4.

[37] For background on discussions regarding the resolution see *Washington Post*, September 13, 2001, p.A3; *CQ Daily Monitor*, September 13, 2001, p.2, 6; *CQ Daily Monitor*, September 14, 2001, p.2; Washington Post, September 14, 2001, p. A30; The New York Times, September 14, 2001, p.A19; *Roll Call*, September 20, 2001, p.17; and Abramowitz, David, "The President, the Congress, and Use of Force: Legal and Political Considerations in Authorizing Use of Force Against International Terrorism," 43 *Harvard International Law Journal* 71 (2002). The debate on S.J.Res. 23 is found in 107 CONG. REC. S9416-S9421 and H5638-H5683 (daily edition September 14, 2001).

[38] P.L. 107-40 (September 18, 2001); 115 Stat. 224.

[39] Statement of the President on September 18, 2001. President Signs Authorization for Use of Military Force bill. Office of the White House Press Secretary. September 18, 2001, available at http://georgewbush-whitehouse.archives.gov/news/releases/2001/09/20010918-10.html.

[40] For a detailed legislative history of the joint resolution addressing its intended scope, see CRS Report RS22357, *Authorization for Use of Military Force in Response to the 9/11 Attacks (P.L. 107-40): Legislative History.*

[41] For an overview of the 2004 Supreme Court decisions regarding the authorization to use military force, see CRS Report RS21884, *The Supreme Court 2003 Term: Summary and Analysis of Opinions Related to Detainees in the War on Terrorism*, by Jennifer K. Elsea.

[42] *See* CRS Report RL31724, *Detention of American Citizens as Enemy Combatants*, by Jennifer K. Elsea. (...continued)

[43] U.S. Department of Justice White Paper on NSA Legal Authorities ("Legal Authorities Supporting the Activities of the National Security Agency Described by the President") ("DOJ White Paper") (January 19, 2006), http://news.findlaw.com/hdocs/docs/nsa/dojnsa11906wp.pdf. For an analysis of the Administration position as presented prior to the DOJ White Paper, see CRS Report R40888, *Presidential Authority to Conduct Warrantless Electronic Surveillance to Gather Foreign Intelligence Information*, by Elizabeth B. Bazan and Jennifer K. Elsea.

[44] Hamdan v. Rumsfeld, 548 U.S. 557 (2006), *rev'g 415* F.3d 33 (D.C. Cir. 2005). For a summary and analysis, see CRS Report RS22466, *Hamdan v. Rumsfeld: Military Commissions in the "Global War on Terrorism"*, by Jennifer K. Elsea.

[45] White House, "President's Remarks at the United Nations General Assembly," press release, September 12, 2002, http://georgewbush-whitehouse.archives.gov/news/releases/2002/09/print/20020912-1.html; White House,

"President Discusses Iraq, Domestic Agenda with Congressional Leaders," press release, September 18, 2002, http://georgewbush-whitehouse.archives.gov/news/releases/2002/09/print/20020918-1.html.

[46] P.L. 107-243; 116 Stat. 1498. For a detailed side-by-side comparison of the House and Senate versions of the authorization of force against Iraq legislation and proposed amendments see CRS Report RL31596, *Iraq: Authorization of Use of U.S. Armed Forces—Side-By-Side Comparison of Public Law 107-243 and Selected Legislative Proposals*, by Dianne E. Rennack.

[47] George W. Bush: "Statement on Signing the Authorization for Use of Military Force Against Iraq Resolution of 2002," October 16, 2002, available online by Gerhard Peters and John T. Woolley, *The American Presidency Project*. http://www.presidency.ucsb.edu/ws/?pid=64386.

[48] In March 2003, President George W. Bush reported to Congress the determination that was required by P.L. 107-243 regarding his exercise of authority for military operations against Iraq. House Document 108-50. March 19, 2003. A report in connection with Presidential Determination under P.L. 107-243. Communication from the President of the United States transmitting a report consistent with Section 3(b) of the Authorization for Use of Military Force Against Iraq Resolution of 2002.

[49] See UNSC Resolution 1511 (October 16, 2003), UNSC Resolution 1546 (June 8, 2004), UNSC Resolution 1637 (November 8, 2005), UNSC Resolution 1723 (November 28, 2006), and UNSC Resolution 1790 (December 18, 2007).

[50] Agreement Between the United States of America and the Republic of Iraq on the Withdrawal of United States Forces from Iraq and the Organization of Their Activities during Their Temporary Presence in Iraq, Article 12, November 17, 2008 [hereinafter *Withdrawal Agreement*], http://www.state.gov/documents/organization/122074.pdf. For a more comprehensive overview of the Withdrawal Agreement, see CRS Report R40011, *U.S.-Iraq Withdrawal/Status of Forces Agreement: Issues for Congressional Oversight*, by R. Chuck Mason.

[51] See, e.g., U.S. Congress, House Committee on International Relations, Subcommittee on Middle East and South Asia and the Subcommittee on International Organizations, Human Rights, and Oversight, 110th Cong., March 4, 2008 (statement of Prof. Oona Hathaway). On this issue, see generally CRS Report RL33837, *Congressional Authority to Limit U.S. Military Operations in Iraq*, by Jennifer K. Elsea, Michael John Garcia, and Thomas J. Nicola.

[52] President Bush vetoed a supplemental appropriations bill to fund the war that would have set conditions and a deadline for ending some military operations, arguing in part that some of its provisions are unconstitutional. H.R. 1591 (110th Cong.). For a description of the vetoed bill, see CRS Report RL33837, *Congressional Authority to Limit U.S. Military Operations in Iraq*, by Jennifer K. Elsea, Michael John Garcia, and Thomas J. Nicola. Other efforts in the 110th Congress included H.R. 1460 (to repeal 2002 resolution); H.R. 1262 (same); S. 679 (to declare that objectives of 2002 resolution had been achieved, and require redeployment of forces from Iraq); S.J.Res. 3 (to establish expiration date for 2002 resolution); S. 670 (to require new military authorization unless certain objectives are met); H.R. 930 (to repeal 2002 resolution); H.R. 508 (same), H.R. 413 (same). Efforts in the 111th Congress included H.R. 335 (to prohibit entry into force of security arrangement with Iraq that was not made with Senate advice and consent), H.R. 66 (to repeal 2002 resolution and require troop withdrawal), H.Res. 72 (sense of the House that the Withdrawal Agreement is not legally binding).

[53] Skubiszewski, Krzysztof, "Peace and War," *Encyclopedia of Public International Law*, Vol 4 (1982), at 74-75.

[54] Hyde, Charles Cheney, *International Law Chiefly as Interpreted and Applied by the United States*, Vol. 3 (1945), at 1686.

[55] von Glahn, Gerhard, *Law Among Nations* (6th ed.) (1992), at 669.

[56] In his treatise *Law of Nations* (1858), at 346, Emmerich de Vattel stated the general principles governing the conduct of war as follows:

As soon, therefore, as we have declared war, we have a right to do against the enemy whatever we find necessary for the attainment of that end—for the purpose of bringing him to reason, and obtaining justice and security from him.

The lawfulness of the end does not give us a real right to anything further than barely the means necessary for the attainment of that end. Whatever we do beyond that, is reprobated by the law of nature, is faulty, and condemnable at the tribunal of conscience. Hence it is that the right to such or such acts of hostility varies according to circumstances. What is just and perfectly innocent in war, in one particular situation, is not always so on other occasions. Right goes hand in hand with necessity and the exigency of the case, but never exceeds them.

[57] Cushman K. Davis, *A Treatise on International Law* (1901), at 141 stated:

War abrogates all treaties between the belligerents; its suspends all commercial intercourse and relations between their respective subjects, and makes them unlawful; it dissolves all partnerships between subjects of the belligerents; it suspends the operation of all executory contracts during the war.... It open a great gulf of non-intercourse between the two nations, and imposes disability upon the subjects of each to do any kind of civil business with those of the other....

[58] Commentators differ on this issue. Grotius claimed that a declaration was a necessary precondition to the existence of a war. *See* Ingrid Detter, *The Law of* War (2000), at 10. Vattel said a declaration communicated to the enemy was demanded by "humanity" prior to the inception of a war, served as an inducement to the enemy to "terminate the difference without the effusion of blood," and was "the constant practice among the powers of Europe." Vattel, *supra* footnote 56, at 315. But he also stated that "there seems to be no absolute necessity for a formal declaration of war to render it legal." *Id.* at 316. *Kent's Commentary on International Law* (1878), at169-171, stated:...

[I]t has become settled by the practice of Europe that war may lawfully exist by a declaration which is unilateral only, or without a declaration on either side. It may begin with mutual hostilities. Since the Peace of Versailles in 1763, formal declarations of war of any kind seem to have been discontinued, and all the necessary and legitimate consequences of war flow at once from a state of public hostilities, duly recognized, and explicitly announced, by a domestic manifesto or State paper."

A legal requirement of a formal declaration of war was included in the Hague Convention (III) Relative to the Opening of Hostilities, negotiated in 1907 and ratified by 42 countries (including the U.S.), which stated as follows:

The Contracting Powers recognize that hostilities between themselves must not commence without previous and explicit warning, in the form either of a reasoned declaration of war or of an ultimatum with conditional declaration of war.

Although this treaty remains in effect for its Parties, its requirement regarding a declaration of war has generally fallen into desuetude; and a declaration generally is no longer regarded as a legal prerequisite to the use of force. Von Glahn, *supra* footnote 55, at 600, states: " ... [G]eneral opinion has sanctioned a commencement of hostilities without issuing a declaration of war or other formal notice of intent to resort to the use of force."

[59] Eagleton, Clyde, "The Form and Function of the Declaration of War," 38 *American Journal of International Law* 19, 21 (1938).

[60] Gray v. United States, 21 Ct.Cl. 340, 373 (1886).

[61] Treaty Providing for the Renunciation of War As an Instrument of National Policy, 46 Stat. 2343 (1929); TS 796; 2 Bevans 732.

[62] *Id.*, Art. I.

[63] The Tribunal stated:

In the opinion of the Tribunal, the solemn renunciation of war as an instrument of national policy necessarily involves the proposition that such a war is illegal in international law; and that those who plan and wage such a war, with its inevitable and terrible consequences, are committing a crime in so doing.

See "International Military Tribunal (Nuremberg): Judgment and Sentences," 41 *American Journal of International Law* 172, 218 (1947).

[64] UN Charter, 59 Stat. 1031, Preamble and Article 2(4).

[65] *Id.* Ch. VII.

[66] The right of self-defense is explicitly recognized in Article 51 of the Charter, which states that "Nothing in the present Charter shall impair the inherent right of individual or collective self-defence if an armed attack occurs against a Member of the United Nations...."

[67] Department of State, *Treaties in Force: A List of Treaties and other International Agreements of the United States in Force on January 1, 2002* (August 2002), at 454.

[68] Dieter Fleck, ed., *The Handbook of Humanitarian Law in Armed Conflicts* (1995), at 39.

[69] The modern codification of the law of diplomatic relations—the Vienna Convention on Diplomatic Relations, 23 UST 3227 (1972)—does not specifically address the effect of a declaration of war or of an authorization for the use of force but does address what is required in cases of "armed conflict." Whenever diplomatic relations are broken, the Convention requires that diplomatic privileges and immunities not cease until the diplomat leaves the country and that the receiving state assist diplomats and their families in leaving "at the earliest possible moment, ... even in case of armed conflict" (Articles 38 and 44). The Convention also requires that a state respect and protect the premises of a diplomatic mission and its property and archives during any time in which diplomatic relations have been broken, including "in the case of armed conflict" (Article 45(a)).

[70] The modern tendency appears to be to deem treaties as remaining in effect to the greatest extent possible. *See generally*, von Glahn, Gerhard, *Law Among Nations* (1992), at 715-716.

[71] *See* The Hague Convention Respecting the Laws and Customs of War on Land, 32 Stat. 1803 (1902); the Hague Convention (III) Relative to the Opening of Hostilities, 36 Stat. 2259 (1910); the Hague Convention (IV) Respecting the Laws and Customs of War on Land, 36 Stat. 2277 (1910); the Hague Convention (V) Respecting the Rights and Duties of Neutral Powers and Persons in Case of War on Land, 36 Stat. 2310 (1910); the Hague Convention (VII) Relative to the Laying of Automatic Submarine Contact Mines, 36 Stat. 2332 (1910); the Hague Convention (IX) Concerning Bombardment by Naval Forces in Time of War, 36 Stat. 2351 (1910); the Hague Convention (XI) Relative to Certain Restrictions With Regard to the Exercise of the Right of Capture in Naval War, 36 Stat. 2396 (1910); the Hague Convention (XIII) Concerning the Rights and Duties of Neutral Powers in Naval War, 36 Stat. 2415 (1910); The Protocol for the Prohibition of the Use in

War of Asphyxiating, Poisonous or other Gases, and of Bacteriological Methods of Warfare, 26 UST 571 (1975) and The Convention on the Prohibition of Military or Any Other Hostile Use of Environmental Modification Techniques, 31 UST 333 (1980). The United States is a Party to all of these conventions.

[72] The four Geneva Conventions apply to the treatment of those in the armed forces who are wounded and sick in the field, those who are shipwrecked, prisoners of war, and civilian populations. *See* Convention (I) for the Amelioration of the Condition of the Wounded and Sick in Armed Forces in the Field, 6 UST 3114 (1956); Convention (II) for the Amelioration of the Condition of the Wounded, Sick, and Shipwrecked Members of Armed Forces at Sea, 6 UST 3217 (1956); Convention (III) Relative to the Treatment of Prisoners of War, 6 UST 3316 (1956); and Convention (IV) Relative to the Protection of Civilian Persons in Time of War, 6 UST 3516 (1956).

[73] Alexander Hamilton, "The Examination No. 1," (December 17, 1801), reprinted in 25 *The Papers of Alexander Hamilton* 455 (Syrett, ed., 1977), quoted in J. Gregory Sidak, "To Declare War," 41 *Duke Law Journal* 27 (1991), at 62. The full quote reads: "War, of itself, gives to the parties a mutual right to kill in battle.... This is a rule of natural law; a necessary and inevitable consequence of the state of war."

[74] *Id.* at 203.

[75] U.S. (4 Dall.) 37, 40 (1800).

[76] *Id.*

[77] *Id.* at 43.

[78] *See, e.g.*, P.L. 107-40 (September 18, 2001) (authorizing the President to use "all necessary and appropriate force against those nations, organizations, or persons he determines planned, authorized, committed, or aided the terrorist attacks that occurred on September 11, 2001....") and P.L. 107-243 (October 16, 2002) (authorizing the President to the use the armed forces "as he determines to be necessary and appropriate in order to—(1) defend the national security of the United States against the continuing threat posed by Iraq; and (2) enforce all relevant United Nations Security Council resolutions regarding Iraq."

[79] *See Hamdi v. Rumsfeld*, 542 U.S. 507, 518 (2004) (O'Connor, J., plurality opinion); *id.* at588-589 (Thomas, J., dissenting). The plurality interpreted the AUMF as authorizing the detention of a U.S. citizen captured in Afghanistan as a "fundamental incident of waging war," and was thus a statute authorizing detention within the meaning of the Non-Detention Act, 18 U.S.C.A. §4001(a), which prohibits the detention of any citizen absent an act of Congress.

[80] *Hamdi*, 542 at 519.

[81] For a historical overview of wartime detention in the United States, see CRS Report R42337, *Detention of U.S. Persons as Enemy Belligerents*, by Jennifer K. Elsea.

[82] 18 U.S.C. §4001(a) provides that "No citizen shall be imprisoned or otherwise detained by the United States except pursuant to an Act of Congress." The 4th Circuit Court of Appeals validated the detention of a U.S. citizen on the basis of his presence during hostilities in Afghanistan, but the government transferred the petitioner to federal court for trial on terrorism charges before the Supreme Court could take the case on appeal. *Padilla v. Hanft*, 423 F.3d 386 (4th Cir.), *motion to vacate denied* 432 F.3d 582 (4th Cir. 2005), *cert. denied* 547 U.S. 1062 (2006). A plurality of the 4th circuit sitting *en banc* upheld the detention of a non-citizen suspected of being a "sleeper agent" for Al Qaeda, although the court did not agree on a definition of "enemy combatant," or individual subject to detention. The Supreme Court vacated the decision at the request of the government after the petitioner was transferred to federal court for trial on terrorism charges. *Al-Marri v. Pucciarelli*, 534 F.3d 213 (4th Cir. 2008)(per curiam), *vacated and remanded sub nom. Al-Marri v. Sapagone*, 129 s.Ct. 1545 (2009). For more background on these cases, see CRS Report R41156, *Judicial Activity Concerning Enemy Combatant Detainees: Major Court Rulings*, by Jennifer K. Elsea and Michael John Garcia; CRS Report R42337, *Detention of U.S. Persons as Enemy Belligerents*, by Jennifer K. Elsea.

[83] The Bush Administration argued that intelligence collection is authorized as an incident to the use of force, and that restrictions under FISA therefore did not apply to electronic surveillance conducted for anti-terrorism purposes because section 109 of FISA provides an exception to the criminal prohibition against electronic surveillance unless "authorized by statute." (50 U.S.C.A. §1809, prior to 2008 amendment to clarify meaning of "authorized by statute"). Congress passed the Protect America Act , P.L. 110-55, to provide additional authority for electronic surveillance.

[84] 50 U.S.C.A. §1541 *et seq.*

[85] *Id.*, §1544(b).

[86] 50 U.S.C. App. §§1 *et seq.*

[87] 50 U.S.C. §§1701 *et seq.*

[88] 50 U.S.C.A. Appx. §5(b).

[89] 50 U.S.C.A. §1702, as amended by P.L. 107-56, Title I, §106 (October 26, 2001).

[90] *See* 50 U.S.C.A. Appx. §5(b). For an overview of TWEA and IEEPA and how their authorities compare, see Staff of the House Ways and Means Committee, 111th Cong., *Overview and Compilation of U.S. Trade Statutes*, ch. 5 (WMCP 111-6, 2010).

[91] P.L. 107-56, Title I, §106 (October 26, 2001).

[92] P.L. 107-297, Title II, §201 (November 26, 2002).

[93] 10 U.S.C.A. §2538.
[94] 16 U.S.C.A. §831s.
[95] 10 U.S.C.A. §2644.
[96] 10 U.S.C.A. §2663(a).
[97] 43 U.S.C.A. §1314(b).
[98] 47 U.S.C.A. §606(a).
[99] 7 U.S.C.A. §5712(c).
[100] 50 U.S.C. §§21 *et seq.*
[101] *Johnson v. Eisentrager*, 339 U.S. 763, 774 (1950).
[102] 50 U.S.C. §21.
[103] *Id.*
[104] *See* J. Gregory Sindak, War, Liberty, and Enemy Aliens, 67 *N.Y.U.L. Rev.* 1402, 1412-1419 (1992). President Roosevelt also ordered thousands of Japanese-American citizens interned; but he did not rely explicitly on the Alien Enemy Act to do so.
[105] 8 U.S.C. §§1101 *et seq. See, e.g.,* 8 U.S.C. §240.
[106] *See Ludecke v. Watkins*, 335 U.S. 160 (1948) ("The very nature of the President's power to order the removal of all enemy aliens rejects the notion that courts may pass judgment upon the exercise of his discretion.").
[107] 50 U.S.C.A. §22.
[108] This list is intended to provide examples, rather than to be exhaustive.
[109] It should be noted that other espionage provisions in 18 U.S.C.A. §§793-799 do not explicitly require a state or time of war to apply, but would presumably apply in wartime as well as peacetime. Unlawful communication of, receipt of, tampering with, or disclosure of restricted data with respect to special nuclear material is addressed in 42 U.S.C.A. §§2274-77. Here again, wartime is not distinguished from other times in the application of these provisions.
[110] The provisions noted in this paragraph are intended as examples, rather than as an exhaustive list.
[111] There are also a number of provisions in 18 U.S.C.A. §§958-67 that may be triggered by conduct during wars involving other nations with whom the United States is at peace or during wars in which the United States is neutral. These deal, for example, with: enlisting in the service of a foreign government to serve in war against a nation with whom the United States is at peace; taking part in or facilitating a military or naval expedition against a friendly nation; strengthening the armed vessel of a foreign nation which is at war with a nation with whom the United States is at peace; arming a vessel to be used against a friendly nation; authorizing the taking out or attempting to take out of a U.S. port a detained vessel of a belligerent nation; delivering an armed vessel to a belligerent nation in a conflict in which the United States is neutral; or authorizing the taking out or attempting to take out of a U.S. port a vessel the departure of which has been prohibited in aid of neutrality.
[112] Some of these statutes are among a number of federal statutes which implicitly or explicitly have extraterritorial application. This raises a question as to whether or to what extent the existence of a state of open hostilities or a declaration of war would affect the availability of extraterritorial application of such provisions. An exploration of this issue is beyond the scope of this report. For a general discussion of extraterritorial application of federal criminal law, including appendices addressing federal criminal laws which enjoy express extraterritorial application and federal crimes subject to federal prosecution when committed overseas, see, CRS Report 94-166, *Extraterritorial Application of American Criminal Law*, by Charles Doyle.
[113] United States v. Shelton, 816 F. Supp. 1132, 1135 (W.D. Tex. 1993). A later case held that the authorizations to use force in connection with Iraq and Afghanistan sufficed to toll the limitations period, United States v. Prosperi, 573 F. Supp. 2d 436, 442 (D. Mass. 2008), applying a four-part test to determine whether the United States was "at war" within the meaning of the statute:

1) the extent of the authorization given by Congress by the President to act; 2) whether the conflict is deemed a "war" under accepted definitions of the term and the rules of international law; 3) the size and scope of the conflict (including the cost of the related procurement effort); and 4) the diversion of resources that might have been expended on investigating frauds against the government.

Id. at 449.

The *Prosperi* court determined that the war in Iraq ended on May 1, 2003, when President Bush declared that "major combat operations" had ended there. *Prosperi*, 573 F. Supp. 2d at 455.
[114] U.S. Congress, Senate Committee on the Judiciary, *Wartime Enforcement of Fraud Act of 2008*, Report to Accompany S. 2892, 110th Cong., 2nd sess., July 25, 2008, S.Rept. 110-431. The Report explains that:

Technically, Section 3287 only applies to declared wars, not circumstances where Congress has authorized the use of military force, as in the recent wars in Iraq and Afghanistan. The amendment to Section 3287 specifically tracks the text of the Congressional authorizations for the use of the Armed Forces in Iraq and Afghanistan and refers only to those authorizations described in the War Powers Resolution (50 U.S.C. 1544(b)). As a result, only significant military actions requiring Congressional action would trigger this suspension of the statute of limitations. This amendment is not intended to apply to peacekeeping missions under the auspices of the United Nations or military actions not specifically authorized by Congress pursuant to the War Powers resolution. This language is intended to apply the suspension of statute of limitations to the wars in Iraq and Afghanistan.

Id. at 5.

The language of S. 2892 (110th Cong.) was later incorporated into the Consolidated Security, Disaster Assistance, and Continuing Appropriations Act, 2009, H.R. 2638, and Duncan Hunter National Defense Authorization Act for Fiscal Year 2009, S. 3001. Both were enacted, but the later-enacted version was subsequently repealed retroactively, P.L. 111-84, Div. A, Title VIII, §1073(c)(7) (repealing §855 of P.L. 110-417).

115 P.L. 110-329, title VIII, §8117. The amended provision also requires notice to Congress if hostilities are ended pursuant to presidential proclamation.

116 In a case subsequent to the enactment of the amendment but involving offenses that occurred earlier, the court dismissed some counts of a complaint as time-barred based on the absence of a formal declaration of war. *United States v. Western Titanium, Inc.*, 2010 WL 2650224 (S.D. Cal. 2010). The court explained that its initial inclination was to adopt the *Prosperi* approach to determine whether the United States was at war when the offenses were committed, it ultimately concluded that the "extensive post-hoc factual determinations required by *Prosperi* render its application too ambiguous and uncertain in the context of a criminal statute of limitation." *Id.* at *3. The court further remarked that:

Whatever Congress intended by the phrase "at war" in the WSLA, it cannot have meant a definition not capable of determination until a court conducts a subjective analysis years after the commission of an offense.

Id.

117 Moreover, by operation of the Military Extraterritorial Jurisdiction Act of 2000, 18 U.S.C.A. §§3261-3267, contractors and other civilians who accompany American armed forces overseas are subject to federal prosecution for the commission of various common law crimes such as murder (18 U.S.C.A. §1111), rape (18 U.S.C.A. §2241), assault (18 U.S.C.A. §113), kidnaping (18 U.S.C.A. §1201), and the like.

118 Electronic surveillance under FISA is addressed at 50 U.S.C.A. §§1801 *et seq.*; foreign intelligence physical searches are addressed at 50 U.S.C. §§1821 *et seq.*; and pen registers and trap and trace devices under FISA are dealt with at 50 U.S.C. §§1841 *et seq.*

119 The Bush Administration took the position that the authorization to use force in response to the 9/11 attacks, P.L. 107-40, implicitly authorized wiretaps without judicial order without time limits as a fundamental incident of waging war, notwithstanding the existence of these provisions. *See* DOJ White Paper, *supra* footnote 43; CRS Report R40888, *Presidential Authority to Conduct Warrantless Electronic Surveillance to Gather Foreign Intelligence Information*, by Elizabeth B. Bazan and Jennifer K. Elsea.

120 For pertinent criteria and procedures applicable to such emergency situations, see 50 U.S.C. §§1805(e) (electronic surveillance), 1824(e) (physical search), or 1843 (pen register or trap and trace device. This authority is applicable only to gathering foreign intelligence information not concerning a United States person or information to protect against international terrorism or clandestine intelligence activities, provided that such an investigation of a U.S. person may not be conducted solely on the basis of First Amendment protected activities).

121 *See, e.g.,* 50 U.S.C. §1802 (electronic surveillance directed solely at acquisition of communications, not involving U.S. persons, of a foreign government or governments or components thereof, factions of a foreign nation or nations not substantially composed of U.S. persons, or entities openly acknowledged to be directed and controlled by a foreign government or governments, without a court order for periods up to one year in specific circumstances; this provision also covers electronic surveillance directed solely at acquisition of technical intelligence, other than spoken communications of individuals, from property or premises of such foreign governments, factions, or entities). For a more detailed discussion of FISA, see CRS Report RL30465, *The Foreign Intelligence Surveillance Act: An Overview of the Statutory Framework and U.S. Foreign Intelligence Surveillance Court and U.S. Foreign Intelligence Surveillance Court of Review Decisions*, by Elizabeth B. Bazan.

122 50 U.S.C.A. App. §§2061 *et seq.*

123 Titles II, IV, V, and VI pertained to Korean War-era economic stabilization measures (controlling prices, wages, credit, etc.).

124 P.L. 111-67, §2 (September 30, 2009) extended the sunset date for these provisions from September 30, 2009 to September 30, 2014.

125 50 U.S.C.A. App. §2062.

126 *Id.* §§2071-2078.

127 Similar authority to require the priority performance of defense contracts, including those for the Nuclear Regulatory Commission, if the President determines that "it is in the interest of national security" to do so, is conferred by 50 U.S.C.A. App. §468. That statute also authorizes the President to take immediate possession of any plant, mine, or other facility that fails to honor such a priority requirement, including steel production facilities that fail to honor priority directives regarding the apportionment of steel to entities producing steel products or materials for the armed forces.

[128] *Id.* §§2077 and 2091-2099.

[129] *Id.*, §§2151- 2170.

[130] For a more extensive discussion of the act, *see* CRS Report RS20587, *Defense Production Act: Purpose and Scope*, by Daniel H. Else (available upon request).

[131] There is an older line of cases in which courts apply a technical meaning to the term "war" to hold that only formally and constitutionally declared wars meet the definition. *See* 10A COUCH ON INSURANCE CONTRACTS §152:3 (2012).

[132] Under New York law, insurance policies are to be interpreted in accordance with their terms. *See Continental Insurance Company v. Arkwright Mutual Insurance Company*, 102 F.3d 30 (2d Cir. 1996). *See also Shneiderman v. Metropolitan Casualty*, 14 A.D.2d 284 (N.Y. 1961) (holding that "an insurance policy is generally a contract with the average man who presumably is unfamiliar with the existence of a state of war from the strictly political, military and/or legal standpoint.")

[133] *See, e.g., Hammond v. National Life and Accident Insurance Co.*, 243 So.2d 902 (La. App.), *cert. den.*, 258 La. 347, 246 So.2d 196 (La. 1971) (war exclusion clauses in two accidental death policies held not to preclude payment of double indemnity benefits for the death of a U.S. sailor on board an aircraft carrier in the Tonkin Gulf caused by crew error rather than hostile action on the grounds the phrase "in time of war" in the policies was ambiguous and, therefore, should be construed against the insurer).

[134] 505 F.2d 989 (2nd Cir. 1974).

[135] *Id.* at 1009. Jefferey W. Stempel, LAW OF INSURANCE CONTRACT DISPUTES §1.02[a] (2001)

[136] *Pan Am*, 505 F.2d at 1006. See also *Kimmins Indus. Service Corp. v. Reliance Ins. Co.*, 19 F.3d 78, 81 (2nd Cir. 1994), *Album Realty Co. v. American Home Assurance Co.*, 176 A.D.2d at 514, *quoting Home Insurance Co. v. American Insurance Co.*, 147 A.D.2d 353, 354 (1989).

[137] *Pan Am*, 505 F.2d at 1006.

[138] *Id.*

[139] For an overview, see CRS Report RS21979, *Terrorism Risk Insurance: An Overview*, by Baird Webel.

[140] Part IV of the Manual for Courts-Martial implements the punitive articles of the UCMJ; Part IV implements non-judicial punishment under art. 15, UCMJ.

[141] See Joseph Romero, "Of War and Punishment: 'Time of War' In Military Jurisprudence and a Call for Congress to Define its Meaning," 51 *Naval Law Review* 1, 8-38 (2005).

[142] 10 U.S.C.A. §843(a) eliminates the statute of limitations for absence without leave or missing movement in time of war. Under 10 U.S.C.A. §843(e),the President may extend the statute of limitations for any offense until six months after hostilities end by certifying to the Secretary of Defense that a trial would be "detrimental to the prosecution of the war or inimical to the national security."

[143] Military courts have not required a declaration of war in order for the suspension to apply, but rather, have applied various tests to determine probable congressional intent in the context of the statute.

[144] *United States v. Bancroftt,* 3 C.M.A. 3 (C.M.A. 1953) (Korean conflict counted as "time of war" in order to make sleeping on post a capital offense); *United States v. Ayers*, 4 C.M.A. 220 (C.M.A. 1953) (statute of limitations tolled for absence without leave in time war where offense was committed in the continental United States during the Korean conflict); *United States v. Taylor*, 4 C.M.A. 232 (C.M.A. 1954) (statute of limitations tolled during Korean conflict with respect to charge of fraud against the United States under 10 U.S.C.A. §843(f).

[145] *Robb v. United States*, 456 F.2d 768 (Ct. Cl. 1972); *United States v. Averette*, 41 C.M.R. 363 (C.M.A. 1968),

[146] P.L. 109-364, §552 (October 17, 2006). "Contingency operation" is defined under 10 U.S.C. §101(a)(13) to mean a military operation that:

(A) is designated by the Secretary of Defense as an operation in which members of the armed forces are or may become involved in military actions, operations, or hostilities against an enemy of the United States or against an opposing military force; or

(B) results in the call or order to, or retention on, active duty of members of the uniformed services under section 688, 12301 (a), 12302, 12304, 12305, or 12406 of [title 10], chapter 15 of [title 10], or any other provision of law during a war or during a national emergency declared by the President or Congress.

[147] *See* Press Release, Multi-National Corps—Iraq PAO *Civilian contractor convicted at a court-martial*, June 23, 2008, available online at http://www.mnf-iraq.com/index.php?option =com_content&task= view&id=20671&Itemid= 128. The defendant was sentenced to five months' confinement (time served) for wrongful appropriation of a knife, obstruction of justice, and making a false official statement to military investigators.

[148] Military Extraterritorial Jurisdiction Act of 2000 (MEJA), P.L. 106-523, 114 Stat. 2488 (2000), *codified at* 18 U.S.C. §3261-67. For more information about criminal jurisdiction over civilian contractors in connection with military operations, see CRS Report R40991, *Private Security Contractors in Iraq and Afghanistan: Legal Issues*, by Jennifer K. Elsea.

[149] *See* CRS Report RL31191, *Terrorism and the Law of War: Trying Terrorists as War Criminals before Military Commissions*, by Jennifer K. Elsea (providing a general background of U.S. history of military commissions).

[150] *See Ex parte* Milligan, 71 U.S. (4 Wall.) 2 (1866).

[151] 10 U.S.C.A. §948b.
[152] 10 U.S.C.A. §948d.
[153] 10 U.S.C.A. §948a.
[154] The language "if Congress so directs in the declaration" was added by P.L. 109-241 (2006).
[155] For a list of "periods of war," see CRS Report RS21405, *U.S. Periods of War and Dates of Current Conflicts*, by Barbara Salazar Torreon. For information about requirements to qualify for veterans' benefits, see CRS Report R42324, *"Who is a Veteran?"—Basic Eligibility for Veterans' Benefits*, by Umar Moulta-Ali.
[156] 50 U.S.C.A. §1601 *et seq.*
[157] *Id.* §§1621 and 1631.
[158] Proclamation 7463 (September 14, 2001); 66 *Federal Register* 48199 (September 18, 2001).
[159] 50 U.S.C.A. §1622.
[160] These lists was compiled based on several LEXIS searches using the search terms "national w/2 emergency," "state or time w/2 war," and "declaration w/2 war," compared to, and supplemented by, a study done under contract for the Office of Mobilization Preparedness in the Federal Emergency Management Agency in 1992 by the System Planning Corporation—*Emergency Executive Authorities* (Contract EMW-91-C-3644). The lists were revised and updated based on a Westlaw search (NATIONAL W/2 EMERGENCY) ((DUR* STATE TIME DECLAR!) W/5 (WAR HOSTILITIES)) and are current as of December 18, 2012.
[161] 42 U.S.C.A. §§5121 *et seq.*
[162] For purposes of this authority, "national emergency" is defined to mean "a general declaration of emergency with respect to the national defense made by the President or by the Congress. 50 U.S.C.A. §58h-3.
[163] It might be noted that 21 U.S.C.A. Section 1901(a) states as a congressional finding that "[t]here is a national emergency resulting from the activities of international narcotics traffickers and their organizations that threatens the national security, foreign policy, and economy of the United States"; but it is not clear whether any special authorities are intended to be triggered by this provision.
[164] This section, as amended by P.L. 111-148, was held unconstitutional as not severable by Florida ex rel. Bondi v. U.S. Dept. Of Health And Human Services, 2011 WL 285683, *1, (N.D.Fla. January31, 2011).
[165] P.L. 93-148. 87 Stat. 555 *et. seq.* 50 U.S.C. §§1541 *et. seq.*
[166] Wm. Holmes Brown, *House Practice: A Guide to the Rules, Precedents and Procedures of the House.* Washington, U.S. Govt. Print. Off., 1996, p. 692.
[167] The House floor discussion on April 4, 1917, concerning procedures for considering H.J.Res. 24, supports this interpretation by implication.
[168] These expedited procedures are ambiguous in several respects. The description presented here should not be considered a substitute for consultations with the House or Senate Parliamentarian.
[169] Other examples of rule-making provisions of law are the various congressional procedures enacted as part of the Congressional Budget and Impoundment Control Act of 1974 and related laws, and the "fast-track" provisions found in the Trade Act of 1974 and related laws.
[170] Presidential reports also are required under two other conditions enumerated in Sec. 4(a).
[171] Prior to 1983, the WPR provided that Congress could mandate the removal of U.S. armed forces by adopting a concurrent resolution. Given the virtual certainty that this procedure was unconstitutional following the Supreme Court's decision in June, 1983, in INS v. Chadha, 462 U.S. 919 (1983), Congress added a new provision to the War Powers Resolution later in 1983 providing for expedited procedures for a bill or joint resolution to require the removal of U.S. armed forces. *See* 50 U.S.C.A. §1546a.
[172] A subsequent section of the WPR mandates expedited procedures for House and Senate consideration of a bill or joint resolution requiring the removal of U.S. armed forces. *See* 50 U.S.C.A. §1546a.

In: Enactment of War and the Use of Military Force
Editor: Craig Perez
ISBN: 978-1-63482-987-8

Chapter 2

U.S. PERIODS OF WAR AND DATES OF RECENT CONFLICTS*

Barbara Salazar Torreon

SUMMARY

Many wars or conflicts in U.S. history have federally designated "periods of war," dates marking their beginning and ending. These dates are important for qualification for certain veterans' pension or disability benefits. Confusion can occur because beginning and ending dates for "periods of war" in many nonofficial sources are often different from those given in treaties and other official sources of information, and armistice dates can be confused with termination dates. This report lists the beginning and ending dates for "periods of war" found in Title 38 of the *Code of Federal Regulations*, dealing with the Department of Veterans Affairs (VA). It also lists and differentiates other beginning dates given in declarations of war, as well as termination of hostilities dates and armistice and ending dates given in proclamations, laws, or treaties. The dates for the recent conflicts in Afghanistan and Iraq are included along with the official end date for Operation New Dawn in Iraq on December 15, 2011, and Operation Enduring Freedom on Afghanistan on December 28, 2014.

WAR DATES

Congress, usually through a declaration of war, has often been the first governmental authority to designate the beginning date of a war or armed conflict. The President, or executive branch officials responsible to him, through proclamation, or Congress, through legislation, has been responsible for designating the war's termination date.[1] In some cases, later legislation is enacted to extend these beginning and ending dates for the purpose of broadening eligibility for veterans' benefits.[2] This report notes the variations in the dates cited in the *Code of Federal Regulations* (CFR) "periods of war" and those dates given in the

* This is an edited, reformatted and augmented version of a Congressional Research Service publication RS21405, prepared for Members and Committees of Congress, dated February 27, 2015.

declarations of war beginning and the proclamations, laws, or treaties terminating such conflicts.[3] Adding to the confusion, during World War II, wars were declared and terminated with six individual combatant countries. Moreover, armistice dates are also often confused with termination dates.[4]

Title 38, Part 3, Section 3.2 of the *Code of Federal Regulations*, dealing with the Department of Veterans Affairs (VA), lists official beginning and termination dates for most war periods from the Indian Wars to the present to be used in determining the availability of veterans' benefits.[5] The material below summarizes these dates. Where applicable, a summary of the Department of Veterans Affairs official beginning and termination dates is provided followed by a citation to the lettered CFR section. For some entries, this initial summary is followed by an explanatory note or declaration, armistice, cease-fire, or termination dates cited by other official sources. Also included are dates for the recent conflicts in Iraq and Afghanistan.

Indian Wars

January 1, 1817, through December 31, 1898, inclusive. Service must have been rendered with U.S. military forces against Indian tribes or nations. *Code of Federal Regulations*, 3.2 (a).

Spanish-American War

April 21, 1898, through July 4, 1902, inclusive. If the veteran served with the U.S. military forces engaged in hostilities in the Moro Province, the ending date is July 15, 1903. The Philippine Insurrection and the Boxer Rebellion are included for the purposes of benefit determination under this CFR section. *Code of Federal Regulations*, 3.2 (b).

Declared by an act of Congress April 25, 1898 (30 Stat. 364, ch. 189). An armistice signed August 12, 1898. Terminated by Treaty signed at Paris, December 10, 1898 (30 Stat. 1754), ratified and proclaimed April 11, 1899.

Mexican Border Period

May 9, 1916, through April 5, 1917. In the case of a veteran who during such period served in Mexico, on the borders thereof, or in the adjacent waters thereto. *Code of Federal Regulations*, 3.2 (h).

World War I

April 6, 1917, through November 11, 1918, inclusive. If the veteran served with the U.S. military forces in Russia, the ending date is April 1, 1920. Service after November 11, 1918, and before July 2, 1921, is considered World War I service if the veteran served in the active military, naval, or air service after April 5, 1917, and before November 12, 1918. *Code of Federal Regulations*, 3.2 (c).

World War I Against Germany

Declared by Joint Resolution of Congress of April 6, 1917 (40 Stat. 429, ch. 1). Armistice signed near Compiègne, France, November 11, 1918. Terminated July 2, 1921, by Joint Resolution of Congress (42 Stat. 105, ch. 40, 1).

World War I Against Austria-Hungary

Declared by Joint Resolution of Congress, December 7, 1917 (40 Stat. 429, ch. 1). An armistice signed near Compiègne, France, November 11, 1918. Terminated July 2, 1921, by Joint Resolution of Congress (42 Stat. 106, ch. 40, 3).

World War II

December 7, 1941, through December 31, 1946, inclusive. If the veteran was in service on December 31, 1946, continuous service before July 26, 1947, is considered World War II service. *Code of Federal Regulations*, 3.2 (d).

Note: During World War II, war was officially declared against six separate countries. The war with each was not over until the effective date of the Treaty of Peace. Note also the confusion cited below over which day is the official Victory in Europe Day (V-E Day)[6] and Victory Over Japan Day (V-J Day).[7]

World War II with Germany

Declared by Joint Resolution of Congress, December 11, 1941 (55 Stat. 796, ch. 564). German representative Colonel General Alfred Jodl signed the unconditional act of surrender to Allied representatives in a Reims, France schoolhouse on May 7, 1945. A second German surrender ceremony was held on May 8 in Berlin at the insistence of the U.S.S.R. Cessation of hostilities declared as of noon, December 31, 1946, by presidential proclamation of December 31, 1946 (Proc. no. 2714, 61 Stat. 1048). State of war with the "government of Germany" terminated October 19, 1951, by Joint Resolution of Congress of that date (65 Stat. 451, ch. 519), by Presidential Proclamation 2950, October 24, 1951. No peace treaty with Germany was signed.

World War II with Japan

Declared by Joint Resolution of Congress, December 8, 1941 (55 Stat. 795, ch. 561). Japanese representatives publicly sign unconditional surrender document on the deck of the *U.S.S. Missouri* anchored in Tokyo Bay on September 2, 1945. President Truman proclaimed this date Victory over Japan Day or V-J Day. Cessation of hostilities declared as of 12 noon, December 31, 1946, by presidential proclamation of December 31, 1946 (Proc. no. 2714, 61 Stat. 1048). Terminated by Multilateral Treaty of Peace with Japan, signed at San Francisco, September 8, 1951 (3 UST 3329), and ratified March 20, 1952, effective April 28, 1952.

World War II with Italy

Declared by Joint Resolution of Congress, December 11, 1941 (55 Stat. 797, ch. 565). Cessation of hostilities declared as of noon December 31, 1946, by presidential proclamation of December 31, 1946 (Proc. no. 2714, 61 Stat. 1048). Terminated by Treaty of Peace dated at Paris, February 10, 1947 (61 Stat. 1247), effective September 15, 1947.

World War II with Bulgaria

Declared by Joint Resolution of Congress, June 5, 1942 (56 Stat. 307, ch. 323). Cessation of hostilities declared as of noon December 31, 1946, by presidential proclamation of December 31, 1946 (Proc. no. 2714, 61 Stat. 1048). Terminated by Treaty of Peace dated at Paris, February 10, 1947 (61 Stat. 1915), effective September 15, 1947.

World War II with Hungary

Declared by Joint Resolution of Congress, June 5, 1942 (56 Stat. 307, ch. 324). Cessation of hostilities declared as of noon December 31, 1946, by presidential proclamation (Proc. no. 2714, 61 Stat. 1048). Terminated by Treaty of Peace dated at Paris, February 10, 1947 (61 Stat. 1757), effective September 15, 1947.

World War II with Romania

Declared by Joint Resolution of Congress, June 5, 1942 (56 Stat. 307, ch. 325). Cessation of hostilities declared as of noon December 31, 1946, by presidential proclamation of December 31, 1946 (Proc. no. 2714, 61 Stat. 1048). Terminated by Treaty of Peace dated at Paris, February 10, 1947 (61 Stat. 1757), effective September 15, 1947.

KOREAN CONFLICT

June 27, 1950, through January 31, 1955, inclusive. *Code of Federal Regulations*, 3.2 (e).

On June 25, 1950, North Korean Communist forces attacked South Korean positions south of the 38th parallel, leading to an immediate United Nations (U.N.) Security Council resolution calling for a cease-fire and withdrawal of the North Korean forces. On June 26, President Truman ordered U.S. air and sea forces in the Far East to aid South Korea. On June 27, the U.N. Security Council adopted a resolution asking U.N. members for assistance in repelling the North Korean armed attack and in restoring peace and security in the area. On June 30, the President stated that he had authorized the use of certain U.S. air and ground units wherever necessary. No declaration of war was requested of Congress and no authorization for use of force, by statute, was requested or enacted. An armistice signed at Panmunjom, Korea, on July 27, 1953, between U.N. and Communist representatives (4 UST 234; TIAS 2782). No peace treaty was ever signed.

VIETNAM ERA

The period beginning on February 28, 1961, and ending on May 7, 1975, inclusive, in the case of a veteran who served in the Republic of Vietnam during that period. The period beginning on August 5, 1964, and ending on May 7, 1975, inclusive, in all other cases. *Code of Federal Regulations*, 3.2 (f).

Tonkin Gulf Resolution

No declaration of war was requested of Congress. Instead, there was a Joint Resolution of Congress to promote the maintenance of international peace and security in Southeast Asia stated in part that the Congress "approves and supports the determination of the President, as Commander in Chief, to take all necessary measures to repel any armed attack against the forces of the United States and to prevent any further aggression." H.J. Res. 1145, P.L. 88-408, August 10, 1964 (78 Stat. 384). The Tonkin Gulf Resolution was formally repealed on January 12, 1971, by P.L. 91-672, (84 Stat. 2055). The Agreement Ending the War and Restoring Peace in Vietnam signed in Paris, January 27, 1973 (TIAS 7674). Joint communiqué implementing the agreement and protocols of January 27, 1973, signed at Paris and entered into force, June 13, 1973.

CONFLICTS IN LEBANON 1982-1983 AND GRENADA 1983

U.S. Marines deployed on August 21, 1982 and September 29, 1982, were part of a temporary multinational force in Lebanon. S. 639, P.L. 98-43 (Lebanon Emergency Assistance Act of 1983). On October 25, 1983, U.S. troops were deployed to Grenada "to restore law and order" and to protect American lives at the request of the members of the Organization of Eastern Caribbean States.

PERSIAN GULF WAR

August 2, 1990, through April 6, 1991, when Iraq officially accepted cease-fire terms. Congress passed H.J.Res. 77, Authorizing the Use of Military Force Against Iraq, the same day it was introduced (January 12, 1991), and it was signed by the President on January 14, 1991 (P.L. 102- 1). Operation Desert Storm and the air war phase began at 3 a.m. January 17, 1991 (January 16, 7 p.m. Eastern Standard Time). Allied ground assault began at 4 a.m. February 24 (February 23, 8 p.m. EST). Cease-fire declared at 8:01 a.m. February 28, 1991 (12:01 a.m. EST).[8] Cease-fire terms negotiated at Safwan, Iraq, March 1, 1991.[9] Iraq officially accepted cease-fire terms, April 6, 1991.[10] Cease-fire took effect April 11, 1991. Currently, the *Code of Federal Regulations*, 3.2 (i) does not list an official end date.[11]

RECENT CONFLICTS: AFGHANISTAN AND IRAQ

Shortly after the terrorist attacks in the United States on September 11, 2001, President George W. Bush called on Afghanistan's leaders to hand over Osama bin Laden and other al Qaeda leaders and close their terrorist training camps. He also demanded the return of all detained foreign nationals and the opening of terrorist training sites to inspection.[12] These demands were rejected. The Administration sought international support from the United Nations (U.N.) for military action against Afghanistan. U.N. Security Council Resolution 1368 of September 12, 2001, stated that the Council "Expresses its readiness to take all necessary steps to respond to the terrorist attacks of September 11, 2001 ... "[13] This resolution was interpreted by many as U.N. authorization for military action in response to the 9/11 attacks. As a result, Congress passed S.J.Res. 23, "Authorization for Use of Military Force," on September 14, 2001. This bill was signed by President George W. Bush on September 18, 2001, as P.L. 107-40, and it authorized the President to use "all necessary and appropriate force against those nations, organizations, or persons he determines planned, authorized, committed, or aided the terrorist attacks that occurred on September 11, 2001, or harbored such organizations or persons.... "[14] Operations in the region began with U.S. military forces deployed to the region on October 7, 2001.

Afghanistan—Operation Enduring Freedom

Operations began with U.S. military forces deployed to Afghanistan to combat terrorism on October 7, 2001, and designated Operation Enduring Freedom (OEF).

On March 27, 2009, President Barack Obama announced a new strategy in Afghanistan and Pakistan and ordered the deployment of 17,000 troops that had been previously requested by General David McKiernan.[15] In President Obama's "Address to the Nation on the Way Forward in Afghanistan and Pakistan" at West Point on December 1, 2009, he stated that "it is in our vital national interest to send an additional 30,000 U.S. troops to Afghanistan. After 18 months, our troops will begin to come home. These are the resources that we need to seize the initiative, while building the Afghan capacity that can allow for a responsible transition of our forces out of Afghanistan."[16]

On June 22, 2011, President Obama again addressed the American people about the way forward in Afghanistan: "We will begin the drawdown of U.S. troops from a position of strength. We have exceeded our expectations on our core goal of defeating al-Qaeda killing 20 of its top 30 leaders, including Osama bin Laden. We have broken the Taliban's momentum, and trained over 100,000 Afghan National Security Forces."[17] As a result, U.S. forces began the withdrawal of 10,000 troops from Afghanistan.

On December 28, 2014, after 13 years of combat operations, President Obama and Secretary of Defense Chuck Hagel announced the end of OEF, a conflict that claimed the lives of more than 2,200 American troops, and the beginning of a follow-on mission on January 1, 2015.[18] A transition ceremony was held at the International Security and Assistance Force headquarters in Kabul, Afghanistan, attended by U.S. commanders and allied troops from the North Atlantic Treaty Organization (NATO).

Afghanistan—Operation Freedom's Sentinel

Effective January 1, 2015, Secretary of Defense Hagel announced that the new U.S. mission in Afghanistan will focus on training, advising, and assisting Afghan security forces and designated as Operation Freedom's Sentinel.[19] About 13,500 U.S. troops are expected in Afghanistan through 2015 and will be assisted by troops from NATO allies.

Iraq—Operation Iraqi Freedom

In mid-2002, the Bush Administration began deploying U.S. troops to Kuwait.[20] During the 107th session (2001-2002), Congress debated whether to send U.S. troops to Iraq, and on October 16, 2002, H.J.Res. 114 was signed into law as P.L. 107-243, Authorization for the use of Military Force Against Iraq Resolution of 2002. This law authorized the President to use military force to "defend the national security of the United States against the continuing threat posed by Iraq" and "to enforce all relevant U.N. Security Council resolutions against Iraq."[21]

On November 8, 2002, the U.N. Security Council adopted Resolution 1441. This resolution found Iraq in breach of past U.N. resolutions prohibiting stockpiling and importing weapons of mass destruction (WMDs).[22] The Hussein government in Iraq continued to be uncooperative with U.N. investigators, which heightened the situation through spring 2003.

In an address to the nation on March 17, 2003, President George W. Bush gave Iraqi President Saddam Hussein and his sons a 48-hour ultimatum to leave Iraq.[23] On March 19, 2003, President Bush announced to the nation that the early stages of military operations against Iraq had begun and designated Operation Iraqi Freedom (OIF).[24]

On May 1, 2003, in an address to the nation, President Bush declared that "major military combat actions in Iraq have ended,"[25] yet U.S. troops remained in Iraq for almost seven years.

A ceremony at Camp Victory in Baghdad on January 1, 2010, marked the end of the Multinational Forces - Iraq (MNF-I) and the beginning of United States Forces - Iraq (USF-I), which merged five major command groups into one single headquarters command.[26] As General David Petraeus, then head of U.S. Central Command (CENTCOM), noted "this ceremony marks another significant transition here in Iraq. It represents another important milestone in the continued drawdown of American Forces."[27] Troops from 30 countries served in MNF-I since 2003.

On August 31, 2010, President Obama announced that the American combat mission in Iraq had ended. A transitional force of U.S. troops remained in Iraq with a different mission: advising and assisting Iraq's security forces, supporting Iraqi troops in targeted counterterrorism missions, and protecting U.S. civilians.[28]

Iraq—Operation New Dawn

Effective September 1, 2010, the military operations in Iraq acquired a new official designation: Operation New Dawn (OND). A short ceremony marked the transfer in which Army General Ray Odierno passed command of USF-I to Army General Lloyd J. Austin. On December 15, 2011, U.S. Armed Forces in Baghdad marked the official end of the war in Iraq. The Chairman of the Joint Chiefs of Staff and other top U.S. military leaders observed the official end of U.S. Forces Iraq's mission after nearly nine years of conflict that claimed the lives of nearly 4,500 U.S. troops.[29] On the military side of Baghdad International Airport, Army General Martin E. Dempsey, Defense Secretary Leon E. Panetta, Army General Lloyd J. Austin III, commanding general of U.S. Forces Iraq, and U.S. Ambassador to Iraq James F. Jeffrey addressed U.S. and Iraqi officials and more than 150 troops and media from around the world.[30]

End Notes

[1] For background on the War Powers Act and use of military force abroad, see the following: CRS Report RL31133, Declarations of War and Authorizations for the Use of Military Force: Historical Background and Legal Implications, by Jennifer K. Elsea and Matthew C. Weed, and CRS Report R42738, Instances of Use of United States Armed Forces Abroad, 1798-2015, by Barbara Salazar Torreon.

[2] The American Legion also follows these dates closely in determining who is eligible for membership; the Veterans of Foreign Wars has its own much more elaborate list of dates.

[3] Code of Federal Regulation (CFR) Title 38, Part 3, §3.2 Periods of war, at http://www.ecfr.gov/cgi-bin/text-idx?rgn= div5&node=38:1.0.1.1.4.

[4] Armistice—"In International law, a suspension or temporary cessation of hostilities by agreement between belligerent powers." Department of Defense Dictionary of Military and Associated Terms, Joint Publication 1-02, Department of Defense, November 8, 2010, as amended through November 15, 2014, at http://www.dtic.mil/doctrine/dod_dictionary/index.html?zoom_query=armistice&zoom_sort=0&zoom_per_page=10&zoom_and=1. See also the more detailed definition in the Parry and Grant Encyclopaedic Dictionary of International Law (New York: Oceana Publications, Inc., 1986), p. 30.

[5] Title 38 of the CFR, titled "Pensions, Bonuses and Veterans' Relief," is not to be confused with Title 38 of the United States Code, titled "Veterans Benefits." Laws enacted in each Congress are first collected as session laws, published in the Statutes at Large for each session. These laws are then codified by subject and published in the United States Code. The general guidance given by these laws results in the issuance of more detailed regulations to implement these laws. Such regulations are first published in the Federal Register and are then codified by subject in the CFR.

[6] May 7, 1945, is listed as V-E day in commentary about signing the first German surrender document in Historic Documents of World War II by Walter Consuelo Langsam (Westport, CT: Greenwood Press, 1958), p. 144. However, May 8, 1945, is cited as V-E day in The Encyclopedia of American Facts and Dates, p. 528; as the "Official V-E Day" in Louis L. Snyder, Louis L. Snyder's Historical Guide to World War Two (Westport, CT: Greenwood, 1982), p. 736; and the World Almanac of World War II, ed. Brigadier Peter Young (New York:

Pharos Books, 1981), p. 347, states in its chronology for May 8, "The British and Americans celebrate VE Day (Victory in Europe Day). Truman, Churchill and King George VI all make special broadcasts." Although President Truman did not officially proclaim May 7 as V-E (Victory in Europe) Day, he did proclaim Sunday, May 13, 1945, a day of prayer. To make for more confusion, his May 8, 1945, Proclamation 2651, proclaiming May 13 as a day of prayer, is titled, "Victory in Europe; Day of Prayer" (3 CFR, 1943-1948 Comp.), p. 55. In addition, his May 8 news conference in which he proclaims May 13 a day of prayer is titled, "The President's News Conference on V-E Day"—Public Papers of the Presidents of the United States. Harry S. Truman, 1945 (Washington: GPO, 1961), p. 43.

[7] In his news conference of August 14, 1945, announcing news of the Japanese government's complete acceptance of terms of surrender, President Truman states, "Proclamation of V-J Day must wait upon the formal signing of the surrender terms by Japan."—Public Papers, p. 216. The proclamation of September 2 as V-J Day was given in his September 1, 1945, "Speech to the American People after the Signing of the Terms of Unconditional Surrender by Japan."—Public Papers, p. 254. However, no formal, numbered proclamation was apparently issued. Both August 14, the day of President Truman's announcement of the Japanese surrender, and September 2, the official day proclaimed by President Truman in his speech, are cited as V-J Day in Chase's Calendar of Events 2002 (New York: McGraw-Hill, 2002), pp. 421 and 555. August 15 is cited as V-J Day by The Encyclopedia of American Facts and Dates, 9th ed., by Gordon Carruth (New York: Harper Collins, 1993), p. 530. August 15, on which the Japanese Emperor made his historic broadcast to the Japanese people telling of Japan's surrender, is cited as V-J Day in The World Almanac of World War II, p. 353.

[8] Cease fire—"A command given to any unit or individual firing any weapon to stop engaging the target." Department of Defense Dictionary, p. 65.

[9] This agreement is actually a transcript of the discussion held at Safwan Airfield, Iraq, between Coalition participants, U.S. Gen. M. Norman Schwarzkopf and Lt. Gen. Khalid of the Joint Arab Forces, and Iraqi participants, Lt. Gen. Sultan Kasim Ahmad, Chief of Staff of the Ministry of Defense, and Lt. Gen. Sala Abud Mahmud, III Corps Commander.

[10] Acceptance is in the form of a letter to the U.N. Security Council accepting the terms of U.N. Resolution 687 (U.N. document S22485, April 11, 1991).

[11] Code of Federal Regulation (CFR) Title 38, Part 3, §3.2 Periods of war at http://www.ecfr.gov/cgi-bin/text-idx?rgn= div5&node=38:1.0.1.1.4). Note: Section (i) for the Persian Gulf War lists "August 2, 1990, through date to be prescribed by Presidential proclamation or law." No specific end date is listed as of the date of this report.

[12] President George W. Bush, Address Before A Joint Session of Congress on the United States Response to the Terrorist Attacks of September 11, September 24, 2001.

[13] United Nations, Security Council Resolution 1368 (2001), adopted by the Security Council at its 4370th meeting, on September 12, 2001, at http://daccess-dds-ny.un.org/doc/UNDOC/GEN/N01/533/82/PDF/N0153382.pdf?OpenElement.

[14] P.L. 107-40, "To authorize the use of United States Armed Forces against those responsible for the recent attacks launched against the United State," at http://www.gpo.gov/fdsys/pkg/PLAW-107publ40/pdf/PLAW-107publ40.pdf.

[15] The White House, Office of the Press Secretary, "Remarks by the President on a New Strategy for Afghanistan and Pakistan," press release, March 27, 2009, at http://www.whitehouse.gov/the_press_office/Remarks-by-the-Presidenton-a-New-Strategy-for-Afghanistan-and-Pakistan.

[16] The White House, Office of the Press Secretary, "Remarks by the President in Address to the Nation on the Way Forward in Afghanistan and Pakistan," press release, December 1, 2009, at http://www.whitehouse.gov/the-pressoffice/remarks-president-address-nation-way-forward-afghanistan-and-pakistan.

[17] The White House, Office of the Press Secretary, "Remarks by the President on the Way Forward in Afghanistan," press release, June 22, 2011, at http://www.whitehouse.gov/the-press-office/2011/06/22/remarks-president-wayforward-afghanistan.

[18] U.S. Department of Defense (DOD), News Release, "Obama, Hagel Mark End of Operation Enduring Freedom," news release, December 28, 2014, at http://www.defense.gov/news/newsarticle.aspx?id=123887.

[19] DOD, "Statement by Secretary of Defense Chuck Hagel on Operation Enduring Freedom and Operation Freedom's Sentinel," news release, December 28, 2014, at http://www.defense.gov/ releases/release.aspx?releaseid=17091.

[20] CRS Report RL31339, Iraq: Post-Saddam Governance and Security, by Kenneth Katzman.

[21] P.L. 107-243, "Authorization for the use of Military Force Against Iraq Resolution of 2002," at https://www.congress.gov/107/plaws/publ243/PLAW-107publ243.pdf.

[22] United Nations, Security Council Resolution 1441 adopted on November 8, 2002, at its 4644th meeting at http://www.un.org/Depts/unmovic/documents/1441.pdf.

[23] U.S. President (G.W. Bush), "Address to the Nation on Iraq," Weekly Compilation of Presidential Documents, March 24, 2003, vol. 39, no. 12, pp. 338-341.

[24] Ibid, pp. 342-343.

[25] Ibid, May 5, 2003, vol. 39, no. 18, pp. 516-518.

[26] Staff Sgt. Luke Koladish and Sgt. Kat Briere, "New Command Marks Milestone in Iraq," U.S. Army website, January 2, 2010, at http://www.army.mil/article/32437/New_command_marks_milestone_in_Iraq/.

[27] Ibid.

[28] The White House, Office of the Press Secretary, "Remarks by the President in Address to the Nation on the End of Combat Operations in Iraq," press release, August 31, 2010, at http://www.whitehouse.gov/the-press-office/2010/08/ 31/remarks-president-address-nation-end-combat-operations-iraq.

[29] Cheryl Pellerin, "Dempsey: Iraq Campaign Was worth the Cost," DOD News, December 15, 2011, at http://www.defense.gov/news/newsarticle.aspx?id=66488.

[30] Ibid.

In: Enactment of War and the Use of Military Force
Editor: Craig Perez
ISBN: 978-1-63482-987-8

Chapter 3

INSTANCES OF USE OF UNITED STATES ARMED FORCES ABROAD, 1798-2015*

Barbara Salazar Torreon

SUMMARY

This report lists hundreds of instances in which the United States has used its Armed Forces abroad in situations of military conflict or potential conflict or for other than normal peacetime purposes. It was compiled in part from various older lists and is intended primarily to provide a rough survey of past U.S. military ventures abroad, without reference to the magnitude of the given instance noted. The listing often contains references, especially from 1980 forward, to continuing military deployments, especially U.S. military participation in multinational operations associated with NATO or the United Nations. Most of these post-1980 instances are summaries based on presidential reports to Congress related to the War Powers Resolution. A comprehensive commentary regarding any of the instances listed is not undertaken here.

The instances differ greatly in number of forces, purpose, extent of hostilities, and legal authorization. Eleven times in its history the United States has formally declared war against foreign nations. These 11 U.S. war declarations encompassed 5 separate wars: the war with Great Britain declared in 1812; the war with Mexico declared in 1846; the war with Spain declared in 1898; the First World War, during which the United States declared war with Germany and with Austria-Hungary during 1917; and World War II, during which the United States declared war against Japan, Germany, and Italy in 1941, and against Bulgaria, Hungary, and Rumania in 1942.

Some of the instances were extended military engagements that might be considered undeclared wars. These include the Undeclared Naval War with France from 1798 to 1800; the First Barbary War from 1801 to 1805; the Second Barbary War of 1815; the Korean War of 1950-1953; the Vietnam War from 1964 to 1973; the Persian Gulf War of 1991; global actions against foreign terrorists after the September 11, 2001, attacks on the United States; and the war with Iraq in 2003. With the exception of the Korean War, all of these conflicts received congressional authorization in some form short of a formal declaration of war. Other, more recent instances often involve deployment of U.S.

* This is an edited, reformatted and augmented version of a Congressional Research Service publication R42738, prepared for Members and Committees of Congress, dated January 15, 2015.

military forces as part of a multinational operation associated with NATO or the United Nations.

The majority of the instances listed prior to World War II were brief Marine or Navy actions to protect U.S. citizens or promote U.S. interests. A number were actions against pirates or bandits. Covert actions, disaster relief, and routine alliance stationing and training exercises are not included here, nor are the Civil and Revolutionary Wars and the continual use of U.S. military units in the exploration, settlement, and pacification of the western part of the United States.

INTRODUCTION

The following list reviews hundreds of instances in which the United States has used military forces abroad in situations of military conflict or potential conflict to protect U.S. citizens or promote U.S. interests. The list does not include covert actions or numerous instances in which U.S. forces have been stationed abroad since World War II in occupation forces or for participation in mutual security organizations, base agreements, or routine military assistance or training operations. Because of differing judgments over the actions to be included, other lists may include more or fewer instances.[1]

The instances vary greatly in size of operation, legal authorization, and significance. The number of troops involved ranges from a few sailors or Marines landed to protect American lives and property to hundreds of thousands in Korea and Vietnam and millions in World War II. Some actions were of short duration, and some lasted a number of years. In some instances a military officer acted without authorization; some actions were conducted solely under the President's powers as Chief Executive or Commander in Chief; other instances were authorized by Congress in some fashion. In 11 separate cases (listed in *bold-face type*) the United States formally declared war against foreign nations. For most of the instances listed, however, the status of the action under domestic or international law has not been addressed. Most instances listed since 1980 are summaries of U.S. military deployments reported to Congress by the President as a result of the War Powers Resolution. Several of these presidential reports are summaries of activities related to an ongoing operation previously reported. Note that inclusion in this list does not connote either legality or level of significance of the instance described. This report covers uses of U.S. military force abroad from 1798 to January 2015. It will be revised as circumstances warrant.

LISTING OF NOTABLE DEPLOYMENTS OF U.S. MILITARY FORCES OVERSEAS, 1798-2015

1798-1800 *Undeclared Naval War with France.* This contest included land actions, such as that in the Dominican Republic, city of Puerto Plata, where marines captured a French privateer under the guns of the forts. Congress authorized military action through a series of statutes.

1801-1805 *Tripoli.* The First Barbary War included the USS *George Washington* and *Philadelphia* affairs and the Eaton expedition, during which a few marines landed with United States Agent William Eaton to raise a force against

Tripoli in an effort to free the crew of the *Philadelphia.* Tripoli declared war but not the United States, although Congress authorized U.S. military action by statute.

1806 *Mexico (Spanish territory).* Captain Z. M. Pike, with a platoon of troops, invaded Spanish territory at the headwaters of the Rio Grande on orders from General James Wilkinson. He was made prisoner without resistance at a fort he constructed in present-day Colorado, taken to Mexico, and later released after seizure of his papers.

1806-1810 *Gulf of Mexico.* American gunboats operated from New Orleans against Spanish and French privateers off the Mississippi Delta, chiefly under Captain John Shaw and Master Commandant David Porter.

1810 *West Florida (Spanish territory).* Governor Claiborne of Louisiana, on orders of the President, occupied with troops territory in dispute east of the Mississippi River as far as the Pearl River, later the eastern boundary of Louisiana. He was authorized to seize as far east as the Perdido River.

1812 *Amelia Island and other parts of east Florida, then under Spain.* Temporary possession was authorized by President Madison and by Congress, to prevent occupation by any other power; but possession was obtained by General George Matthews in so irregular a manner that his measures were disavowed by the President.

1812-1815 War of 1812. On June 18, 1812, the United States declared war between the United States and the United Kingdom of Great Britain and Ireland. Among the issues leading to the war were British interception of neutral ships and blockades of the United States during British hostilities with France.

1813 *West Florida (Spanish territory).* On authority given by Congress, General Wilkinson seized Mobile Bay in April with 600 soldiers. A small Spanish garrison gave way. The United States advanced into disputed territory to the Perdido River, as projected in 1810. No fighting.

1813-1814 *Marquesas Islands.* U.S. forces built a fort on the island of Nukahiva to protect three prize ships which had been captured from the British.

1814 *Spanish Florida.* General Andrew Jackson took Pensacola and drove out the British, with whom the United States was at war.

1814-1825 *Caribbean.* Engagements between pirates and American ships or squadrons took place repeatedly, especially ashore and offshore about Cuba, Puerto Rico, Santo Domingo, and Yucatan. Three thousand pirate attacks on merchantmen were reported between 1815 and 1823. In 1822, Commodore James Biddle employed a squadron of two frigates, four sloops of war, two brigs, four schooners, and two gunboats in the West Indies.

1815 *Algiers.* The second Barbary War was declared against the United States by the Dey of Algiers of the Barbary states, an act not reciprocated by the United States. Congress did authorize a military expedition by statutes. A large fleet under Decatur attacked Algiers and obtained indemnities. *Tripoli.* After securing an agreement from Algiers, Decatur demonstrated with his squadron at Tunis and Tripoli, where he secured indemnities for offenses during the War of 1812.

1816	*Spanish Florida.* United States forces destroyed Nicholls Fort, called also Negro Fort, which harbored raiders making forays into United States territory.
1816-1818	*Spanish Florida—First Seminole War.* The Seminole Indians, whose area was a haven for escaped slaves and border ruffians, were attacked by troops under Generals Jackson and Gaines and pursued into northern Florida. Spanish posts were attacked and occupied, British citizens executed. In 1819 the Floridas were ceded to the United States.
1817	*Amelia Island (Spanish territory off Florida).* Under orders of President Monroe, United States forces landed and expelled a group of smugglers, adventurers, and freebooters.
1818	*Oregon.* The USS *Ontario*, dispatched from Washington, landed at the Columbia River and in August took possession of Oregon territory. Britain had conceded sovereignty but Russia and Spain asserted claims to the area.
1820-1823	*Africa.* Naval units raided the slave traffic pursuant to the 1819 act of Congress.
1822	*Cuba.* United States naval forces suppressing piracy landed on the northwest coast of Cuba and burned a pirate station.
1823	*Cuba.* Brief landings in pursuit of pirates occurred April 8 near Escondido; April 16 near Cayo Blanco; July 11 at Siquapa Bay; July 21 at Cape Cruz; and October 23 at Camrioca.
1824	*Cuba.* In October the USS *Porpoise* landed bluejackets near Matanzas in pursuit of pirates. This was during the cruise authorized in 1822. *Puerto Rico (Spanish territory).* Commodore David Porter with a landing party attacked the town of Fajardo which had sheltered pirates and insulted American naval officers. He landed with 200 men in November and forced an apology. Commodore Porter was later court-martialed for overstepping his powers.
1825	*Cuba.* In March cooperating American and British forces landed at Sagua La Grande to capture pirates.
1827	*Greece.* In October and November landing parties hunted pirates on the islands of Argenteire, Miconi, and Androse.
1831-1832	*Falkland Islands.* Captain Duncan of the USS *Lexington* investigated the capture of three American sealing vessels and sought to protect American interests.
1832	*Sumatra.* February 6 to 9. A naval force landed and stormed a fort to punish natives of the town of Quallah Battoo for plundering the American ship *Friendship*.
1833	*Argentina.* October 31 to November 15. A force was sent ashore at Buenos Aires to protect the interests of the United States and other countries during an insurrection.
1835-1836	*Peru.* December 10, 1835, to January 24, 1836, and August 31 to December 7, 1836. Marines protected American interests in Callao and Lima during an attempted revolution.

1836	*Mexico.* General Gaines occupied Nacogdoches (Texas), disputed territory, from July to December during the Texan war for independence, under orders to cross the "imaginary boundary line" if an Indian outbreak threatened.
1838-1839	*Sumatra.* December 24, 1838, to January 4, 1839. A naval force landed to punish natives of the towns of Quallah Battoo and Muckie (Mukki) for depredations on American shipping.
1840	*Fiji Islands.* July. Naval forces landed to punish natives for attacking American exploring and surveying parties.
1841	*Drummond Island, Kingsmill Group.* A naval party landed to avenge the murder of a seaman by the natives. *Samoa.* February 24. A naval party landed and burned towns after the murder of an American seaman on Upolu Island.
1842	*Mexico.* Commodore T.A.C. Jones, in command of a squadron long cruising off California, occupied Monterey, CA, on October 19, believing war had come. He discovered peace, withdrew, and saluted. A similar incident occurred a week later at San Diego.
1843	*China.* Sailors and marines from the *St. Louis* were landed after a clash between Americans and Chinese at the trading post in Canton. *Africa.* November 29 to December 16. Four United States vessels demonstrated and landed various parties (one of 200 marines and sailors) to discourage piracy and the slave trade along the Ivory Coast, and to punish attacks by the natives on American seamen and shipping.
1844	Mexico. President Tyler deployed U.S. forces to protect Texas against Mexico, pending Senate approval of a treaty of annexation. (Later rejected.) He defended his action against a Senate resolution of inquiry.
1846-1848	Mexican War. On May 13, 1846, the United States recognized the existence of a state of war with Mexico. After the annexation of Texas in 1845, the United States and Mexico failed to resolve a boundary dispute and President Polk said that it was necessary to deploy forces in Mexico to meet a threatened invasion.
1849	Smyrna. In July a naval force gained release of an American seized by Austrian officials.
1851	Turkey. After a massacre of foreigners (including Americans) at Jaffa in January, a demonstration by the Mediterranean Squadron was ordered along the Turkish (Levant) coast. Johanns Island (east of Africa). August. Forces from the U.S. sloop of war Dale exacted redress for the unlawful imprisonment of the captain of an American whaling brig.
1852-1853	Argentina. February 3 to 12, 1852; September 17, 1852, to April 1853. Marines were landed and maintained in Buenos Aires to protect American interests during a revolution.
1853	Nicaragua. March 11 to 13. U.S. forces landed to protect American lives and interests during political disturbances.
1853-1854	Japan. Commodore Perry and his naval expedition made a display of force leading to the "opening of Japan." Ryukyu and Bonin Islands. Commodore Perry on three visits before going to Japan and while waiting for a reply from Japan made a naval demonstration, landing marines twice, and secured

a coaling concession from the ruler of Naha on Okinawa; he also demonstrated in the Bonin Islands with the purpose of securing facilities for commerce.

1854 China. April 4 to June 15 to 17. American and English ships landed forces to protect American interests in and near Shanghai during Chinese civil strife. Nicaragua. July 9 to 15. Naval forces bombarded and burned San Juan del Norte (Greytown) to avenge an insult to the American Minister to Nicaragua.

1855 China. May 19 to 21. U.S. forces protected American interests in Shanghai and, from August 3 to 5, fought pirates near Hong Kong. Fiji Islands. September 12 to November 4. An American naval force landed to seek reparations for depredations on American residents and seamen. Uruguay. November 25 to 29. United States and European naval forces landed to protect American interests during an attempted revolution in Montevideo.

1856 Panama, Republic of New Grenada. September 19 to 22. U.S. forces landed to protect American interests during an insurrection. China. October 22 to December 6. U.S. forces landed to protect American interests at Canton during hostilities between the British and the Chinese, and to avenge an assault upon an unarmed boat displaying the United States flag.

1857 Nicaragua. April to May, November to December. In May Commander C.H. Davis of the United States Navy, with some marines, received the surrender of William Walker, who had been attempting to get control of the country, and protected his men from the retaliation of native allies who had been fighting Walker. In November and December of the same year United States vessels Saratoga, Wabash, and Fulton opposed another attempt of William Walker on Nicaragua. Commodore Hiram Paulding's act of landing marines and compelling the removal of Walker to the United States was tacitly disavowed by Secretary of State Lewis Cass, and Paulding was forced into retirement.

1858 Uruguay. January 2 to 27. Forces from two United States warships landed to protect American property during a revolution in Montevideo. Fiji Islands. October 6 to 16. A marine expedition chastised natives for the murder of two American citizens at Waya.

1858-1859 *Turkey.* The Secretary of State requested a display of naval force along the Levant after a massacre of Americans at Jaffa and mistreatment elsewhere "to remind the authorities (of Turkey) of the power of the United States."

1859 *Paraguay.* Congress authorized a naval squadron to seek redress for an attack on a naval vessel in the Parana River during 1855. Apologies were made after a large display of force. *Mexico.* Two hundred United States soldiers crossed the Rio Grande in pursuit of the Mexican bandit Cortina. *China.* July 31 to August 2. A naval force landed to protect American interests in Shanghai.

1860 *Angola, Portuguese West Africa.* March 1. American residents at Kissembo called upon American and British ships to protect lives and property during problems with natives. *Colombia (Bay of Panama).* September 27 to

October 8. Naval forces landed to protect American interests during a revolution.

1863 *Japan.* July 16. The USS *Wyoming* retaliated against a firing on the American vessel *Pembroke* at Shimonoseki.

1864 *Japan.* July 14 to August 3. Naval forces protected the United States Minister to Japan when he visited Yedo to negotiate concerning some American claims against Japan, and to make his negotiations easier by impressing the Japanese with American power. *Japan.* September 4 to 14. Naval forces of the United States, Great Britain, France, and the Netherlands compelled Japan and the Prince of Nagato in particular to permit the Straits of Shimonoseki to be used by foreign shipping in accordance with treaties already signed.

1865 *Panama.* March 9 and 10. U.S. forces protected the lives and property of American residents during a revolution.

1866 *China.* From June 20 to July 7, U.S. forces punished an assault on the American consul at Newchwang. *Mexico.* To protect American residents, General Sedgwick and 100 men in November obtained surrender of Matamoras. After three days he was ordered by U.S. government to withdraw. His act was repudiated by the President.

1867 *Nicaragua.* Marines occupied Managua and Leon. *Formosa.* June 13. A naval force landed and burned a number of huts to punish the murder of the crew of a wrecked American vessel.

1868 *Japan (Osaka, Hiolo, Nagasaki, Yokohama, and Negata).* February 4 to 8, April 4 to May 12, June 12 and 13. U.S. forces were landed to protect American interests during the civil war in Japan. *Uruguay.* February 7 and 8, 19 to 26. U.S. forces protected foreign residents and the customhouse during an insurrection at Montevideo. *Colombia.* April. U.S. forces protected passengers and treasure in transit at Aspinwall during the absence of local police or troops on the occasion of the death of the president of Colombia.

1870 *Mexico.* June 17 and 18. U.S. forces destroyed the pirate ship *Forward*, which had been run aground about 40 miles up the Rio Tecapan. *Hawaiian Islands.* September 21. U.S. forces placed the American flag at half-mast upon the death of Queen Kalama, when the American consul at Honolulu would not assume responsibility for so doing.

1871 *Korea.* June 10 to 12. A U.S. naval force attacked and captured five forts to punish natives for depredations on Americans, particularly for murdering the crew of the *General Sherman* and burning the schooner, and for later firing on other American small boats taking soundings up the Salee River.

1873 *Colombia (Bay of Panama).* May 7 to 22, September 23 to October 9. U.S. forces protected American interests during hostilities between local groups over control of the government of the State of Panama.

1873-1896 *Mexico.* United States troops crossed the Mexican border repeatedly in pursuit of cattle thieves and other brigands. There were some reciprocal pursuits by Mexican troops into border territory. Mexico protested frequently. Notable cases were at Remolina in May 1873 and at Las Cuevas in 1875. Washington orders often supported these excursions. Agreements between

	Mexico and the United States, the first in 1882, finally legitimized such raids. They continued intermittently, with minor disputes, until 1896.
1874	*Hawaiian Islands.* February 12 to 20. Detachments from American vessels were landed to preserve order and protect American lives and interests during the coronation of a new king.
1876	*Mexico.* May 18. An American force was landed to police the town of Matamoras temporarily while it was without other government.
1882	*Egypt.* July 14 to 18. American forces landed to protect American interests during warfare between British and Egyptians and looting of the city of Alexandria by Arabs.
1885	*Panama (Colon).* January 18 and 19. U.S. forces were used to guard the valuables in transit over the Panama Railroad, and the safes and vaults of the company during revolutionary activity. In March, April, and May in the cities of Colon and Panama, the forces helped reestablish freedom of transit during revolutionary activity.
1888	*Korea.* June. A naval force was sent ashore to protect American residents in Seoul during unsettled political conditions, when an outbreak of the populace was expected. *Haiti.* December 20. A display of force persuaded the Haitian government to give up an American steamer which had been seized on the charge of breach of blockade.
1888-1889	*Samoa.* November 14, 1888, to March 20, 1889. U.S. forces were landed to protect American citizens and the consulate during a native civil war.
1889	*Hawaiian Islands.* July 30 and 31. U.S. forces protected American interests at Honolulu during a revolution.
1890	*Argentina.* A naval party landed to protect U.S. consulate and legation in Buenos Aires.
1891	*Haiti.* U.S. forces sought to protect American lives and property on Navassa Island. *Bering Strait.* July 2 to October 5. Naval forces sought to stop seal poaching. *Chile.* August 28 to 30. U.S. forces protected the American consulate and the women and children who had taken refuge in it during a revolution in Valparaiso.
1893	*Hawai.* January 16 to April 1. Marines were landed ostensibly to protect American lives and property, but many believed actually to promote a provisional government under Sanford B. Dole. This action was disavowed by the United States.
1894	*Brazil.* January. A display of naval force sought to protect American commerce and shipping at Rio de Janeiro during a Brazilian civil war. *Nicaragua.* July 6 to August 7. U.S. forces sought to protect American interests at Bluefields following a revolution.
1894-1895	*China.* Marines were stationed at Tientsin and penetrated to Peking for protection purposes during the Sino-Japanese War. *China.* A naval vessel was beached and used as a fort at Newchwang for protection of American nationals.
1894-1896	*Korea.* July 24, 1894, to April 3, 1896. A guard of marines was sent to protect the American legation and American lives and interests at Seoul during and following the Sino-Japanese War.

1895	*Colombia*. March 8 to 9. U.S. forces protected American interests during an attack on the town of Bocas del Toro by a bandit chieftain.
1896	*Nicaragua*. May 2 to 4. U.S. forces protected American interests in Corinto during political unrest.
1898	*Nicaragua*. February 7 and 8. U.S. forces protected American lives and property at San Juan del Sur.
1898	The Spanish-American War. On April 25, 1898, the United States declared war with Spain. The war followed a Cuban insurrection against Spanish rule and the sinking of the USS Maine in the harbor at Havana.
1898-1899	China. November 5, 1898, to March 15, 1899. U.S. forces provided a guard for the legation at Peking and the consulate at Tientsin during contest between the Dowager Empress and her son.
1899	Nicaragua. American and British naval forces were landed to protect national interests at San Juan del Norte, February 22 to March 5, and at Bluefields a few weeks later in connection with the insurrection of General Juan P. Reyes. Samoa. February-May 15. American and British naval forces were landed to protect national interests and to take part in a bloody contention over the succession to the throne.
1899-1901	Philippine Islands. U.S. forces protected American interests following the war with Spain and conquered the islands by defeating the Filipinos in their war for independence.
1900	China. May 24 to September 28. American troops participated in operations to protect foreign lives during the Boxer rising, particularly at Peking. For many years after this experience a permanent legation guard was maintained in Peking, and was strengthened at times as trouble threatened.
1901	Colombia (State of Panama). November 20 to December 4. U.S. forces protected American property on the Isthmus and kept transit lines open during serious revolutionary disturbances.
1902	Colombia. April 16 to 23. U.S. forces protected American lives and property at Bocas del Toro during a civil war. Colombia (State of Panama). September 17 to November 18. The United States placed armed guards on all trains crossing the Isthmus to keep the railroad line open, and stationed ships on both sides of Panama to prevent the landing of Colombian troops.
1903	Honduras. March 23 to 30 or 31. U.S. forces protected the American consulate and the steamship wharf at Puerto Cortez during a period of revolutionary activity. Dominican Republic. March 30 to April 21. A detachment of marines was landed to protect American interests in the city of Santo Domingo during a revolutionary outbreak. Syria. September 7 to 12. U.S. forces protected the American consulate in Beirut when a local Moslem uprising was feared.
1903-1904	Abyssinia. Twenty-five marines were sent to Abyssinia to protect the U.S. Consul General while he negotiated a treaty.
1903-1914	Panama. U.S. forces sought to protect American interests and lives during and following the revolution for independence from Colombia over construction of the Isthmian Canal. With brief intermissions, United States

	Marines were stationed on the Isthmus from November 4, 1903, to January 21, 1914, to guard American interests.
1904	Dominican Republic. January 2 to February 11. American and British naval forces established an area in which no fighting would be allowed and protected American interests in Puerto Plata and Sosua and Santo Domingo City during revolutionary fighting. Tangier, Morocco. "We want either Perdicaris alive or Raisula dead." A squadron demonstrated to force release of a kidnapped American. Marines were landed to protect the consul general. Panama. November 17 to 24. U.S. forces protected American lives and property at Ancon at the time of a threatened insurrection.
1904-1905	Korea. January 5, 1904, to November 11, 1905. A guard of Marines was sent to protect the American legation in Seoul during the Russo-Japanese War.
1906-1909	Cuba. September 1906 to January 23, 1909. U.S. forces sought to restore order, protect foreigners, and establish a stable government after serious revolutionary activity.
1907	Honduras. March 18 to June 8. To protect American interests during a war between Honduras and Nicaragua, troops were stationed in Trujillo, Ceiba, Puerto Cortez, San Pedro, Laguna, and Choloma.
1910	Nicaragua. May 19 to September 4. U.S. forces protected American interests at Bluefields.
1911	Honduras. January 26. American naval detachments were landed to protect American lives and interests during a civil war in Honduras. China. As the nationalist revolution approached, in October an ensign and 10 men tried to enter Wuchang to rescue missionaries but retired on being warned away, and a small landing force guarded American private property and consulate at Hankow. Marines were deployed in November to guard the cable stations at Shanghai; landing forces were sent for protection in Nanking, Chinkiang, Taku, and elsewhere.
1912	Honduras. A small force landed to prevent seizure by the government of an American-owned railroad at Puerto Cortez. The forces were withdrawn after the United States disapproved the action. Panama. Troops, on request of both political parties, supervised elections outside the Canal Zone. Cuba. June 5 to August 5. U.S. forces protected American interests on the Province of Oriente, and in Havana. China. August 24 to 26, on Kentucky Island, and August 26 to 30 at Camp Nicholson. U.S. forces protected Americans and American interests during revolutionary activity. Turkey. November 18 to December 3. U.S. forces guarded the American legation at Constantinople during a Balkan War.
1912-1925	Nicaragua. August to November 1912. U.S. forces protected American interests during an attempted revolution. A small force, serving as a legation guard and seeking to promote peace and stability, remained until August 5, 1925.
1912-1941	China. The disorders which began with the overthrow of the dynasty during Kuomintang rebellion in 1912, which were redirected by the invasion of China by Japan, led to demonstrations and landing parties for the protection of U.S. interests in China continuously and at many points from 1912 on to

1941. The guard at Peking and along the route to the sea was maintained until 1941. In 1927, the United States had 5,670 troops ashore in China and 44 naval vessels in its waters. In 1933 the United States had 3,027 armed men ashore. The protective action was generally based on treaties with China concluded from 1858 to 1901.

1913 Mexico. September 5 to 7. A few marines landed at Ciaris Estero to aid in evacuating American citizens and others from the Yaqui Valley, made dangerous for foreigners by civil strife.

1914 Haiti. January 29 to February 9, February 20 to 21, October 19. Intermittently, U.S. naval forces protected American nationals in a time of rioting and revolution. Dominican Republic. June and July. During a revolutionary movement, United States naval forces by gunfire stopped the bombardment of Puerto Plata, and by threat of force maintained Santo Domingo City as a neutral zone.

1914-1917 Mexico. Undeclared Mexican-American hostilities followed the Dolphin affair and Villa's raids and included capture of Vera Cruz and later Pershing's expedition into northern Mexico.

1915-1934 Haiti. July 28, 1915, to August 15, 1934. U.S. forces maintained order during a period of chronic political instability.

1916 China. American forces landed to quell a riot taking place on American property in Nanking.

1916-1924 Dominican Republic. May 1916 to September 1924. American naval forces maintained order during a period of chronic and threatened insurrection.

1917 China. American troops were landed at Chungking to protect American lives during a political crisis.

1917-1918 World War I. On April 6, 1917, the United States declared war with Germany and on December 7, 1917, with Austria-Hungary. Entrance of the United States into the war was precipitated by Germany's submarine warfare against neutral shipping.

1917-1922 Cuba. U.S. forces protected American interests during an insurrection and subsequent unsettled conditions. Most of the United States Armed Forces left Cuba by August 1919, but two companies remained at Camaguey until February 1922.

1918-1919 Mexico. After withdrawal of the Pershing expedition, U.S. troops entered Mexico in pursuit of bandits at least three times in 1918 and six times in 1919. In August 1918 American and Mexican troops fought at Nogales.

1918-1920 Panama. U.S. forces were used for police duty according to treaty stipulations, at Chiriqui, during election disturbances and subsequent unrest. Soviet Russia. Marines were landed at and near Vladivostok in June and July to protect the American consulate and other points in the fighting between the Bolshevik troops and the Czech Army, which had traversed Siberia from the western front. A joint proclamation of emergency government and neutrality was issued by the American, Japanese, British, French, and Czech commanders in July. In August 7,000 men were landed in Vladivostok and remained until January 1920, as part of an allied occupation force. In September 1918, 5,000 American troops joined the allied intervention force

	at Archangel and remained until June 1919. These operations were in response to the Bolshevik revolution in Russia and were partly supported by Czarist or Kerensky elements.
1919	Dalmatia. U.S. forces were landed at Trau at the request of Italian authorities to police order between the Italians and Serbs. Turkey. Marines from the USS Arizona were landed to guard the U.S. Consulate during the Greek occupation of Constantinople. Honduras. September 8 to 12. A landing force was sent ashore to maintain order in a neutral zone during an attempted revolution.
1920	China. March 14. A landing force was sent ashore for a few hours to protect lives during a disturbance at Kiukiang. Guatemala. April 9 to 27. U.S. forces protected the American legation and other American interests, such as the cable station, during a period of fighting between Unionists and the government of Guatemala.
1920-1922	Russia (Siberia). February 16, 1920, to November 19, 1922. A Marine guard was sent to protect the United States radio station and property on Russian Island, Bay of Vladivostok.
1921	Panama-Costa Rica. American naval squadrons demonstrated in April on both sides of the Isthmus to prevent war between the two countries over a boundary dispute.
1922	Turkey. September and October. A landing force was sent ashore with consent of both Greek and Turkish authorities to protect American lives and property when the Turkish Nationalists entered Smyrna.
1922-1923	China. Between April 1922 and November 1923 marines were landed five times to protect Americans during periods of unrest.
1924	Honduras. February 28 to March 31, September 10 to 15. U.S. forces protected American lives and interests during election hostilities. China. September. Marines were landed to protect Americans and other foreigners in Shanghai during Chinese factional hostilities.
1925	China. January 15 to August 29. Fighting of Chinese factions accompanied by riots and demonstrations in Shanghai brought the landing of American forces to protect lives and property in the International Settlement. Honduras. April 19 to 21. U.S. forces protected foreigners at La Ceiba during a political upheaval. Panama. October 12 to 23. Strikes and rent riots led to the landing of about 600 American troops to keep order and protect American interests.
1926-1933	Nicaragua. May 7 to June 5, 1926; August 27, 1926, to January 3, 1933. The coup d'état of General Chamorro aroused revolutionary activities leading to the landing of American marines to protect the interests of the United States. United States forces came and went intermittently until January 3, 1933.
1926	China. August and September. The Nationalist attack on Hankow brought the landing of American naval forces to protect American citizens. A small guard was maintained at the consulate general even after September 16, when the rest of the forces were withdrawn. Likewise, when Nationalist forces captured Kiukiang, naval forces were landed for the protection of foreigners November 4 to 6.

1927	China. February. Fighting at Shanghai caused American naval forces and marines to be increased. In March a naval guard was stationed at the American consulate at Nanking after Nationalist forces captured the city. American and British destroyers later used shell fire to protect Americans and other foreigners. Subsequently additional forces of marines and naval vessels were stationed in the vicinity of Shanghai and Tientsin.
1932	China. American forces were landed to protect American interests during the Japanese occupation of Shanghai.
1933	Cuba. During a revolution against President Gerardo Machado naval forces demonstrated but no landing was made.
1934	China. Marines landed at Foochow to protect the American Consulate.
1940	Newfoundland, Bermuda, St. Lucia, Bahamas, Jamaica, Antigua, Trinidad, and British Guiana. Troops were sent to guard air and naval bases obtained by negotiation with Great Britain. These were sometimes called lend-lease bases.
1941	Greenland. Greenland was taken under protection of the United States in April. Netherlands (Dutch Guiana). In November the President ordered American troops to occupy Dutch Guiana, but by agreement with the Netherlands government in exile, Brazil cooperated to protect aluminum ore supply from the bauxite mines in Surinam. Iceland. Iceland was taken under the protection of the United States, with consent of its government, for strategic reasons. Germany. Sometime in the spring the President ordered the Navy to patrol ship lanes to Europe. By July U.S. warships were convoying and by September were attacking German submarines. In November, the Neutrality Act was partly repealed to protect U.S. military aid to Britain.
1941-1945	World War II. On December 8, 1941, the United States declared war with Japan, on December 11 with Germany and Italy, and on June 5, 1942, with Bulgaria, Hungary, and Rumania. The United States declared war against Japan after the surprise bombing of Pearl Harbor, and against Germany and Italy after those nations, under the dictators Hitler and Mussolini, declared war against the United States. The United States declared war against Bulgaria, Hungary, and Rumania in response to the declarations of war by those nations against the United States.
1945	China. In October 50,000 U.S. Marines were sent to North China to assist Chinese Nationalist authorities in disarming and repatriating the Japanese in China and in controlling ports, railroads, and airfields. This was in addition to approximately 60,000 U.S. forces remaining in China at the end of World War II.
1946	Trieste. President Truman ordered the augmentation of U.S. troops along the zonal occupation line and the reinforcement of air forces in northern Italy after Yugoslav forces shot down an unarmed U.S. Army transport plane flying over Venezia Giulia. Earlier U.S. naval units had been dispatched to the scene.
1948	Palestine. A marine consular guard was sent to Jerusalem to protect the U.S. Consul General. Berlin. After the Soviet Union established a land blockade

	of the U.S., British, and French sectors of Berlin on June 24, 1948, the United States and its allies airlifted supplies to Berlin until after the blockade was lifted in May 1949.
1948-1949	China. Marines were dispatched to Nanking to protect the American embassy when the city fell to Communist troops, and to Shanghai to aid in the protection and evacuation of Americans.
1950-1953	Korean War. The United States responded to North Korean invasion of South Korea by going to its assistance, pursuant to United Nations Security Council resolutions. U.S. forces deployed in Korea exceeded 300,000 during the last year of the conflict. Over 36,600 U.S. military were killed in action.
1950-1955	Formosa (Taiwan). In June 1950 at the beginning of the Korean War, President Truman ordered the U.S. Seventh Fleet to prevent Chinese Communist attacks upon Formosa and Chinese Nationalist operations against mainland China.
1954-1955	China. Naval units evacuated U.S. civilians and military personnel from the Tachen Islands.
1956	Egypt. A marine battalion evacuated U.S. nationals and other persons from Alexandria during the Suez crisis.
1958	Lebanon. Marines were landed in Lebanon at the invitation of its government to help protect against threatened insurrection supported from the outside. The President's action was supported by a congressional resolution passed in 1957 that authorized such actions in that area of the world.
1959-1960	The Caribbean. 2d Marine Ground Task Force was deployed to protect U.S. nationals during the Cuban crisis.
1962	Thailand. The 3d Marine Expeditionary Unit landed on May 17, 1962, to support that country during the threat of Communist pressure from outside; by July 30 the 5,000 marines had been withdrawn. Cuba. On October 22, President Kennedy instituted "quarantine" on the shipment of offensive missiles to Cuba from the Soviet Union. He also warned the Soviet Union that the launching of any missile from Cuba against any nation in the Western Hemisphere would bring about U.S. nuclear retaliation on the Soviet Union. A negotiated settlement was achieved in a few days.
1962-1975	Laos. From October 1962 until 1975, the United States played an important role in military support of anti-Communist forces in Laos.
1964	Congo. The United States sent four transport planes to provide airlift for Congolese troops during a rebellion and to transport Belgian paratroopers to rescue foreigners.
1964-1973	Vietnam War. U.S. military advisers had been in South Vietnam for a decade, and their numbers had been increased as the military position of the Saigon government became weaker. After citing what he termed were attacks on U.S. destroyers in the Tonkin Gulf, President Johnson asked in August 1964 for a resolution expressing U.S. determination to support freedom and protect peace in Southeast Asia. Congress responded with the Tonkin Gulf Resolution, expressing support for "all necessary measures" the President might take to repel armed attack against U.S. forces and prevent

further aggression. Following this resolution, and following a Communist attack on a U.S. installation in central Vietnam, the United States escalated its participation in the war to a peak of 543,000 military personnel by April 1969.

1965 Dominican Republic. The United States intervened to protect lives and property during a Dominican revolt and sent more troops as fears grew that the revolutionary forces were coming increasingly under Communist control.

1967 Congo. The United States sent three military transport aircraft with crews to provide the Congo central government with logistical support during a revolt.

1970 Cambodia. U.S. troops were ordered into Cambodia to clean out Communist sanctuaries from which Viet Cong and North Vietnamese attacked U.S. and South Vietnamese forces in Vietnam. The object of this attack, which lasted from April 30 to June 30, was to ensure the continuing safe withdrawal of American forces from South Vietnam and to assist the program of Vietnamization.

1974 Evacuation from Cyprus. United States naval forces evacuated U.S. civilians during hostilities between Turkish and Greek Cypriot forces.

1975 Evacuation from Vietnam. On April 3, 1975, President Ford reported U.S. naval vessels, helicopters, and marines had been sent to assist in evacuation of refugees and U.S. nationals from Vietnam.[2] Evacuation from Cambodia. On April 12, 1975, President Ford reported that he had ordered U.S. military forces to proceed with the planned evacuation of U.S. citizens from Cambodia. South Vietnam. On April 30, 1975, President Ford reported that a force of 70 evacuation helicopters and 865 marines had evacuated about 1,400 U.S. citizens and 5,500 third country nationals and South Vietnamese from landing zones near the U.S. embassy in Saigon and the Tan Son Nhut Airfield. Mayaguez incident. On May 15, 1975, President Ford reported he had ordered military forces to retake the SS Mayaguez, a merchant vessel en route from Hong Kong to Thailand with a U.S. citizen crew which was seized by Cambodian naval patrol boats in international waters and forced to proceed to a nearby island.

1976 Lebanon. On July 22 and 23, 1974, helicopters from five U.S. naval vessels evacuated approximately 250 Americans and Europeans from Lebanon during fighting between Lebanese factions after an overland convoy evacuation had been blocked by hostilities. Korea. Additional forces were sent to Korea after two American soldiers were killed by North Korean soldiers in the demilitarized zone between North and South Korea while cutting down a tree.

1978 Zaire. From May 19 through June 1978, the United States utilized military transport aircraft to provide logistical support to Belgian and French rescue operations in Zaire.

1980 Iran. On April 26, 1980, President Carter reported the use of six U.S. transport planes and eight helicopters in an unsuccessful attempt to rescue American hostages being held in Iran.

1981	El Salvador. After a guerilla offensive against the government of El Salvador, additional U.S. military advisers were sent to El Salvador, bringing the total to approximately 55, to assist in training government forces in counterinsurgency. Libya. On August 19, 1981, U.S. planes based on the carrier USS Nimitz shot down two Libyan jets over the Gulf of Sidra after one of the Libyan jets had fired a heat-seeking missile. The United States periodically held freedom of navigation exercises in the Gulf of Sidra, claimed by Libya as territorial waters but considered international waters by the United States.
1982	Sinai. On March 19, 1982, President Reagan reported the deployment of military personnel and equipment to participate in the Multinational Force and Observers in the Sinai. Participation had been authorized by the Multinational Force and Observers Resolution, P.L. 97-132. Lebanon. On August 21, 1982, President Reagan reported the dispatch of 800 marines to serve in the multinational force to assist in the withdrawal of members of the Palestine Liberation force from Beirut. The Marines left September 20, 1982.
1982-1983	Lebanon. On September 29, 1982, President Reagan reported the deployment of 1,200 marines to serve in a temporary multinational force to facilitate the restoration of Lebanese government sovereignty. On September 29, 1983, Congress passed the Multinational Force in Lebanon Resolution (P.L. 98-119) authorizing the continued participation for 18 months.
1983	Egypt. After a Libyan plane bombed a city in Sudan on March 18, 1983, and Sudan and Egypt appealed for assistance, the United States dispatched an AWACS electronic surveillance plane to Egypt.
1983-1989	Honduras. In July 1983 the United States undertook a series of exercises in Honduras that some believed might lead to conflict with Nicaragua. On March 25, 1986, unarmed U.S. military helicopters and crewmen ferried Honduran troops to the Nicaraguan border to repel Nicaraguan troops.
1983	*Chad.* On August 8, 1983, President Reagan reported the deployment of two AWACS electronic surveillance planes and eight F-15 fighter planes and ground logistical support forces to assist Chad against Libyan and rebel forces. *Grenada.* On October 25, 1983, President Reagan reported a landing on Grenada by Marines and Army airborne troops to protect lives and assist in the restoration of law and order and at the request of five members of the Organization of Eastern Caribbean States.
1984	*Persian Gulf.* On June 5, 1984, Saudi Arabian jet fighter planes, aided by intelligence from a U.S. AWACS electronic surveillance aircraft and fueled by a U.S. KC-10 tanker, shot down two Iranian fighter planes over an area of the Persian Gulf proclaimed as a protected zone for shipping.
1985	*Italy.* On October 10, 1985, U.S. Navy pilots intercepted an Egyptian airliner and forced it to land in Sicily. The airliner was carrying the hijackers of the Italian cruise ship *Achille Lauro,* who had killed an American citizen during the hijacking.
1986	*Libya.* On March 26, 1986, President Reagan reported to Congress that, on March 24 and 25, U.S. forces, while engaged in freedom of navigation

exercises around the Gulf of Sidra, had been attacked by Libyan missiles and the United States had responded with missiles. *Libya.* On April 16, 1986, President Reagan reported that U.S. air and naval forces had conducted bombing strikes on terrorist facilities and military installations in Libya. *Bolivia.* U.S. Army personnel and aircraft assisted Bolivia in anti-drug operations.

1987-1988 *Persian Gulf.* After the Iran-Iraq War resulted in several military incidents in the Persian Gulf, the United States increased U.S. joint military forces operations in the Persian Gulf and adopted a policy of reflagging and escorting Kuwaiti oil tankers through the Gulf. President Reagan reported that U.S. Navy ships had been fired upon or struck mines or taken other military action on September 23, October 10, and October 20, 1987, and April 19, July 4, and July 14, 1988. The United States gradually reduced its forces after a cease-fire between Iran and Iraq on August 20, 1988.

1988 *Panama.* In mid-March and April 1988, during a period of instability in Panama and as pressure grew for Panamanian military leader General Manuel Noriega to resign, the United States sent 1,000 troops to Panama, to "further safeguard the canal, U.S. lives, property and interests in the area." The forces supplemented 10,000 U.S. military personnel already in Panama.

1989 *Libya.* On January 4, 1989, two U.S. Navy F-14 aircraft based on the USS *John F. Kennedy* shot down two Libyan jet fighters over the Mediterranean Sea about 70 miles north of Libya. The U.S. pilots said the Libyan planes had demonstrated hostile intentions. *Panama.* On May 11, 1989, in response to General Noriega's disregard of the results of the Panamanian election, President Bush ordered a brigade-sized force of approximately 1,900 troops to augment the estimated 11,000 U.S. forces already in the area. *Andean Initiative in War on Drugs.* On September 15, 1989, President Bush announced that military and law enforcement assistance would be sent to help the Andean nations of Colombia, Bolivia, and Peru combat illicit drug producers and traffickers. By mid-September there were 50-100 U.S. military advisers in Colombia in connection with transport and training in the use of military equipment, plus seven Special Forces teams of 2-12 persons to train troops in the three countries. *Philippines.* On December 2, 1989, President Bush reported that on December 1 U.S. fighter planes from Clark Air Base in the Philippines had assisted the Aquino government to repel a coup attempt. In addition, 100 marines were sent from the U.S. Navy base at Subic Bay to protect the U.S. embassy in Manila.

1989-1990 *Panama.* On December 21, 1989, President Bush reported that he had ordered U.S. military forces to Panama to protect the lives of American citizens and bring General Noriega to justice. By February 13, 1990, all the invasion forces had been withdrawn.

1990 *Liberia.* On August 6, 1990, President Bush reported that a reinforced rifle company had been sent to provide additional security to the U.S. embassy in Monrovia, and that helicopter teams had evacuated U.S. citizens from Liberia. *Saudi Arabia.* On August 9, 1990, President Bush reported that he had ordered the forward deployment of substantial elements of the U.S.

Armed Forces into the Persian Gulf region to help defend Saudi Arabia after the August 2 invasion of Kuwait by Iraq. On November 16, 1990, he reported the continued buildup of the forces to ensure an adequate offensive military option.

1991 *Iraq.* On January 18, 1991, President Bush reported that he had directed U.S. Armed Forces to commence combat operations on January 16 against Iraqi forces and military targets in Iraq and Kuwait, in conjunction with a coalition of allies and U.N. Security Council resolutions. On January 12 Congress had passed the Authorization for Use of Military Force against Iraq Resolution (P.L. 102-1). Combat operations were suspended on February 28, 1991. *Iraq.* On May 17, 1991, President Bush stated in a status report to Congress that the Iraqi repression of the Kurdish people had necessitated a limited introduction of U.S. forces into northern Iraq for emergency relief purposes.

Zaire. On September 25-27, 1991, after widespread looting and rioting broke out in Kinshasa, U.S. Air Force C-141s transported 100 Belgian troops and equipment into Kinshasa. U.S. planes also carried 300 French troops into the Central African Republic and hauled back American citizens and third country nationals from locations outside Zaire.

1992 *Sierra Leone.* On May 3, 1992, U.S. military planes evacuated Americans from Sierra Leone, where military leaders had overthrown the government. *Kuwait.* On August 3, 1992, the United States began a series of military exercises in Kuwait, following Iraqi refusal to recognize a new border drawn up by the United Nations and refusal to cooperate with U.N. inspection teams. *Iraq.* On September 16, 1992, President Bush stated in a status report to Congress that he had ordered U.S. participation in the enforcement of a prohibition against Iraqi flights in a specified zone in southern Iraq, and aerial reconnaissance to monitor Iraqi compliance with the cease-fire resolution. *Somalia.* On December 10, 1992, President Bush reported that he had deployed U.S. Armed Forces to Somalia in response to a humanitarian crisis and a U.N. Security Council Resolution determining that the situation constituted a threat to international peace. This operation, called Operation Restore Hope, was part of a U.S.-led United Nations Unified Task Force (UNITAF) and came to an end on May 4, 1993. U.S. forces continued to participate in the successor United Nations Operation in Somalia (UNOSOM II), which the U.N. Security Council authorized to assist Somalia in political reconciliation and restoration of peace.

1993 *Iraq.* On January 19, 1993, President Bush said in a status report that on December 27, 1992, U.S. aircraft had shot down an Iraqi aircraft in the prohibited zone; on January 13 aircraft from the United States and coalition partners had attacked missile bases in southern Iraq; and further military actions had occurred on January 17 and 18. Administration officials said the United States was deploying a battalion task force to Kuwait to underline the continuing U.S. commitment to Kuwaiti independence. *Iraq.* On January 21, 1993, shortly after his inauguration, President Clinton said the United States would continue the Bush policy on Iraq, and U.S. aircraft fired at targets in

Iraq after pilots sensed Iraqi radar or anti-aircraft fire directed at them. *Bosnia.* On February 28, 1993, the United States began an airdrop of relief supplies aimed at Muslims surrounded by Serbian forces in Bosnia. *Bosnia.* On April 13, 1993, President Clinton reported U.S. forces were participating in a North Atlantic Treaty Organization (NATO) air action to enforce a U.N. ban on all unauthorized military flights over Bosnia-Herzegovina. *Iraq.* In a status report on Iraq of May 24, President Clinton said that on April 9 and April 18 U.S. planes had bombed or fired missiles at Iraqi anti-aircraft sites that had tracked U.S. aircraft. *Somalia.* On June 10, 1993, President Clinton reported that in response to attacks against U.N. forces in Somalia by a factional leader, the U.S. Quick Reaction Force in the area had participated in military action to quell the violence. On July 1 President Clinton reported further air and ground military operations on June 12 and June 17 aimed at neutralizing military capabilities that had impeded U.N. efforts to deliver humanitarian relief and promote national reconstruction, and additional instances occurred in the following months. *Iraq.* On June 28, 1993, President Clinton reported that on June 26 U.S. naval forces had launched missiles against the Iraqi Intelligence Service's headquarters in Baghdad in response to an unsuccessful attempt to assassinate former President Bush in Kuwait in April 1993. *Iraq.* In a status report of July 22, 1993, President Clinton said on June 19 a U.S. aircraft had fired a missile at an Iraqi anti-aircraft site displaying hostile intent. U.S. planes also bombed an Iraqi missile battery on August 19, 1993. *Macedonia.* On July 9, 1993, President Clinton reported the deployment of 350 U.S. soldiers to the former Yugoslav Republic of Macedonia to participate in the U.N. Protection Force to help maintain stability in the area of former Yugoslavia. *Haiti.* On October 20, 1993, President Clinton reported that U.S. ships had begun to enforce a U.N. embargo against Haiti.

1994 *Bosnia.* On February 17, 1994, President Clinton reported that the United States had expanded its participation in United Nations and NATO efforts to reach a peaceful solution to the conflict in former Yugoslavia and that 60 U.S. aircraft were available for participation in the authorized NATO missions. *Bosnia.* On March 1, 1994, President Clinton reported that on February 28 U.S. planes patrolling the "no-fly zone" in former Yugoslavia under NATO shot down four Serbian Galeb planes. *Bosnia.* On April 12, 1994, President Clinton reported that on April 10 and 11, U.S. warplanes under NATO command had fired against Bosnian Serb forces shelling the "safe" city of Gorazde. *Rwanda.* On April 12, 1994, President Clinton reported that combat-equipped U.S. military forces had been deployed to Burundi to conduct possible non-combatant evacuation operations of U.S. citizens and other third-country nationals from Rwanda, where widespread fighting had broken out. By September 30, 1994, all U.S. troops had departed from Rwanda and surrounding nations. In the Defense Appropriations Act for FY1995 (P.L. 103-335, signed September 30, 1994), Congress barred use of funds for U.S. military participation in or around Rwanda after October 7, 1994, except for any action necessary to protect

U.S. citizens. *Macedonia.* On April 19, 1994, President Clinton reported that the U.S. contingent in the former Yugoslav Republic of Macedonia had been augmented by a reinforced company of 200 personnel. *Haiti.* On April 20, 1994, President Clinton reported that U.S. naval forces had continued enforcement of the U.N. embargo in the waters around Haiti and that 712 vessels had been boarded since October 20, 1993. *Bosnia.* On August 22, 1994, President Clinton reported the use on August 5 of U.S. aircraft under NATO to attack Bosnian Serb heavy weapons in the Sarajevo heavy weapons exclusion zone upon request of the U.N. Protection Forces. *Haiti.* On September 21, 1994, President Clinton reported the deployment of 1,500 troops to Haiti to restore democracy in Haiti. The troop level was subsequently increased to 20,000. *Bosnia.* On November 22, 1994, President Clinton reported the use of U.S. combat aircraft on November 21, 1994, under NATO, to attack bases used by Serbs to attack the town of Bihac in Bosnia. *Macedonia.* On December 22, 1994, President Clinton reported that the U.S. Army contingent in the former Yugoslav Republic of Macedonia continued its peacekeeping mission and that the current contingent would soon be replaced by about 500 soldiers from the 3rd Battalion, 5th Cavalry Regiment, and 1st Armored Division from Kirchgons, Germany.

1995 *Somalia.* On March 1, 1995, President Clinton reported that on February 27, 1995, 1,800 combat-equipped U.S. Armed Forces personnel began deployment into Mogadishu, Somalia, to assist in the withdrawal of U.N. forces assigned there to the United Nations Operation in Somalia (UNOSOM II). This mission was completed on March 3, 1995. *Haiti.* On March 21, 1995, President Clinton reported that U.S. military forces in Haiti as part of a U.N. Multinational Force had been reduced to just under 5,300 personnel. He noted that as of March 31, 1995, approximately 2,500 U.S. personnel would remain in Haiti as part of the U.N. Mission in Haiti (UNMIH). *Bosnia.* On May 24, 1995, President Clinton reported that U.S. combat-equipped fighter aircraft and other aircraft continued to contribute to NATO's enforcement of the no-fly zone in airspace over Bosnia-Herzegovina. U.S. aircraft, he noted, were also available for close air support of U.N. forces in Croatia. Roughly 500 U.S. soldiers continued to be deployed in the former Yugoslav Republic of Macedonia as part of the U.N. Preventive Deployment Force (UNPREDEP). U.S. forces continued to support U.N. refugee and embargo operations in this region. *Bosnia.* On September 1, 1995, President Clinton reported that "U.S. combat and support aircraft" had been used beginning on August 29, 1995, in a series of NATO air strikes against Bosnian Serb Army (BSA) forces in Bosnia-Herzegovina that were threatening the U.N.-declared safe areas of Sarajevo, Tuzla, and Gorazde. He noted that during the first day of operations, "some 300 sorties were flown against 23 targets in the vicinity of Sarajevo, Tuzla, Gorazde and Mostar." *Haiti.* On September 21, 1995, President Clinton reported that currently the United States had 2,400 military personnel in Haiti as participants in UNMIH. In addition, 260 U.S. military personnel were assigned to the U.S. Support Group Haiti. *Bosnia.* On December 6, 1995,

President Clinton reported to Congress that he had "ordered the deployment of approximately 1,500 U.S. military personnel" to Bosnia-Herzegovina and Croatia as part of a NATO "enabling force" to lay the groundwork for the prompt and safe deployment of the NATO-led Implementation Force (IFOR)," which would be used to implement the Bosnian peace agreement after its signing. The President also noted that he had authorized deployment of roughly 3,000 other U.S. military personnel to Hungary, Italy, and Croatia to establish infrastructure for the enabling force and the IFOR. *Bosnia.* On December 21, 1995, President Clinton reported to Congress that he had ordered the deployment of approximately 20,000 U.S. military personnel to participate in IFOR in the Republic of Bosnia-Herzegovina, and approximately 5,000 U.S. military personnel would be deployed in other former Yugoslav states, primarily in Croatia. In addition, about 7,000 U.S. support forces would be deployed to Hungary, Italy, and Croatia and other regional states in support of IFOR's mission.

1996 *Haiti.* On March 21, 1996, President Clinton reported to Congress that beginning in January 1996 there had been a "phased reduction" in the number of United States personnel assigned to UNMIH. As of March 21, 309 U.S. personnel remained a part of UNMIH. These U.S. forces were "equipped for combat." *Liberia.* On April 11, 1996, President Clinton reported to Congress that on April 9, 1996, due to the "deterioration of the security situation and the resulting threat to American citizens" in Liberia he had ordered U.S. military forces to evacuate from that country "private U.S. citizens and certain third-country nationals who had taken refuge in the U.S. Embassy compound." *Liberia.* On May 20, 1996, President Clinton reported to Congress the continued deployment of U.S. military forces in Liberia to evacuate both American citizens and other foreign personnel, and to respond to various isolated "attacks on the American Embassy complex" in Liberia. The President noted that the deployment of U.S. forces would continue until there was no longer any need for enhanced security at the embassy and a requirement to maintain an evacuation capability in the country. *Central African Republic.* On May 23, 1996, President Clinton reported to Congress the deployment of U.S. military personnel to Bangui, Central African Republic, to conduct the evacuation from that country of "private U.S. citizens and certain U.S. Government employees," and to provide "enhanced security for the American Embassy in Bangui." *Bosnia.* On June 21, 1996, President Clinton reported to Congress that United States forces totaling about 17,000 remain deployed in Bosnia "under NATO operational command and control" as part of the NATO Implementation Force (IFOR). In addition, about 5,500 U.S. military personnel were deployed in Hungary, Italy, and Croatia, and other regional states to provide "logistical and other support to IFOR." The President noted that it was the intention that IFOR would complete the withdrawal of all troops in the weeks after December 20, 1996, on a schedule "set by NATO commanders consistent with the safety of troops and the logistical requirements for an orderly withdrawal." He also noted that a U.S. Army contingent (of about 500 U.S. soldiers) remained in the Former Yugoslav Republic of Macedonia as part of the United Nations Preventive Deployment Force (UNPREDEP). *Rwanda and Zaire.* On December 2, 1996, President Clinton reported to Congress that to support the humanitarian efforts of the United Nations regarding refugees in Rwanda and the Great Lakes Region of Eastern Zaire, he had authorized the use of U.S. personnel and aircraft, including AC-130U planes to help in surveying the region in support of humanitarian operations, although fighting still was occurring in the area, and U.S. aircraft had been subject to fire when on flight duty. *Bosnia.* On December 20, 1996, President Clinton reported to Congress that he had authorized U.S. participation in an IFOR follow-on force in Bosnia, known as SFOR (Stabilization Force), under NATO command. The President said the U.S. forces contribution to SFOR was to be "about 8,500" personnel whose primary mission is to deter or prevent a resumption of hostilities or new threats to peace in Bosnia. SFOR's duration in Bosnia was expected to be 18 months, with progressive reductions and eventual withdrawal.

1997 *Albania.* On March 15, 1997, President Clinton reported to Congress that on March 13, 1997, he had utilized U.S. military forces to evacuate certain U.S. government employees and private U.S. citizens from Tirana, Albania, and to enhance security for the U.S. embassy in that city. *Congo and Gabon.* On March 27, 1997, President Clinton reported to Congress that, on March 25, 1997, a standby evacuation force of U.S. military personnel had been deployed to Congo and Gabon to provide enhanced security for American private citizens, government employees, and selected third country nationals in Zaire, and to be available for any necessary evacuation operation. *Sierra Leone.* On May 30, 1997, President Clinton reported to Congress that on May 29 and May 30, 1997, U.S. military personnel were deployed to Freetown, Sierra Leone, to prepare for and undertake the evacuation of certain U.S. government employees and private U.S. citizens. *Bosnia.* On June 20, 1997, President Clinton reported to Congress that U.S. Armed Forces continued to support peacekeeping operations in Bosnia and other states in the region in support of the NATO-led Stabilization Force (SFOR). He reported that currently most U.S. military personnel involved in SFOR were in Bosnia, near Tuzla, and about 2,800 U.S. troops were deployed in Hungary, Croatia, Italy, and other regional states to provide logistics and other support to SFOR. A U.S. Army contingent of about 500 also remained in the Former Yugoslav Republic of Macedonia as part of the UNPREDEP. *Cambodia.* On July 11, 1997, President Clinton reported to Congress that in an effort to ensure the security of American citizens in Cambodia during a period of domestic conflict there, he had deployed a Task Force of about 550 U.S. military personnel to Utapao Air Base in Thailand. These personnel were to be available for possible emergency evacuation operations in Cambodia as deemed necessary. *Bosnia.* On December 19, 1997, President Clinton reported to Congress that he intended "in principle" to have the United States participate in a security presence in Bosnia when the NATO SFOR contingent withdrew in the summer of 1998.

1998 *Guinea-Bissau.* On June 12, 1998, President Clinton reported to Congress that, on June 10, 1998, in response to an army mutiny in Guinea-Bissau endangering the U.S. embassy, U.S. government employees, and U.S. citizens in that country, he had deployed a standby evacuation force of U.S. military personnel to Dakar, Senegal, to remove such individuals, as well as selected third country nationals, from the city of Bissau. The deployment continued until the necessary evacuations were completed. *Bosnia.* On June 19, 1998, President Clinton reported to Congress regarding activities in the last six months of combat-equipped U.S. forces in support of NATO's SFOR in Bosnia and surrounding areas of former Yugoslavia. *Kenya and Tanzania.* On August 10, 1998, President Clinton reported to Congress that he had deployed, on August 7, 1998, Joint Task Force of U.S. military personnel to Nairobi, Kenya, to coordinate the medical and disaster assistance related to the bombings of the U.S. Embassies in Kenya and Tanzania. He also reported that teams of 50-100 security personnel had arrived in Nairobi, Kenya, and Dar es Salaam, Tanzania, to enhance the security of the U.S. Embassies and citizens there. *Albania.* On August 18, 1998, President Clinton reported to Congress that he had, on August 16, 1998, deployed 200 U.S. Marines and 10 Navy SEALS to the U.S. embassy compound in Tirana, Albania, to enhance security against reported threats against U.S. personnel. *Afghanistan and Sudan.* On August 21, 1998, by letter, President Clinton reported to Congress that he had authorized airstrikes on August 20 against camps and installations in Afghanistan and Sudan used by the Osama bin Laden terrorist organization. The President did so based on what he viewed as convincing information that the bin Laden organization was responsible for the bombings, on August 7, 1998, of the U.S. Embassies in Kenya and Tanzania. *Liberia.* On September 29, 1998, President Clinton reported to Congress that on September 27, 1998, he had, due to political instability and civil disorder in Liberia, deployed a stand-by response and evacuation force of 30 U.S. military personnel to augment the security force at the U.S. embassy in Monrovia, and to provide for a rapid evacuation capability, as needed, to remove U.S. citizens and government personnel from the country. *Iraq.* During the period from December 16-23, 1998, the United States, together with the United Kingdom, conducted a bombing campaign, termed Operation Desert Fox, against Iraqi industrial facilities deemed capable of producing weapons of mass destruction, and against other Iraqi military and security targets.

1998-1999 *Iraq.* Beginning in late December 1998, and continuing during 1999, the United States, together with forces of the coalition enforcing the "no-fly" zones over Iraq, conducted military operations against the Iraqi air defense system on numerous occasions in response to actual or potential threats against aircraft enforcing the "no-fly" zones in northern and southern Iraq.

1999 *Bosnia.* On January 19, 1999, President Clinton reported to Congress that he was continuing to authorize the use of combat-equipped U.S. Armed Forces in Bosnia and other states in the region as participants in and supporters of the NATO-led Stabilization Force (SFOR). He noted that the U.S. SFOR military personnel totaled about 6,900, with about 2,300 U.S. military personnel deployed to Hungary, Croatia, Italy, and other regional states. Also, some 350 U.S. military personnel remain deployed in the Former Yugoslav Republic of Macedonia (FYROM) as part of UNPREDEP. *Kenya.* On February 25, 1999, President Clinton reported to Congress that he was continuing to deploy U.S. military personnel in that country to assist in providing security for the U.S. embassy and American citizens in Nairobi, pending completion of renovations of the American embassy facility in Nairobi, subject of a terrorist bombing in August 1998. *Yugoslavia.* On March 26, 1999, President Clinton reported to Congress that, on March 24, 1999, U.S. military forces, at his direction, and in coalition with NATO allies, had commenced air strikes against Yugoslavia in response to the Yugoslav government's campaign of violence and repression against the ethnic Albanian population in Kosovo. *Yugoslavia/Albania.* On April 7, 1999, President Clinton reported to Congress that he had ordered additional U.S. military forces to Albania, including rotary wing aircraft, artillery, and tactical missiles systems to enhance NATO's ability to conduct effective air operations in Yugoslavia. About 2,500 soldiers and aviators are to be deployed as part of this task force. The President also reported the deployment of U.S. military forces to Albania and Macedonia to support humanitarian disaster relief operations for Kosovar refugees. *Yugoslavia/Albania.* On May 25, 1999, President Clinton reported to Congress, "consistent with the war Powers Resolution," that he had directed "deployment of additional aircraft and forces to support NATO's ongoing efforts [against Yugoslavia], including several thousand additional U.S. Armed Forces personnel to Albania in support of the deep strike force located there." He also directed that additional U.S. forces be deployed to the region to assist in "humanitarian operations." *Yugoslavia/Kosovo.* On June 12, 1999, President Clinton reported to Congress, "consistent with the War Powers Resolution," that he had directed the deployment of about "7,000 U.S. military personnel as the U.S. contribution to the approximately 50,000-member, NATO-led security force (KFOR)" currently being assembled in Kosovo. He also noted that about "1,500 U.S. military personnel, under separate U.S. command and control, will deploy to other countries in the region, as our national support element, in support of KFOR." *Bosnia.* On July 19, 1999, President Clinton reported to Congress, "consistent with the War Powers Resolution," that about 6,200 U.S. military personnel were continuing to participate in the NATO-led Stabilization Force (SFOR) in Bosnia, and that another 2,200 personnel were supporting SFOR operations from Hungary, Croatia, and Italy. He also noted that U.S. military personnel remain in the Former Yugoslav Republic of Macedonia to support the international security presence in Kosovo (KFOR). *East Timor.* On October 8, 1999, President Clinton reported to Congress "consistent with the War Powers Resolution" that he had directed the deployment of a limited number of U.S. military forces to East Timor to support the U.N. multinational force (INTERFET) aimed at restoring peace to East Timor.

U.S. support has been limited initially to "communications, logistics, planning assistance and transportation." The President further noted that he had authorized deployment of the amphibious ship USS *Belleau Wood*, together with its helicopters and her complement of personnel from the 31st Marine Expeditionary Unit (Special Operations Capable) (MEU SOC), to the East Timor region, to provide helicopter airlift and search and rescue support to the multinational operation. U.S. participation was anticipated to continue until the transition to a U.N. peacekeeping operation was complete. *Yugoslavia/Kosovo.* On December 15, 1999, President Clinton reported to Congress "consistent with the War Powers Resolution" that U.S. combat-equipped military personnel continued to serve as part of the NATO-led security force in Kosovo (KFOR). He noted that the American contribution to KFOR in Kosovo was "approximately 8,500 U.S. military personnel." U.S. forces were deployed in a sector around Urosevac in the eastern portion of Kosovo." For U.S. KFOR forces, "maintaining public security is a key task." Other U.S. military personnel are deployed to other countries in the region to serve in administrative and logistics support roles for U.S. forces in KFOR. Of these forces, about 1,500 U.S. military personnel are in Macedonia and Greece, and occasionally in Albania.

1999-2000 *Iraq.* At various times during 1999, and continuing throughout 2000, the United States, together with forces of the coalition enforcing the "no-fly" zones over Iraq, conducted military operations against the Iraqi air defense system on numerous occasions in response to actual or potential threats against aircraft enforcing the "no-fly" zones in northern and southern Iraq.

2000 *Bosnia.* On January 25, 2000, President Clinton reported to Congress "consistent with the War Powers Resolution" that the United States continued to provide combat-equipped U.S. Armed Forces to Bosnia-Herzegovina and other states in the region as part of the NATO led Stabilization Force (SFOR). The President noted that the U.S. force contribution was being reduced from "approximately 6,200 to 4,600 personnel," with the U.S. forces assigned to Multinational Division, North, around the city of Tuzla. He added that approximately 1,500 U.S. military personnel were deployed to Hungary, Croatia, and Italy to provide "logistical and other support to SFOR" and U.S. forces continue to support SFOR in "efforts to apprehend persons indicted for war crimes." *East Timor.* On February 25, 2000, President Clinton reported to Congress "consistent with the War Powers Resolution" that he had authorized the participation of a small number of U.S. military personnel in support of the United Nations Transitional Administration in East Timor (UNTAET), which has a mandate to maintain law and order throughout East Timor, and to facilitate establishment of an effective administration there, delivery of humanitarian assistance, and support the building of self-government. The President reported that the U.S. contingent was small: three military observers, and one judge advocate. To facilitate and coordinate U.S. military activities in East Timor, the President also authorized the deployment of a support group (USGET), consisting of 30 U.S. personnel. U.S. personnel would be temporarily deployed to East Timor, on a rotational basis, and through periodic ship visits, during which U.S. forces would conduct "humanitarian and assistance activities throughout East Timor." Rotational activities should continue through the summer of 2000. *Sierra Leone.* On May 12, 2000, President Clinton, "consistent with the War Powers Resolution," reported to Congress that he had ordered a U.S. Navy patrol craft to deploy to Sierra Leone to be ready to support evacuation operations from that country if needed. He also authorized a U.S. C-17 aircraft to deliver "ammunition, and other supplies and equipment" to Sierra Leone in support of United Nations peacekeeping operations there. *Yugoslavia/Kosovo.* On June 16, 2000, President Clinton reported to Congress, "consistent with the War Powers Resolution," that the United States was continuing to provide military personnel to the NATO-led KFOR security force in Kosovo. U.S. forces were numbered at 7,500, but were scheduled to be reduced to 6,000 when ongoing troop rotations were completed. U.S. forces in Kosovo are assigned to a sector centered near Gnjilane in eastern Kosovo. Other U.S. military personnel are deployed to other countries serving in administrative and logistics support roles, with approximately 1,000 U.S. personnel in Macedonia, Albania, and Greece. *Bosnia.* On July 25, 2000, President Clinton reported to Congress, "consistent with the War Powers Resolution," that combat-equipped U.S. military personnel continued to participate in the NATO-led Stabilization Force (SFOR) in Bosnia-Herzegovina, being deployed to Bosnia and other states in the region in support of peacekeeping efforts in former Yugoslavia. U.S. military personnel levels have been reduced from 6,200 to 4,600. Apart from the forces in Bosnia, approximately 1,000 U.S. personnel continue to be deployed in support roles in Hungary, Croatia, and Italy. *East Timor.* On August 25, 2000, President Clinton reported to Congress, "consistent with the War Powers Resolution," that the United States was currently contributing three military observers to the United Nations Transitional Administration in East Timor (UNTAET) that is charged by the U.N. with restoring and maintaining peace and security there. He also noted that the United States was maintaining a military presence in East Timor separate from UNTAET, comprised of about 30 U.S. personnel who facilitate and coordinate U.S. military activities in East Timor and rotational operations of U.S. forces there. U.S. forces currently conduct humanitarian and civic assistance activities for East Timor's citizens. U.S. rotational presence operations in East Timor are presently expected, the President said, to continue through December 2000. *Yemen.* On October 14, 2000, President Clinton reported to Congress, "consistent with the War Powers Resolution," that on October 12, 2000, in the wake of an attack on the USS *Cole* in the port of Aden, Yemen, he had authorized deployment of about 45 military personnel from U.S. Naval Forces Central Command to Aden to provide "medical, security, and disaster response assistance." The President further reported that on October 13, 2000, about 50 U.S. military security personnel arrived in Aden, and that additional "security elements" may be deployed to the area, to enhance the ability of the U.S. to ensure the security of the USS *Cole* and the personnel responding to the incident. In addition, two U.S. Navy surface combatant vessels are operating in or near Yemeni territorial waters to provide communications and other support, as required. *Yugoslavia/Kosovo.* On December 18, 2000, President Clinton reported to Congress, "consistent with the War Powers Resolution," that the United States was continuing to provide approximately 5,600 U.S. military personnel in support of peacekeeping efforts in Kosovo as part of KFOR. An additional 500 U.S. military personnel are deployed as the National Support Element in Macedonia, with an occasional presence in Albania and Greece. U.S. forces are assigned to a sector around Gnjilane in the eastern portion of Kosovo. The President noted that the mission for these U.S. military forces is maintaining a safe and secure environment through conducting "security patrols in urban areas and in the countryside throughout their sector."

2001 *East Timor.* On March 2, 2001, President George W. Bush reported to Congress, "consistent with the War Powers Resolution," that U.S. Armed Forces were continuing to support the United Nations peacekeeping effort in East Timor aimed at providing security and maintaining law and order in East Timor, coordinating delivery of humanitarian assistance, and helping establish the basis for self-government in East Timor. The United States currently has three military observers attached to UNTAET. The United States also has a separate military presence, the U.S. Support Group East Timor (USGET), of approximately 12 U.S. personnel, including a security detachment, which "facilitates and coordinates" U.S. military activities in East Timor. *Yugoslavia/Kosovo.* On May 18, 2001, President George W. Bush reported to Congress, "consistent with the War Powers Resolution," that the United States was continuing to provide approximately 6,000 U.S. military personnel in support of peacekeeping efforts in Kosovo as part of KFOR. An additional 500 U.S. military personnel are deployed as the National Support Element in Macedonia, with an occasional presence in Greece and Albania. U.S. forces in Kosovo are assigned to a sector around Gnjilane in the eastern portion. President Bush noted that the mission for these U.S. military forces is maintaining a safe and secure environment through conducting security patrols in urban areas and in the countryside through their sector. *Bosnia.* On July 25, 2001, President George W. Bush reported to Congress, "consistent with the War Powers Resolution," that about 3,800 combat-equipped U.S. Armed Forces continued to be deployed in Bosnia-Herzegovina and other regional states as part of SFOR. Most were based at Tuzla in Bosnia. About 500 others were based in Hungary, Croatia, and Italy, providing logistical and other support. *Iraq.* At various times throughout 2001, the United States, together with forces of the coalition enforcing the "no-fly" zones over Iraq, conducted military operations against the Iraqi air defense system on numerous occasions in response to actual or potential threats against aircraft enforcing the "no-fly" zones in northern and southern Iraq. *East Timor.* On August 31, 2001, President George W. Bush reported to Congress, "consistent with the War Powers Resolution," that U.S. Armed Forces were continuing to support the United Nations peacekeeping effort in East Timor aimed at providing security and maintaining law and order in East Timor, coordinating delivery of humanitarian assistance, and helping establish the basis for self-government in East Timor. The United States currently has three military observers attached to UNTAET. The United States also has a separate military presence, USGET, of approximately 20 U.S. personnel, including a security detachment, which "facilitates and coordinates" U.S. military activities in East Timor, as well as a rotational presence of U.S. forces through temporary deployments to East Timor. The President stated that U.S. forces would continue a presence through December 2001, while options for a U.S. presence in 2002 are being reviewed, with the President's objective being redeployment of USGET personnel, as circumstances permit. *Terrorism threat.* On September 24, 2001, President George W. Bush reported to Congress, "consistent with the War Powers Resolution" and "Senate Joint Resolution 23," that in response to terrorist attacks on the World Trade Center and the Pentagon he had ordered the "deployment of various combat-equipped and combat support forces to a number of foreign nations in the Central and Pacific Command areas of operations." The President noted in efforts to "prevent and deter terrorism" he might find it necessary to order "additional forces into these and other areas of the world." He stated that he could not now predict "the scope and duration of these deployments," or the "actions necessary to counter the terrorist threat to the United States." *Afghanistan.* On October 9, 2001, President George W. Bush reported to Congress, "consistent with the War Powers Resolution" and "Senate Joint Resolution 23," that on October 7, 2001, U.S. Armed Forces "began combat action in Afghanistan against Al Qaida terrorists and their Taliban supporters." The President stated that he had directed this military action in response to the September 11, 2001, attacks on U.S. "territory, our citizens, and our way of life, and to the continuing threat of terrorist acts against the United States and our friends and allies." This military action was "part of our campaign against terrorism" and was "designed to disrupt the use of Afghanistan as a terrorist base of operations." *Yugoslavia/Kosovo.* On November 19, 2001, President George W. Bush reported to Congress, "consistent with the War Powers Resolution," that the United States was continuing to provide approximately 5,500 U.S. military personnel in support of peacekeeping efforts in Kosovo as part of KFOR. An additional 500 U.S. military personnel are deployed as the National Support Element in Macedonia, with an occasional presence in Greece and Albania. U.S. forces in Kosovo are assigned to a sector around Gnjilane in the eastern portion. President Bush noted that the mission for these U.S. military forces is maintaining a safe and secure environment through conducting security patrols in urban areas and in the countryside through their sector.

2002 *Bosnia.* On January 21, 2002, President George W. Bush reported to Congress, "consistent with the War Powers Resolution," that about 3,100 combat-equipped U.S. Armed Forces continued to be deployed in Bosnia-Herzegovina and other regional states as part of the NATO-led Stabilization

Force (SFOR). Most American forces were based at Tuzla in Bosnia. About 500 others were based in Hungary, Croatia, and Italy, providing logistical and other support. *East Timor.* On February 28, 2002, President George W. Bush reported to Congress, "consistent with the War Powers Resolution," that U.S. Armed Forces were continuing to support the United Nations peacekeeping effort in East Timor aimed at providing security and maintaining law and order in East Timor, coordinating delivery of humanitarian assistance, and helping establish the basis for self-government in East Timor. The United States currently has three military observers attached to UNTAET. The United States also has a separate military presence, USGET, composed of approximately 10 U.S. personnel, including a security detachment, which "facilitates and coordinates" U.S. military activities in East Timor, as well as a rotational presence of U.S. forces through temporary deployments to East Timor. The President stated that U.S. forces would continue a presence through 2002. The President noted his objective was to gradually reduce the "rotational presence operations," and to redeploy USGET personnel, as circumstances permitted. *Terrorism threat.* On March 20, 2002, President George W. Bush reported to Congress, "consistent with the War Powers Resolution," on U.S. efforts in the "global war on Terrorism." He noted that the "heart of the al-Qaeda training capability" had been "seriously degraded," and that the remainder of the Taliban and the al-Qaeda fighters were being "actively pursued and engaged by the U.S., coalition and Afghan forces." The United States was also conducting "maritime interception operations ... to locate and detain suspected al-Qaeda or Taliban leadership fleeing Afghanistan by sea." At the Philippine government's invitation, the President had ordered deployed "combat-equipped and combat support forces to train with, advise, and assist" the Philippines' Armed Forces in enhancing their "existing counterterrorist capabilities." The strength of U.S. military forces working with the Philippines was projected to be 600 personnel. The President noted that he was "assessing options" for assisting other nations, including Georgia and Yemen, in enhancing their "counterterrorism capabilities, including training and equipping their armed forces." He stated that U.S. combat-equipped and combat support forces would be necessary for these efforts, if undertaken. *Yugoslavia/Kosovo.* On May 17, 2002, President George W. Bush reported to Congress, "consistent with the War Powers Resolution," that the U.S. military was continuing to support peacekeeping efforts of KFOR. He noted that the current U.S. contribution was about 5,100 military personnel, and an additional 468 personnel in Macedonia, with an occasional presence in Albania and Greece. *Bosnia.* On July 22, 2002, President George W. Bush reported to Congress, "consistent with the War Powers Resolution," that the U.S. military was continuing to support peacekeeping efforts of SFOR in Bosnia-Herzegovina and other regional states. He noted that the current U.S. contribution was "approximately 2,400 personnel." Most U.S. forces in Bosnia-Herzegovina are assigned to the Multinational Division, North, headquartered in Tuzla. An additional 60 U.S. military personnel are deployed to Hungary and Croatia to provide logistical and other support. *Terrorism threat.* On September 20, 2002, President Bush reported to Congress "consistent with the War Powers Resolution," that U.S. "combat-equipped and combat support forces" had been deployed to the Philippines since January 2002 to train with, assist, and advise the Philippines' Armed Forces in enhancing their "counterterrorist capabilities." He added that U.S. forces were conducting maritime interception operations in the Central and European Command areas to combat movement, arming, or financing of "international terrorists." He also noted that U.S. combat personnel had been deployed to Georgia and Yemen to help enhance the "counterterrorist capabilities" of their armed forces. *Cote d'Ivoire.* On September 26, 2002, President Bush reported to Congress "consistent with the War Powers Resolution," that in response to a rebellion in Cote d'Ivoire he had on September 25, 2002, sent U.S. military personnel into Cote d'Ivoire to assist in the evacuation of American citizens and third country nationals from the city of Bouake; and otherwise assist in other evacuations as necessary. *Yugoslavia/Kosovo.* On November 15, 2002, the President reported to Congress "consistent with the War Powers Resolution" that the United States was continuing to deploy combat equipped military personnel as part of KFOR. Currently there are approximately 4,350 U.S. military personnel in Kosovo, with an additional 266 military personnel in Macedonia. The United States also has an occasional presence in Albania and Greece, associated with the KFOR mission.

2003 *Bosnia.* On January 21, 2003, President George W. Bush reported to Congress, "consistent with the War Powers Resolution," that about 1,800 U.S. Armed Forces personnel continued to be deployed in Bosnia-Herzegovina, and other regional states as part of SFOR. Most were based at Tuzla in Bosnia. About 80 others were based in Hungary and Croatia, providing logistical and other support. *Terrorism threat.* On March 20, 2003, President Bush reported to Congress, "consistent with the War Powers Resolution," as well as P.L. 107-40, and "pursuant to" his authority as Commander-in-Chief, that he had continued a number of U.S. military operations globally in the war against terrorism. These military operations included ongoing U.S. actions against al-Qaeda fighters in Afghanistan; collaborative anti-terror operations with forces of Pakistan in the Pakistan/Afghanistan border area; "maritime interception operations on the high seas" in areas of responsibility of the Central and European Commands to prevent terrorist movement and other activities; and military support for the armed forces of Georgia and Yemen in counter-terrorism operations. *Iraq War.* On March 21, 2003, President Bush reported to Congress, "consistent with the War Powers Resolution," as well as P.L. 102-1 and P.L. 107-243, and "pursuant to" his authority as Commander-in-Chief, that he had "directed U.S. Armed Forces, operating with other coalition forces, to commence operations on March 19, 2003, against Iraq." He further stated that it was not possible to know at present the duration of active combat operations or the scope necessary to accomplish the goals of the operation "to disarm Iraq in pursuit of peace, stability, and security both in the Gulf region and in the United States." *Yugoslavia/Kosovo.* On May 14, 2003, President Bush reported to Congress, "consistent with the War Powers Resolution," that combat-equipped U.S. military personnel continued to be deployed as part of KFOR. He noted that about 2,250 U.S. military personnel were deployed in Kosovo, and additional military personnel operated, on occasion, from Macedonia, Albania, and Greece in support of KFOR operations. *Liberia.* On June 9, 2003, President Bush reported to Congress, "consistent with the War Powers Resolution," that on June 8 he had sent about 35 combat-equipped U.S. military personnel into Monrovia, Liberia, to augment U.S. embassy security forces, to aid in the possible evacuation of U.S. citizens if necessary. The President also noted that he had sent about 34 combat-equipped U.S. military personnel to help secure the U.S. embassy in Nouakchott, Mauritania, and to assist in evacuation of American citizens if required. They were expected to arrive at the U.S. embassy by June 10, 2003. Back-up and support personnel were sent to Dakar, Senegal, to aid in any necessary evacuation from either Liberia or Mauritania. *Bosnia.* On July 22, 2003, President Bush reported to Congress, "consistent with the War Powers Resolution," that the United States continued to provide about 1,800 combat-equipped military personnel in Bosnia-Herzegovina in support of NATO's SFOR and its peacekeeping efforts in this country. *Liberia.* On August 13, 2003, President Bush reported to Congress, "consistent with the War Powers Resolution," that in response to conditions in Liberia, on August 11, 2003, he had authorized about 4,350 U.S. combat-equipped military personnel to enter Liberian territorial waters in support of U.N. and West African States efforts to restore order and provide humanitarian assistance in Liberia. *Terrorism threat.* On September 19, 2003, President Bush reported to Congress "consistent with the War Powers Resolution," that U.S. "combat-equipped and combat support forces" continue to be deployed at a number of locations around the world as part of U.S. anti-terrorism efforts. American forces support anti-terrorism efforts in the Philippines, and maritime interception operations continue on the high seas in the Central, European, and Pacific Command areas of responsibility, to "prevent the movement, arming, or financing of international terrorists." He also noted that "U.S. combat equipped and support forces" had been deployed to Georgia and Djibouti to help in enhancing their "counterterrorist capabilities." *Yugoslavia/Kosovo.* On November 14, 2003, the President reported to Congress "consistent with the War Powers Resolution" that the United States was continuing to deploy combat equipped military personnel as part of the NATO-led international security force in Kosovo (KFOR). Currently there are approximately 2,100 U.S. military personnel in Kosovo, with additional American military personnel operating out of Macedonia, Albania and Greece, in support of KFOR operations.

2004 *Bosnia.* On January 22, 2004, the President reported to Congress "consistent with the War Powers Resolution" that the United States was continuing to deploy combat equipped military personnel Bosnia and Herzegovina in support of NATO's SFOR and its peacekeeping efforts in this country. About 1,800 U.S. personnel are participating. *Haiti.* On February 25, 2004, the President reported to Congress "consistent with the War Powers Resolution" that, on February 23, he had sent a combat-equipped "security force" of about "55 U.S. military personnel from the U.S. Joint Forces Command" to Port-au-Prince, Haiti, to augment the U.S. embassy security forces there and to protect American citizens and property in light of the instability created by the armed rebellion in Haiti. *Haiti.* On March 2, 2004, the President reported to Congress "consistent with the War Powers Resolution" that on February 29 he had sent about "200 additional U.S. combat-equipped, military personnel from the U.S. Joint Forces Command" to Port-au-Prince, Haiti, for a variety of purposes, including preparing the way for a U.N. Multinational Interim Force, and otherwise supporting U.N. Security Council Resolution 1529 (2004). *Terrorism/Bosnia and Haiti.* On March 20, 2004, the President reported to Congress "consistent with the War Powers Resolution," a consolidated report giving details of multiple on-going United States military deployments and operations "in support of the global war on terrorism (including in Afghanistan)," as well as operations in Bosnia and Herzegovina, Kosovo, and Haiti. In this report, the President noted that U.S. anti-terror related activities were underway in Georgia, Djibouti, Kenya, Ethiopia, Yemen, and Eritrea. He further noted that U.S. combat-equipped military personnel continued to be deployed in Kosovo as part of the NATO-led KFOR (1,900 personnel); in Bosnia and Herzegovina as part of the NATO-led SFOR (about 1,100 personnel); and approximately 1,800 military personnel were deployed in Haiti as part of the U.N. Multinational Interim Force. *Terrorism threat/Horn of Africa/Kosovo/Bosnia/Iraq.* On November 4, 2004, the President sent to Congress, "consistent with the War Powers Resolution," a consolidated report giving details of multiple ongoing United States military deployments and operations "in support of the global war on terrorism." These deployments, support or military operations include activities in Afghanistan, Djibouti, as well as Kenya, Ethiopia, Eritrea, Bosnia and Herzegovina, and Kosovo. In this report, the President noted that U.S. anti-terror related activities were underway in Djibouti, Kenya, Ethiopia, Yemen, and Eritrea. He further noted that U.S. combat-equipped military personnel continued to be deployed in Kosovo as part of the NATO-led KFOR (1,800 personnel); and in Bosnia and Herzegovina as part of the NATO-led SFOR (about 1,000 personnel). Meanwhile, he stated that the United States continued to deploy more than 135,000 military personnel in Iraq.

2005 *Terrorism threat/Horn of Africa/Kosovo/Bosnia.* On May 20, 2005, the President sent to Congress "consistent with the War Powers Resolution," a consolidated report giving details of multiple ongoing United States military deployments and operations "in support of the global war on terrorism," as well as operations in Iraq, where about 139,000 U.S. military personnel were deployed. U.S. forces are also deployed in Kenya, Ethiopia, Yemen, Eritrea, and Djibouti assisting in "enhancing counterterrorism capabilities" of these nations. The President further noted that U.S. combat-equipped military personnel continued to be deployed in Kosovo as part of the NATO-led KFOR (1,700 personnel). Approximately 235 U.S. personnel are also deployed in Bosnia and Herzegovina as part of the NATO Headquarters-Sarajevo who assist in defense reform and perform operational tasks, such as counter-terrorism and supporting the International Criminal Court for the Former Yugoslavia. *Terrorism threat/Horn of Africa/Kosovo/Bosnia/Iraq.* On December 7, 2005, the President sent to Congress "consistent" with the War Powers Resolution, a consolidated report giving details of multiple ongoing United States military deployments and operations "in support of the global war on terrorism," and in support of the Multinational Force in Iraq, where about 160,000 U.S. military personnel were deployed. U.S. forces were also deployed in the Horn of Africa region—Kenya, Ethiopia, Yemen, and Djibouti—assisting in "enhancing counter-terrorism capabilities" of these nations. The President further noted that U.S. combat-equipped military personnel continued to be deployed in Kosovo as part of the NATO-led KFOR (1,700 personnel). Approximately 220 U.S. personnel were also deployed in Bosnia and Herzegovina as part of the NATO Headquarters-Sarajevo who assist in defense reform and perform operational tasks, such as "counter-terrorism and supporting the International Criminal Court for the Former Yugoslavia."

2006 *Terrorism threat/Kosovo/Bosnia/Iraq.* On June 15, 2006, the President sent to Congress, "consistent" with the War Powers Resolution, a consolidated report giving details of multiple ongoing United States military deployments and operations "in support of the war on terror," and in Kosovo, Bosnia and Herzegovina, and as part of the Multinational Force (MNF) in Iraq. About 131,000 military personnel were deployed in Iraq. U.S. forces were also deployed in the Horn of Africa region, and in Djibouti to support necessary operations against al-Qaida and other international terrorists operating in the region. U.S. military personnel continue to support the NATO-led KFOR. The U.S. contribution to KFOR was about 1,700 military personnel. The NATO Headquarters-Sarajevo was established in November 22, 2004, as a successor to its stabilization operations in Bosnia-Herzegovina to continue to assist in implementing the peace agreement. Approximately 250 U.S. personnel were assigned to the NATO Headquarters-Sarajevo to assist in defense reform and perform operational tasks, such as "counter-terrorism and supporting the International Criminal Court for the Former Yugoslavia." *Lebanon.* On July 18, 2006, the President reported to Congress "consistent" with the War Powers Resolution, that in response to the security threat posed in Lebanon to U.S. embassy personnel and citizens and designated third country personnel, he had deployed combat-equipped military helicopters and military personnel to Beirut to assist in the departure of the persons under threat from Lebanon. The President noted that additional combat-equipped U.S. military forces may be deployed "to Lebanon, Cyprus and other locations, as necessary" to assist further departures of persons from

Lebanon and to provide security. He further stated that once the threat to U.S. citizens and property has ended, the U.S. military forces would redeploy. *Terrorism threat/Horn of Africa/Kosovo/Bosnia.* On December 15, 2006, the President sent to Congress, "consistent" with the War Powers Resolution, a consolidated report giving details of multiple ongoing United States military deployments and operations "in support of the war on terror," in Kosovo, Bosnia and Herzegovina, and as part of the Multinational Force (MNF) in Iraq. About 134,000 military personnel are deployed in Iraq. U.S. forces were also deployed in the Horn of Africa region, and in Djibouti to support necessary operations against al-Qaida and other international terrorists operating in the region, including Yemen. U.S. military personnel continue to support the NATO-led KFOR. The U.S. contribution to KFOR was about 1,700 military personnel. The NATO Headquarters-Sarajevo was established in November 22, 2004, as a successor to its stabilization operations in Bosnia-Herzegovina to continue to assist in implementing the peace agreement. Approximately 100 U.S. personnel were assigned to the NATO Headquarters-Sarajevo to assist in defense reform and perform operational tasks, such as "counter-terrorism and supporting the International Criminal Court for the Former Yugoslavia."

2007 *Terrorism threat/Kosovo/Afghanistan.* On June 15, 2007, the President sent to Congress, "consistent" with the War Powers Resolution, a consolidated report giving details of ongoing United States military deployments and operations "in support of the war on terror," and in support of the NATO-led KFOR. The President reported that various U.S. "combat-equipped and combat-support forces" were deployed to "a number of locations in the Central, Pacific, European (KFOR), and Southern Command areas of operation" and were engaged in combat operations against al-Qaida terrorists and their supporters. The United States is currently "pursuing and engaging remnant al-Qaida and Taliban fighters in Afghanistan." U.S. forces in Afghanistan currently total approximately 25,945. Of this total, "approximately 14,340 are assigned to the International Security Assistance Force (ISAF) in Afghanistan." The U.S. military continues to support peacekeeping operations in Kosovo, specifically the NATO-led KFOR. Currently, the U.S. contribution to KFOR in Kosovo is approximately 1,584 military personnel. *Terrorism threat/Kosovo/Afghanistan.* On December 14, 2007, the President sent to Congress "consistent with the War Powers Resolution," a consolidated report giving details of ongoing United States military deployments and operations "in support of the war on terror," and in support of the NATO-led Kosovo Force (KFOR). The President reported that various U.S. "combat-equipped and combat-support forces" were deployed to "a number of locations in the Central, Pacific, European, and Southern Command areas of operation" and were engaged in combat operations against al-Qaida terrorists and their supporters. The United States is currently "pursuing and engaging remnant alQaida and Taliban fighters in Afghanistan." U.S. forces in Afghanistan currently total approximately 25,900. Of this total, "approximately 15,180 are assigned to the International Security Assistance Force (ISAF) in Afghanistan." The U.S. military continues to support peacekeeping operations in Kosovo, specifically, the NATO-led KFOR. Currently, the U.S. contribution to KFOR in Kosovo is approximately 1,498 military personnel.

2008 *Terrorism threat/Kosovo/Afghanistan.* On June 13, 2008, the President sent to Congress, "consistent with the War Powers Resolution," a consolidated report giving details of ongoing United States military deployments and operations "in support of the war on terror," and in support of the NATO-led KFOR. The President reported that various U.S. "combat-equipped and combat-support forces" were deployed to "a number of locations in the Central, Pacific, European, and Southern Command areas of operation" and were engaged in combat operations against al-Qaida terrorists and their supporters. The United States is actively "pursuing and engaging remnant al-Qaida and Taliban fighters in Afghanistan." U.S. forces in Afghanistan currently total approximately 31,122. Of this total, "approximately 14,275 are assigned to the International Security Assistance Force (ISAF) in Afghanistan." The U.S. military continues to support peacekeeping operations in Kosovo, specifically, the NATO-led KFOR. Currently, the U.S. contribution to KFOR in Kosovo is approximately 1,500 military personnel. *Terrorism threat/Kosovo/Afghanistan.* On December 16, 2008, the President sent to Congress, "consistent with the War Powers Resolution," a consolidated report giving details of ongoing United States military deployments and operations "in support of the war on terror," and in support of the NATO-led KFOR. The President reported that various U.S. "combat-equipped and combat-support forces" were deployed to "a number of locations in the Centrol, Pacific, European, Southern, and Africa Command areas of operation" and were engaged in combat operations against al-Qaida and their supporters. The United States is "actively pursuing and engaging remnant al-Qaida and Taliban fighters in Afghanistan." U.S. forces in Afghanistan total approximately 31,000. Of this total, "approximately 13, 000 are assigned to the International Security Assistance Force (ISAF) in Afghanistan." The U.S. military continues to support peacekeeping operations in Kosovo, specifically the NATO-led KFOR. The current U.S. contribution to KFOR in Kosovo is about 1,500 military personnel.

2009 *Terrorism threat/Afghanistan/Iraq/Kosovo.* On June 15, 2009, the President sent to Congress, "consistent with the War Powers Resolution," a supplemental consolidated report, giving details of "ongoing contingency operations overseas." The report noted that the total number of U.S. forces in Afghanistan was "approximately 58,000," of which approximately 20,000 are assigned to the International Security Assistance Force (ISAF) in Afghanistan. The United States continues to pursue and engage "remaining al-Qa'ida and Taliban forces in Afghanistan." The United States also continues to deploy military forces in support of the Multinational Force (MNF) in Iraq. The current U.S. contribution to this effort is "approximately 138,000 U.S. military personnel." U.S. military operations continue in Kosovo, as part of the NATO-led KFOR. Presently the United States contributes approximately 1,400 U.S. military personnel to KFOR. In addition, the United states continues to deploy "U.S. combat-equipped forces to help enhance the counterterrorism capabilities of our friends and allies" not only in the Horn of Africa region, but globally through "maritime interception operations on the high seas" aimed at blocking the "movement, arming and financing of international terrorists." *Terrorism threat/Afghanistan/Iraq/Kosovo.* On December 5, 2009, the President sent to Congress "consistent with the War Powers Resolution," a consolidated report, giving details of "global deployments of U.S. Armed Forces equipped for combat." The report detailed "ongoing U.S. contingency operations overseas." The report noted that the total number of U.S. forces in Afghanistan was "approximately 68,000," of which approximately 34,000 are assigned to the International Security Assistance Force (ISAF) in Afghanistan. The United States continues to pursue and engage "remaining al-Qa'ida and Taliban forces in Afghanistan." The United States has deployed "various combat-equipped forces to a number of locations in the Central, Pacific, European, Southern and African Command areas of operation" in support of anti-terrorist and anti-al-Qa'ida actions. The United States also continues to deploy military forces in Iraq to "maintain security and stability" there. These Iraqi operations continue pursuant to the terms of a bilateral agreement between the United States and Iraq, which entered into force on January 1, 2009. The current U.S. force level in Iraq is "approximately 116,000 U.S. military personnel." U.S. military operations continue in Kosovo, as part of the NATO-led KFOR. Presently the United States contributes approximately 1,475 U.S. military personnel to KFOR. In addition, the United States continues to deploy "U.S. combat-equipped forces to assist in enhancing the counterterrorism capabilities of our friends and allies" not only in the Horn of Africa region, but globally through "maritime interception operations on the high seas" aimed at blocking the "movement, arming and financing of international terrorists."

2010 *Terrorism threat/Afghanistan/Iraq/Kosovo.* On June 15, 2010, the President sent to Congress, "consistent with the War Powers Resolution," a consolidated report giving details of "deployments of U.S. Armed Forces equipped for combat." The report noted that the total number of U.S. forces in Afghanistan was "approximately 87,000," of which over 62,000 are assigned to the International Security Assistance Force (ISAF) in Afghanistan. The United States continues combat operations "against al-Qa'ida terrorists and their Taliban supporters" in Afghanistan. The United States has deployed "combat-equipped forces to a number of locations in the U.S. Central, Pacific, European, Southern and African Command areas of operation" in support of anti-terrorist and anti-al-Qa'ida actions. The United States also continues to deploy military forces in Iraq to "maintain security and stability" there. These Iraqi operations continue pursuant to the terms of a bilateral agreement between the United States and Iraq, which entered into force on January 1, 2009. The current U.S. force level in Iraq is "approximately 95,000 U.S. military personnel." U.S. military operations continue in Kosovo, as part of the NATO-led KFOR. Presently, the United States contributes approximately 1,074 U.S. military personnel to KFOR. In addition, the United States continues to "conduct maritime interception operations on the high seas" directed at "stopping the movement, arming and financing of international terrorist groups." *Terrorism threat/Afghanistan/Iraq/Kosovo.* On December 15, 2010, the President submitted to Congress "consistent with the War Powers Resolution," a consolidated report, detailing "deployments of U.S. Armed Forces equipped for combat." The report noted that the total number of U.S. forces in Afghanistan was "approximately 97,500," of which over 81,500 were assigned to the International Security Assistance Force (ISAF) in Afghanistan. The United States is continuing combat operations "against al-Qa'ida terrorists and their Taliban supporters" in Afghanistan. The United States has deployed "combat-equipped forces to a number of locations in the U.S. Central, Pacific, European, Southern and African Command areas of operation" in support of anti-terrorist and anti-al-Qa'ida actions. In addition, the United States continues to conduct "maritime interception operations on the high seas in the areas of responsibility of the geographic combatant commands" directed at "stopping the movement, arming and financing of international terrorist groups." The United States also continues to deploy military forces in Iraq in support of Iraqi efforts to "maintain security and stability" there. These Iraqi operations continue pursuant to the terms of a bilateral agreement between the United States and Iraq, which entered into force on January 1, 2009. The current U.S. force level in Iraq is "approximately 48,400 U.S. military personnel." U.S. military operations also continue in Kosovo, as part of the NATO-led KFOR. The United States currently contributes approximately 808 U.S. military personnel to KFOR.

2011 *Terrorism threat/Afghanistan/Libya/Kosovo.* On June 15, 2011, the President sent to Congress, "consistent with the War Powers Resolution," a supplemental consolidated report giving details of "global deployments of U.S. Armed Forces equipped for combat." The report detailed ongoing U.S. contingency operations overseas. The report noted that the total number of U.S. forces in Afghanistan was "approximately 99,000," of which approximately 83,000 are assigned to the International Security Assistance Force (ISAF) in Afghanistan. The United States continues to pursue and engage "remaining al-Qa'ida and Taliban fighters in Afghanistan." The United States has deployed various "combat-equipped forces" to a number of locations in the Central, Pacific, European, Southern and African Command areas of operation in support of anti-terrorist and anti-al-Qa'ida actions. This includes the deployment of U.S. military forces globally to assist in enhancing the counterterrorism capabilities of our friends and allies through maritime interception operations on the high seas "aimed at stopping the movement, arming and financing of certain international terrorist groups." A combat-equipped security force of about "40 U.S. military personnel from the U.S. Central Command" was deployed to Cairo,

Egypt, on January 31, 2011, for the sole purpose of "protecting American citizens and property." That force remains at the U.S. embassy in Cairo. The United States also continues to deploy military forces in Iraq to help it "maintain security and stability" there. These Iraqi operations continue pursuant to the terms of a bilateral agreement between the United States and Iraq, which entered into force on January 1, 2009. The current U.S. force level in Iraq is "approximately 45,000 U.S. military personnel." In Libya, since April 4, 2011, the United States has transferred responsibility for military operations there to NATO, and U.S. involvement "has assumed a supporting role in the coalition's efforts." U.S. support in Libya has been limited to "intelligence, logistical support, and search and rescue assistance." The U.S. military aircraft have also been used to assist in the "suppression and destruction of air defenses in support of the no-fly zone" over Libya. Since April 23, 2011, the United States has supported the coalition effort in Libya through use of "unmanned aerial vehicles against a limited set of clearly defined targets" there. Except in the case of operations to "rescue the crew of a U.S. aircraft" on March 21, 2011, "the United States has deployed no ground forces to Libya." U.S. military operations continue in Kosovo, as part of the NATO-led KFOR. Presently the United States contributes approximately 800 U.S. military personnel to KFOR. *Libya.* On March 21, 2011, the President submitted to Congress "consistent with the War Powers Resolution," a report stating that at "approximately 3:00 p.m. Eastern Daylight Time, on March 19, 2011," he had directed U.S. military forces to commence "operations to assist an international effort authorized by the United Nations (U.N.) Security Council and undertaken with the support of European allies and Arab partners, to prevent a humanitarian catastrophe and address the threat posed to international peace and security by the crisis in Libya." He further stated that U.S. military forces, "under the command of Commander, U.S. Africa Command (AFRICOM) began a series of strikes against air defense systems and military airfields for the purposes of preparing a no-fly zone." These actions were part of "the multilateral response authorized under U.N. Security Council Resolution 1973," and the President added that "these strikes will be limited in their nature, duration, and scope. Their purpose is to support an international coalition as it takes all necessary measures to enforce the terms of U.N. Security Council Resolution 1973. These limited U.S. actions will set the stage for further action by other coalition partners." The President noted that United Nations Security Council Resolution 1973 authorized Member States, under Chapter VII of the U.N. Charter, to take all necessary measures to protect civilians and civilian populated areas under threat of attack in Libya, including the establishment and enforcement of a "no-fly zone" in the airspace of Libya. United States military efforts are discrete and focused on employing unique U.S. military capabilities to set the conditions for our European allies and Arab partners to carry out the measures authorized by the U.N. Security Council Resolution. The President stated further that the "United States has not deployed ground forces into Libya. United States forces are conducting a limited and well-defined mission in support of international efforts to protect civilians and prevent a humanitarian disaster." Accordingly, he added, "U.S. forces have targeted the Qadhafi regime's air defense systems, command and control structures, and other capabilities of Qadhafi's armed forces used to attack civilians and civilian populated areas." It was the intent of the United States, he said, to "seek a rapid, but responsible, transition of operations to coalition, regional, or international organizations that are postured to continue activities as may be necessary to realize the objectives of U.N. Security Council Resolutions 1970 and 1973." The President said that the actions he had directed were "in the national security and foreign policy interests of the United States." He took them, the President stated, "pursuant to my constitutional authority to conduct U.S. foreign relations and as Commander in Chief and Chief Executive." *Central Africa.* On October 14, 2011, the President submitted to Congress, "consistent with the War Powers Resolution," a report stating that "he had authorized a small number of combat-equipped U.S. forces to deploy to central Africa to provide assistance to regional forces that are working toward the removal of Joseph Kony," leader of the Lord's Resistance Army (LRA), from the battlefield. For over two decades the LRA has murdered, kidnapped, and raped tens of thousands of men, women, and children throughout central Africa, and has continued to commit atrocities in South Sudan, the Democratic Republic of the Congo, and the Central African Republic. The U.S. Armed Forces, the President noted, would be a "significant contribution toward counter-LRA efforts in central Africa." The President stated that on "October 12, 2011, the initial team of U.S. military personnel with appropriate combat equipment deployed to Uganda." In the "next month, additional forces will deploy, including a second combat-equipped team and associated headquarters, communications, and logistics personnel." The President further stated that the "total number of U.S. military personnel deploying for this mission is approximately 100. These forces will act as advisors to partner forces that have the goals of removing from the battlefield Joseph Kony and other senior leadership of the LRA." U.S. forces "will provide information, advice, and assistance to select partner nation forces." With the approval of the respective host nations, "elements of these U.S. forces will deploy into Uganda, South Sudan, the Central African Republic, and the Democratic Republic of the Congo. The support provided by U.S. forces will enhance regional efforts against the LRA." The President emphasized that even though the "U.S. forces are combat-equipped, they will only be providing information, advice, and assistance to partner nation forces, and they will not themselves engage LRA forces unless necessary for self-defense. All appropriate precautions have been taken to ensure the safety of U.S. military personnel during their deployment." The President took note in his report that Congress had previously "expressed support for increased, comprehensive U.S. efforts to help mitigate and eliminate the threat posed by the LRA to civilians and regional stability" through the passage of the Lord's Resistance Army Disarmament and Northern Uganda Recovery Act of 2009, P.L. 111-172, enacted May 24, 2010. *Terrorism threat/Afghanistan/Libya/Iraq/Kosovo.* On December 15, 2011, the President submitted to Congress, "consistent with the War Powers Resolution," a supplemental consolidated report, giving details of "deployments of U.S. Armed Forces equipped for combat." The report detailed ongoing U.S. contingency operations overseas. The report noted that the total number of U.S. forces in Afghanistan was "approximately 93,000," of which approximately 78,000 are assigned to the International Security Assistance Force (ISAF) in Afghanistan. The United States continues to pursue and engage "remaining al-Qa'ida and Taliban fighters in Afghanistan." The United States has deployed various "combat-equipped forces" to a number of locations in the Central, Pacific, European, Southern, and African Command areas of operation in support of anti-terrorist and anti-al-Qa'ida actions. This includes the deployment of U.S. military forces globally: "including special operations and other forces" for "sensitive operations" in various places, as well as forces to assist in enhancing the counterterrorism capabilities of our friends and allies. U.S. forces also have engaged in maritime interception operations on the high seas "aimed at stopping the movement, arming and financing of certain international terrorist groups." The United States continued to deploy military forces in Iraq to help it "maintain security and stability" there. These Iraqi operations were undertaken pursuant to the terms of a bilateral agreement between the United States and Iraq, which entered into force on January 1, 2009. The U.S. force level in Iraq on October 28, 2011, was "36,001 U.S. military personnel." The United States was committed to withdraw U.S. forces from Iraq by December 31, 2011. (This occurred, as scheduled, after this report was submitted.) In Libya, after April 4, 2011, the United States transferred responsibility for military operations there to NATO, and U.S. involvement "assumed a supporting role in the coalition's efforts." U.S. support in Libya was limited to "intelligence, logistical support, and search and rescue assistance." The U.S. military aircraft were also used to assist in the "suppression and destruction of air defenses in support of the no-fly zone" over Libya. After April 23, 2011, the United States supported the coalition effort in Libya through use of "unmanned aerial vehicles against a limited set of clearly defined targets" there. Except in the case of operations to "rescue the crew of a U.S. aircraft" on March 21, 2011, and deploying 16 U.S. military personnel to aid in re-establishing the U.S. embassy in Tripoli in September 2011, "the U.S. deployed no ground forces to Libya." On October 27, 2011, the United Nations terminated the "no-fly zone" effective October 31, 2011. NATO terminated its mission during this same time. U.S. military operations continue in Kosovo, as part of the NATO-led KFOR. Presently the United States contributes approximately 800 U.S. military personnel to KFOR.

2012 *Somalia.* On January 26, 2012, the President submitted to Congress, "consistent with the War Powers Resolution," a report detailing a successful U.S. Special Operations Forces operation in Somalia of January 24, 2012, to rescue Ms. Jessica Buchanan, a U.S. citizen who had been kidnapped by a group linked to Somali pirates and financiers. This operation was undertaken "by a small number of joint combat-equipped U.S. forces" following receipt of reliable intelligence establishing her location in Somalia. A Danish national, Poul Hagen Thisted, kidnapped with Ms. Buchanan, was also rescued with her. *Terrorism threat/Afghanistan/Somalia/Yemen/Central Africa/Kosovo.* On June 15, 2012, the President reported to Congress "consistent with" the War Powers Resolution, a consolidated report regarding various deployments of U.S. Armed Forces equipped for combat. In the efforts in support of U.S. counterterrorism (CT) objectives against al-Qa'ida, the Taliban and, associated forces, he noted that U.S. forces engaged in Afghanistan in the above effort were "approximately 90,000." With regard to other counter-terrorism operations, the President stated that the United States had deployed "U.S. combat-equipped forces to assist in enhancing the CT capabilities of our friends and allies including special operations and other forces for sensitive operations in various locations around the world." He noted that the "U.S. military has taken direct action in Somalia against members of al-Qa'ida, including those who are also members of al-Shabaab, who are engaged in efforts to carry out terrorist attacks against the United States and our interests." The President further stated that the U.S. military had been "working closely with the Yemeni government to operationally and ultimately eliminate the terrorist threat posed by al-Qa-ida in the Arabian Peninsula (AQAP), the most active and dangerous affiliate of al-Qa'ida today." He added that these "joint efforts have resulted in direct action against a limited number of AQAP operatives and senior leaders in that country who posed a terrorist threat to the United States and our interests." The President noted that he would direct "additional measures against al-Qa'ida, the Taliban, and associated forces to protect U.S. citizens and interests." Further information on such matters is provided in a "classified annex to this report." Other military operations reported by the President include the "deployment of U.S. combat-equipped military personnel to Uganda to serve as advisors to regional forces that are working to apprehend or remove Joseph Kony and other senior Lord's Resistance Army (LRA) leaders from the battlefield and to protect local populations." The total number of U.S. military personnel deployed for this mission is "approximately 90," and elements of these U.S. forces have been sent to "forward locations in the LRA-affected areas of the Republic of South Sudan, the Democratic Republic of the Congo, and the Central African Republic." These U.S. forces "will not engage LRA forces except in self-defense." The President also reported that presently the United States was contributing approximately 817 military personnel to the NATO-led KFOR in Kosovo. He also reported that the United States remained prepared to engage in "maritime interception operations" intended to stop the "movement, arming, and financing of certain international terrorist groups," as well as stopping "proliferation by sea of weapons of mass destruction and related materials." Additional details about these efforts are included in "the classified annex" to this report. *Libya/Yemen.* On September 14, 2012, the

President reported to Congress, "consistent with" the War Powers Resolution, that on September 12, 2012, he ordered deployed to Libya "a security force from the U.S. Africa Command" to "support the security of U.S. personnel in Libya." This action was taken in response to the attack on the U.S. "diplomatic post in Benghazi, Libya," that had killed four America citizens, including U.S. Ambassador John Christopher Stevens. The President added on September 13, 2012, that "an additional security force arrived in Yemen in response to security threats there." He further stated that: "Although these security forces are equipped for combat, these movements have been undertaken solely for the purpose of protecting American citizens and property." These security forces will remain in Libya and in Yemen, he noted, "until the security situation becomes such that they are no longer needed." *Southern Philippines Humanitarian Assistance for Typhoon Bopha.* On December 17, 2012, U.S. Pacific Command (PACOM) reported all DOD humanitarian assistance and military-to-military search and rescue assistance had been completed in the southeastern Philippines following Typhoon Bopha. According to Pentagon Press Secretary George Little at the time, "U.S. forces provided planning, coordination, personnel, water purification teams, and aircraft assets that flew 24 sorties to deliver 756,800 pounds of relief supplies, flew 56 hours in support of search and rescue operations and provided 60 hours of search and rescue coverage. PACOM forces are returning back to their home stations or are proceeding to follow-on taskings."

2013 *Afghanistan.* On January 31, 2013, DOD identified three major units to deploy as part of the ongoing rotation of forces operating in Afghanistan. The scheduled rotation involved one Infantry Brigade Combat Team (IBCT) with roughly 2,250 personnel from the 4th Infantry Brigade Combat Team, 3rd Infantry Division, Fort Stewart, Georgia; a Combat Aviation Brigade (CAB) with roughly 2,200 personnel from the 10th Combat Aviation Brigade, 10th Mountain Division, Fort Drum, New York; and a corps headquarters with roughly 500 personnel from the III Corps Headquarters, Fort Hood, Texas, in spring 2013. *Niger.* On February 22, 2013, the President reported in a letter dated February 20 to congressional leaders, that "the last 40 of the approximately 100 military personnel had arrived in Niger and were deployed with weapons for the purpose of providing their own force protection and security." President Obama further stated, "This deployment will provide support for intelligence collection and will also facilitate intelligence sharing with French forces conducting operations in Mali, and with other partners in the region." *Afghanistan.* On April 10, 2013, DOD identified four major units to deploy as part of the upcoming rotation of forces operating in Afghanistan. The scheduled rotation is ongoing and involves one cavalry regiment, the 2nd Cavalry Regiment from Vilseck, Germany, with roughly 3,000 personnel; one armored brigade combat team (ABCT) with roughly 3,200 personnel from the 2nd Armored Brigade Combat Team, 1st Cavalry Division, Fort Hood, Texas; one infantry brigade combat team (IBCT) with roughly 2,200 personnel from the 3rd Infantry

Brigade Combat Team, 1st Infantry Division, Fort Knox, Kentucky; and a division headquarters with roughly 450 personnel from the 4th Infantry Division Headquarters, Fort Carson, Colorado, to rotate in summer 2013. *Jordan*. Defense Secretary Chuck Hagel ordered the deployment of more American troops to Jordan. He announced the deployment on April 17, 2013, in a statement on Syria before the Senate Armed Services Committee. He said that U.S. troops will work alongside Jordanian forces to "improve readiness and prepare for a number of scenarios." The troops, which number up to 200, are from the headquarters of the 1st Armored Division at Fort Bliss, Texas, according to DOD sources. *Terrorism threat/Afghanistan/Somalia/Yemen/Central Africa*. On June 14, 2013, President Obama sent Congress a letter "consistent with" the War Powers Resolution, on U.S. military operations against al-Qa'ida, the Taliban, and associated forces, and in support of related U.S. counterterrorism objectives in Afghanistan and elsewhere. There are approximately 62,000 U.S. forces in Afghanistan of which 49,000 of these forces are assigned to the NATO-led International Security Assistance Force (ISAF). Further directed reduction of forces will continue to the 34,000 level by February 12, 2014. *Jordan*. President Obama sent Congress a letter on June 21, 2013, regarding a combat-equipped detachment of 700 U.S. troops remaining in Jordan following training exercises that ended on June 20. This was at the request of the government of Jordan and in furtherance of U.S. national security and foreign policy interests. *Afghanistan*. On July 11, 2013, DOD identified three units to deploy as part of the upcoming rotation of forces in Afghanistan. The scheduled rotation involves elements of one infantry brigade combat team (IBCT) with roughly 2,000 personnel; and elements of two combat aviation brigades, one with roughly 1,450 personnel and one with roughly 2,100 personnel, to rotate in Fall 2013 in support of the combatant commander's mission requirements. The deploying units include the 3rd Infantry Brigade Combat Team, 10th Mountain Division, Fort Drum, New York; the 1st Cavalry Division Combat Aviation Brigade, Fort Hood, Texas; and the 1st Infantry Division Combat Aviation Brigade, Fort Riley, Kansas. *Afghanistan*. On September 24, 2013, DOD identified six units to deploy as part of the upcoming rotation of forces operating in Afghanistan. The scheduled rotation involves elements of two infantry brigade combat teams (IBCT)—one with roughly 1,830 personnel (4th Infantry Brigade Combat Team, 4th Infantry Division) and one with roughly 2,000 personnel (2nd Brigade Combat Team, 101st Airborne Division); elements of one armored brigade combat team (ABCT) with roughly 1,160 personnel (3rd Armored Brigade Combat Team, 1st Armored Division); elements of one combat aviation brigade with roughly 1,800 personnel (159th Combat Aviation Brigade, 101st Airborne Division); a division headquarters element with roughly 630 personnel (10th Mountain Division Headquarters); and a corps headquarters element with roughly 560 personnel (XVIII Airborne Corps Headquarters) to rotate in winter 2013-2014 in support of the combatant commander's mission requirements. The deploying units include

Brigade Combat Teams/Combat Aviation Brigades: 2nd Brigade Combat Team, 101st Airborne Division, Fort Campbell, KY; 4th Infantry Brigade Combat Team, 4th Infantry Division, Fort Carson, CO; 3rd Armored Brigade Combat Team, 1st Armored Division, Fort Bliss, TX; and 159th Combat Aviation Brigade, 101st Airborne Division, Fort Campbell, KY; Division Headquarters: 10th Mountain Division Headquarters, Fort Drum, NY; and Corps Headquarters: XVIII Airborne Corps Headquarters, Fort Bragg, NC. *Leyte, Philippines Humanitarian Assistance for Typhoon Haiyan.* On November 9, 2013, the Defense Secretary directed the U.S. Pacific Command to support humanitarian relief operations in the Philippines after Typhoon Haiyan (Yolanda). The aircraft carrier USS *George Washington* (CVN 73) and other U.S. Navy ships were ordered to the Philippines. The aircraft carrier, which carries 5,000 sailors and more than 80 aircraft, was in Hong Kong for a port visit. In addition to the carrier were the cruisers USS *Antietam* (CG 54) and USS *Cowpens* (CG 63), the destroyers USS *Mustin* (DDG 89) and USS *Lassen* (DDG 82), and the supply ship USNS *Charles Drew* (T-AKE-10). Embarked on board the USS *George Washington* was Carrier Air Wing Five (CVW-5), a collection of aircraft designed to perform various functions including disaster relief. Included were the "Golden Falcons" of Helicopter Sea Combat Squadron 12 flying the MH-60S Seahawk and the "Saberhawks" of Helicopter Maritime Strike Squadron 77 flying the MH-60R Seahawk. *Burundi and Central African Republic.* A small U.S. Air Force support team and two C-17 Globemaster III aircraft began airlift operations on December 12, 2013, in response to a French request for airlift support. The U.S. airmen conducted 16 flights from Burundi to the Central African Republic transporting 857 Burundian troops, 73 pallets of equipment, and 18 Burundian military vehicles. Fewer than 10 Americans remained on the ground serving as liaisons with the French military when operations were completed on December 30, 2013. *Afghanistan.* On December 13, 2013, DOD identified five units to deploy as part of the upcoming rotation of forces operating in Afghanistan. The scheduled rotation involves elements of one infantry brigade combat team (IBCT) with roughly 3,200 personnel (1st Brigade, 82nd Airborne Division); elements of one cavalry regiment (CR) with roughly 2,050 personnel (3rd Cavalry Regiment); elements of two combat aviation brigades—one with roughly 1,700 personnel and the other with roughly 1,000 personnel (16th Combat Aviation Brigade and 12th Combat Aviation Brigade), and a division headquarters element with roughly 350 personnel (1st Cavalry Division Headquarters) to rotate in spring 2014 in support of the combatant commander's mission requirements. The deploying units include Brigade Combat Teams/Combat Aviation Brigades: 1st Brigade, 82nd Airborne Division, Fort Bragg, NC; 3rd Cavalry Regiment, Fort Hood, TX; 16th Combat Aviation Brigade, Joint Base Lewis-McChord, WA; and 12th Combat Aviation Brigade, Ansbach, Germany, and Division Headquarters: 1st Cavalry Division Headquarters, Fort Hood, TX. *South Sudan.* On December 18, 2013, at the request of the U.S. State Department, DOD directed two U.S. C-130 aircraft to evacuate 120 personnel from the embassy in Juba, the capital of South Sudan, to Nairobi, Kenya. In President Obama's report to the Congress on December 19, 2013, he provided information on the deployment of U.S. forces to support the security of U.S. citizens and personnel at the U.S. embassy in South Sudan consistent with the War Powers Resolution (P.L. 93- 148). On December 21, 2013, 46 additional U.S. military personnel deployed by military aircraft to the area of Bor, South Sudan, to conduct an operation to evacuate U.S. citizens and personnel. After the aircraft came under fire, the operation was curtailed due to security considerations and the aircraft and all military personnel onboard departed without completing the evacuation.

2014 *South Korea.* On January 7, 2014, DOD announced the rotational deployment of the U.S. Army's 1st Battalion, 12th Cavalry Regiment, 1st U.S. Cavalry Division from Fort Hood, TX, to Camps Hovey and Stanley, Republic of Korea, on February 1, 2014. Comprised of approximately 800 soldiers, this combined arms battalion will deploy to conduct operations in support of U.S. Forces Korea and the Eighth Army. This action supports the U.S defense commitment to the Republic of Korea as specified by the mutual defense treaty and presidential agreements. *Uganda, South Sudan, the Democratic Republic of the Congo, and the Central African Republic.* President Obama announced on March 23, 2014, the deployment of U.S. aircraft, aircrews, and support personnel to central Africa. The total number of U.S. military personnel deployed for this mission is about 280 and may increase to as many as 300. According to the president's letter to Congress, "The aircraft and personnel providing the enhanced air mobility support will deploy to the Lord's Resistance Army-affected areas of central Africa episodically, as they are available, and consistent with other Department of Defense requirements."[3] *Iraq.* On June 19, 2014, President Obama announced his decision to deploy 300 U.S. military personnel to advise the Iraqi security forces. These special operators will secure the U.S. embassy and personnel operating inside Iraq, assess the situation on the ground, help evaluate gaps in Iraqi security forces, and increase these forces' capacity to counter the threat posed by the Islamic State of Iraq and the Levant (ISIL).[4] *Iraq.* June 30, 2014, President Obama ordered an additional 200 military personnel deployed to Iraq to reinforce security at the U.S. embassy in Baghdad and other U.S. facilities as well as at the city's international airport.[5] *Ukraine.* On August 6, 2014, at the request of the U.S. State Department, a dozen American troops from U.S. European Command arrived in Kiev, Ukraine, to help investigate the downing of the Malaysian airliner MH17 that killed all 298 passengers aboard.[6] These specialists will assist State Department personnel in Kiev and not visit the crash site in eastern Ukraine, where there is fighting between the Ukrainian forces of the central government and separatists backed by Russia. *Iraq.* On August 13, 2014, Defense Secretary Hagel announced that President Obama had ordered 130 new assessors to deploy to Erbil, Iraq, to assess the scope of the humanitarian mission and develop additional humanitarian assistance options in support of displaced Iraqi civilians trapped on Sinjar Mountain by the ISIL.[7] *Poland.* DOD announced on August 13, 2014, that 600 soldiers from the 1st Brigade, 1st Cavalry Division, Fort Hood, TX, will rotate to Poland as the next unit to participate in the reassurance initiative. The brigade will be the next unit to take part in ongoing land forces exercises that fall under the umbrella of Operation Atlantic Resolve. According to Pentagon officials, "the United States is demonstrating its continued commitment to collective security through a series of actions designed to reassure NATO allies and partners of America's dedication to enduring peace and stability in the region, in light of the Russian intervention in Ukraine."[8] *Iraq.* On September 2, 2014, President Barack Obama approved an increase of 350 additional military personnel on the ground in Baghdad providing security at the U.S. embassy compound and its support facilities.[9] On September 10, Pentagon Press Secretary Navy Rear Adm. John Kirby announced that "approximately 475 additional service members will be deployed to Iraq to conduct the following missions: advise and assist the Iraqi security forces in order to help them go on the offense against ISIL, conduct intelligence, surveillance and reconnaissance flights to increase U.S. capacity to target ISIL, and coordinate the activities of the U.S. military across Iraq.[10] *Liberia, West Africa.* President Obama announced on September 16, 2014, a major increase in the U.S. response to the current Ebola outbreak in West Africa. U.S. Africa Command set up a Joint Force Command headquartered in Monrovia, Liberia, to provide regional command-and-control support to U.S. military activities and facilitate coordination with U.S. government and international relief efforts.[11] An estimated 3,000 U.S. forces are to be involved in the upcoming months. Pentagon spokesman Army Col. Steve Warren announced that as of September 29, 2014, about 150 U.S. service members were in the Liberian capital Monrovia, conducting a range of activities in support of the U.S. Agency for International Development, as U.S. Africa Command sets up a joint force command headquarters there to support U.S. military activities.[12] *Liberia and Senegal, West Africa.* On October 1, 2014, Defense Secretary Hagel authorized the deployment of 700 soldiers from the 101st Airborne Division headquarters to Liberia to help with the Ebola epidemic. By October 3, there were 205 U.S. service members in Liberia, with another 26 in neighboring Senegal to establish a cargo-processing hub in support of Operation United Assistance, the international effort to battle Ebola in West Africa.[13] On October 29, a 20-member team of Air Force medical trainers arrived in Monrovia, Liberia, to train non-U.S. medical personnel as part of Operation United Assistance. On October 31, a team of soldier-scientists who are part of an Army expeditionary laboratory unit based in Aberdeen, MD, deployed to Liberia for up to a year to establish four labs outside Monrovia and contribute to the U.S. effort to halt Ebola outbreaks in West Africa.[14] *Dakar, Senegal.* On November 10, 2014, 35 airmen and two Air Force C-130 Hercules aircraft from Dyess Air Force Base, TX, joined forces with more than 70 airmen from the Kentucky Air National Guard's 123rd Contingency Response

Group who have been operating a cargo hub at the International Airport in Dakar since October 5 as part of Operation United Assistance.[15] *Senegal and Liberia, West Africa.* On November 14, 2014, Secretary of Defense Chuck Hagel signed an order authorizing the involuntary mobilization of approximately 2,100 Army Reserve and Army National Guard soldiers to support Operation United Assistance.[16] These troops will replace forces in Senegal and Liberia who are supporting the U.S response to the Ebola outbreak. *Vilnius, Lithuania.* On November 24, 2014, Lt. Gen. Ben Hodges, the commander of U.S. Army Europe, stated that soldiers of the 1st Cavalry Division and later replacement units will rotate to locations in Eastern Europe through the end of next year as part of Operation Atlantic Resolve. Those rotations could continue beyond 2015.[17] *Iraq.* On December 19, 2014, Pentagon Press Secretary Navy Rear Adm. John Kirby announced that up to 1,300 more U.S. troops, including approximately 1,000 soldiers from the Army's 82nd Airborne Division, will deploy to Iraq in late January 2015 to "to train, advise and assist Iraqi security forces."[18]

2015 *Liberia and Senegal, West Africa.* On January 8, 2015, Pentagon spokesman Army Col. Steve Warren announced that 2,367 DOD personnel are involved in the battle to stop the spread of Ebola. Most of those personnel (2,174) are based in Liberia's capital, Monrovia, and the remaining 193 personnel are Marine Corps members and port operations personnel operating in Dakar, Senegal. The Pentagon noted that U.S. military personnel are not involved in treating patients with Ebola. Instead, U.S. military personnel provide continuing logistical support and training for health care workers, testing medical samples, and constructing treatment units.[19]

Sources

In addition to the historical resources listed in the "Introduction," below are official government websites that serve as authoritative sources of information for this report.

Central Intelligence Agency (CIA), News & Information
https://www.cia.gov/news-information/index.html
Department of Defense (DOD), News Releases
http://www.defense.gov/releases/default.aspx
DOD, Secretary of Defense Speeches
http://www.defense.gov/speeches/secdefmedia.aspx
DOD, Transcripts
http://www.defense.gov/transcripts/
Operation Atlantic Resolve, America's Commitment to European Security
http://www.defense.gov/home/features/2014/0514_atlanticresolve/?source=GovDelivery
Open Source, Military Issues and Global Issues
https://www.opensource.gov/
Department of State, Bureau of Public Affairs: Office of Press Relations

http://www.state.gov/r/pa/prs/
The White House Briefing Room, Speeches and Remarks
http://www.whitehouse.gov/briefing-room/speeches-and-remarks
The White House Briefing Room Statements and Press Releases
http://www.whitehouse.gov/briefing-room/statements-and-releases

End Notes

[1] Other lists include Sen. Barry Goldwater, "War without Declaration: A Chronological List of 199 U.S. Military Hostilities Abroad without a Declaration of War. 1798-1972," Congressional Record, vol. 119, July 20, 1973: S14174- S14183; U.S. Department of State, "Armed Actions Taken by the United States Without a Declaration of War, 1789- 1967," Research Project 806A, Historical Studies Division, Bureau of Public Affairs; John M. Collins, America's Small Wars (New York: Brassey's, 1990). For a discussion of the evolution of lists of military actions and legal authorization for various actions, see Francis D. Wormuth and Edwin B. Firmage, To Chain the Dog of War; the War Power of Congress in History and Law (Dallas: Southern Methodist University Press, 1986), pp. 133-149.

[2] This and subsequent mentions of presidential reports or notifications refer to reports the President submitted to Congress related to the War Powers Resolution (P.L. 91-148, November 7, 1973). Background information on the discussion of the War Powers Resolution and various types of reports required under it was included in CRS Report RL33532, War Powers Resolution: Presidential Compliance, and CRS Report R42699, The War Powers Resolution: After Thirty-Eight Years, both by Richard F. Grimmett, specialist in International Security, who is retired.

[3] The White House, Office of the Press Secretary, "Letter from the President -- IDLs -- War Powers Resolution," March 25, 2014, at http://www.whitehouse.gov/the-press-office/2014/03/25/letter-president-idls-war-powers-resolution.

[4] The White House, Office of the Press Secretary, "Remarks by the President on the Situation in Iraq," June 19, 2014, at http://www.whitehouse.gov/the-press-office/2014/06/19/remarks-president-situation-iraq.

[5] DOD News, "Additional Troops Sent to Bolster Security at U.S. Embassy in Baghdad," June 30, 2014, at http://www.defense.gov/news/newsarticle.aspx?id=122581&source=GovDelivery.

[6] Richard Sisk, "US Military Deploys Team of Troops to Ukraine," August 6, 2014, Military.com at http://www.military.com/daily-news/2014/08/06/us-military-deploys-team-of-troops-to-ukraine.html?ESRC=eb.nl.

[7] Jim Garamone, "President Sends More Assessors to Iraq," DOD News, Defense Media Activity, August 13, 2014, at http://www.defense.gov/news/newsarticle.aspx?id=122911&source=GovDelivery.

[8] Army Sgt.1st Class Tyrone C. Marshall Jr., "DOD Announces Operation Atlantic Resolve Brigade Rotation," DOD News, Defense Media Activity, August 13, 2014, at http://www.defense.gov/ news/newsarticle.aspx?id=122917.

[9] "Statement from Pentagon Press Secretary Rear Admiral John Kirby on Security Personnel in Iraq," DOD News Release, September 2, 2014, at http://www.defense.gov/Releases/Release.aspx?ReleaseID=16913.

[10] Jim Garamone, "U.S. Sending 475 More Service Members to Iraq," DOD News, September 10, 2014, at http://www.defense.gov/news/newsarticle.aspx?id=123127.

[11] The White House, Office of the Press Secretary, "FACT SHEET: U.S. Response to the Ebola Epidemic in West Africa," September 16, 2014, at http://www.whitehouse.gov/the-press-office/2014/09/16/fact-sheet-us-response-ebolaepidemic-west-africa.

[12] Cheryl Pellerin, "Operation United Assistance Helps in Liberian Ebola Fight," DOD News, Sept. 29, 2014, at http://www.defense.gov/news/newsarticle.aspx?id=123289.

[13] Jim Garamone, "DoD May Deploy up to 4,000 Troops to Combat Ebola," DOD News, October 3, 2014, at http://www.defense.gov/news/newsarticle.aspx?id=123336.

[14] Cheryl Pellerin, "Army Expeditionary Laboratory Team to Deploy to Liberia," DOD News, October 31, 2014, at http://www.defense.gov/news/newsarticle.aspx?id=123537.

[15] Dale Greer, "Troops Establish Air Bridge for Ebola Response," DOD News, November 10, 2014, at http://www.defense.gov/news/newsarticle.aspx?id=123603.

[16] "Hagel Mobilizes Reserve Forces in Support of Operation United Assistance," DOD News, November 14, 2014, at http://www.defense.gov/news/newsarticle.aspx?id=123640.

[17] David Vergun, "Eastern Europe Troop Rotations Could Continue, Commander Says," DOD News, Army News Service, November 24, 2014, at http://www.defense.gov/news/newsarticle.aspx?id=123716.

[18] Jake Richmond, "Hagel Authorizes Up to 1,300 Additional Troops to Deploy to Iraq," DOD News, December 19, 2014, at http://www.defense.gov/news/newsarticle.aspx?id=123863.

[19] Claudette Roulo, "DoD Releases Breakdown of Ebola Response Effort," DOD News, January 8, 2015, at http://www.defense.gov/news/newsarticle.aspx?id=123935.

INDEX

C

D

N

O

P

T

U

V

W

Y